For Erica,

I hope this useful in our joint endeavors for HRE!

— Sanita

Pennsylvania Studies in Human Rights

Bert B. Lockwood, Series Editor

A complete list of books in the series is available from the publisher.

Human Rights Education

Human Rights Education

Forging an Academic Discipline

Sarita Cargas

PENN

UNIVERSITY OF PENNSYLVANIA PRESS

PHILADELPHIA

Published by
University of Pennsylvania Press
Philadelphia, Pennsylvania 19104-4112
www.upenn.edu/pennpress

Printed in the United States of America
on acid-free paper

10 9 8 7 6 5 4 3 2 1

A Cataloging-in-Publication record is available from the Library of Congress
ISBN 978-0-8122-5179-1

For Harry James Cargas (1932–1998)

Peace in deed.

Contents

Preface

Most of us teaching human rights to undergraduates are self-taught. We did not earn degrees in the field, because there were no doctorates in human rights to be had. Some people studied topics closely related to human rights and have PhDs in political science, international relations, international studies, or human rights law. But I do not have such a degree. Mine is in theology from Oxford University. I came to human rights education because someone asked me to teach a course even before I had my diploma in hand. I needed the work and reasoned that my research on war and the Holocaust wasn't wholly unrelated to human rights. But the person who hired me to teach in a newly formed bachelor's degree provided no guidance—not even an old syllabus to follow. Fresh from years of study in the UK, and not yet acquainted with anyone in the Midwestern university department where I landed, I called my dear friend from Oxford, Antonio Buti, a human rights lawyer (and now statesman) in Australia, and asked advice. He suggested the unwieldy tome that Henry Steiner, Philip Alston, and Ryan Goodman wrote for law students, *International Human Rights in Context: Law, Politics, Morals*. I taught it and my passion for the subject was ignited. (Though I quickly substituted the book with Paul Gordon Lauren's *The Evolution of International Human Rights* and Jack Donnelly's *International Human Rights*.)

Soon into my career I became associate dean and was immediately tasked with "branding" our college of arts and sciences with human rights. The dean thought we ought to showcase our somewhat unique degree program, as it fit nicely with our history as a Catholic college with a social justice mission (which had long since secularized). We would name a rights-based theme for the college each year (e.g., "the year of the right to food"). The dean sent a book on that year's theme to each incoming freshman, and we scheduled community events around the theme.

I was somewhat reticent about our efforts at first, because I did not know exactly what a brand-worthy human rights degree should look like. Thus began the decade-long journey that has led to this book. I started by gathering every available detail about the eight human rights bachelor's degree programs in the US and the two in England. At every opportunity, I visited colleges and universities that taught human rights to any extent and began collecting syllabi for courses with "human rights" in the title by scouring the Internet. (That stack is now more than a foot tall.)

Meanwhile, faculty from throughout the university would offer to teach their course as part of the human rights program, even when I was fairly certain they weren't even versed on the Universal Declaration of Human Rights (UDHR). It was not on their syllabi. And while the syllabi with "human rights" in their course titles that I was collecting from around the world demonstrated a fair amount of consistency in the general topics they were presenting, the eight colleges and universities that offered a bachelor's degree in human rights did not have a single course in common. Not all offer an introductory course, a history course, or a theories course; in fact, some have none of these three. Therefore, it is likely that there is not only a lot of variety among the programs—which is reasonable to some degree— but there is also a lack of consensus about what is foundational in a human rights education. Not teaching foundational topics to undergraduates is doing them a disservice. Unfortunately, there is little consistency among any of the English-language undergraduate degrees in human rights in Canada, the UK, and the US.

Despite the lack of consistency among the programs, there is a great deal of coherence in how knowledgeable people teach and write about human rights. I argued with the dean of my college that we should treat human rights as a discipline within our university even though the faculty who taught in our program hailed from a hodgepodge of other academic fields. He said human rights was too interdisciplinary a topic to be a discipline, and we actively debated for five years until I moved across the country to pursue full-time research and teaching on human rights pedagogy. Many people I have spoken with since have echoed the dean's assertion that human rights is inherently interdisciplinary and therefore cannot be taught or administered at universities in the way of fields with narrower scope. What follows is my argument that for the good of the students, practitioners, and the field itself, human rights can and should be disciplined.

Though one could surmise that to define and put parameters around human rights is to constrain it in the academy, I expect to demonstrate the opposite. Some faculty may fear over-disciplining the field. However, there is also freedom in discipline. By examining the defining characteristics of what can be considered requisite in human rights education, we will provide it with structure, enabling colleges and universities everywhere to provide a best-practice human rights education. Along the way, I will promote the notion that human rights education (HRE) is fundamental to the purpose of higher education—namely, educating and equipping the next generation with critical thinking in order to thrive as advocates for the common good within a pluralistic democracy.

Human rights in academia is evolving beyond its nascent stage. Samuel Moyn credits the Carter administration for bringing human rights into public discourse in the 1970s.[1] It is certainly the case that from the 1970s on, books with "human rights" in the title were published with much greater frequency, according to a Google Ngram search. In the 1990s, more faculty were offering courses with a human rights focus. Donnelly's groundbreaking books *Universal Human Rights in Theory and Practice* and *International Human Rights* were first published in 1989 and 1993, respectively.[2] Lauren's seminal *The Evolution of Human Rights: Visions Seen* followed in 1998.[3] Also in 1998, the first three BA degrees in human rights were inaugurated at the University of Dayton, in Ohio; Trinity College, in Hartford, Connecticut; and the University of Essex, in England. Courses in human rights are now offered in numerous fields, including anthropology, business, history, international relations, law, medicine, philosophy, political science, psychology, religious studies, and sociology. It is likely that thousands of postsecondary courses in human rights are being offered across the world.

In addition to the eight BAs on offer in the US, there are at least forty programs designed as minors, certificates, or concentrations in human rights. There are approximately another fifty BAs in other universities across the globe. Master's degrees in human rights are more prevalent, and there are now a few doctoral programs as well. With the advent of two new journals devoted to HRE in higher education, special journal issues devoted to HRE, several new edited volumes about HRE, new web resources, and a consortium for HRE in higher education, one could argue that there is an organic upsurge of HRE occurring in the twenty-first century.

And yet little has been written thus far analyzing the pedagogy of human rights, and there has been no systematic analysis. In this book, after providing some critique, I propose a critical pedagogy of human rights. Other scholars have mentioned the need for a critical pedagogy for HRE, but it has not been fleshed out to the extent done here. I define HRE in the first chapter and provide specific tools for using it throughout the second half of the book (Chapters 4 to 6).

Also, as mentioned, there is little consistency in the structure of the extant curricula in the US. Some allow students to select from a list of courses rather than requiring even a single specific course. On hearing that a graduate has earned a degree in human rights, one cannot be sure what information and skills the curriculum has imparted. This is especially troubling for the tens of thousands of organizations that require staff with human rights knowledge. This book addresses that problem with the intent to advance the field of human rights education by offering a framework for structuring curricula and teaching courses, thereby facilitating replication and growth as an academic discipline.

Though discussed at length later, mention of what kind of discipline human rights should be is called for here. Disciplines fall on a continuum; some must be taught in a more scaffolded and hierarchical manner, where topics and skills are learned sequentially. Others require certain material be covered but don't require a particular sequence. Some departments housing a discipline have faculty with a range of different PhDs in their ranks who teach courses required for the major in that discipline. Some disciplines allow only faculty with PhDs in the same or closely related fields to teach in the discipline.

Human rights would benefit in having some scaffolding of content and skills—the UDHR at the beginning and an advocacy course later in a curriculum, for example. The skills involved in critical pedagogy, such as critical thinking, should follow the pedagogical best practice of first being introduced, then reinforced, followed by working toward competence. HRE may not need as much structure as a hard science requires, but this text demonstrates how students, activists, researchers, and, ultimately, society will benefit from a disciplined HRE. I argue that the field of religious studies provides a useful model of what a human rights discipline should look like. Both have relationships with many of the same related disciplines, and both have a world of practice that is different from that of academia. In contrast, research in chemistry is similar if done in a government or university lab. Yet to be religious in one's life differs from the study of religion, which may or may not involve faith. Likewise for human rights, fieldwork and the academic study of human rights are two different realms of activity.

After framing human rights as a discipline, recommendations are outlined for majors, minors, and certificates. Thus, the first part of this book makes the argument for disciplining human rights, and the second part is a handbook for designing curricula to support human rights education using a critical pedagogy. Though focused on higher education in the US, much of the research and recommendations provided are applicable elsewhere, because, like other disciplines, most of the content and skills necessary for an education in human rights will not change due to location. Although some content will vary due to regional problems, laws, and legal regimes, the majority will not.

Chapter 1 explains how HRE fits in with the arc of human rights history in general. We are at a moment in the history of the movement when HRE must be codified to become more pervasive. Chapter 1 also presents the many reasons why we need more HRE in higher education. The price a populace pays when largely unversed in human rights is too high. In this vein, it's important to note that many people are already engaged in human rights work, though often they are not aware that their social justice efforts have anything to do with human rights, and they are working with vulnerable populations who deserve the skill of individuals who are well trained to help and to prevent further harm in the process. Also, for the global community to live into its full potential, human rights advocacy must increase in both skill and volume. By the same token, HRE has much to learn from the methods of those doing human rights fieldwork. Helping marginalized communities often involves a participatory approach sometimes called participatory action research (PAR), which includes education about one's rights and the cocreation of knowledge.[4] As can be seen when the chapter makes the argument for critical pedagogy, the participatory aspect is essential.

Chapter 2 presents a survey of the current state of HRE globally. After illustrating the wide variety of HRE offerings, I examine the commonalities in existing curricula, formal and informal, and the most popular texts to describe and highlight an emergent consensus. Then, in Chapter 3, I advance the argument for recognizing and teaching human rights as an academic discipline as opposed to an interdisciplinary field, demonstrating that current HRE practice is actually multidisciplinary (lacking the integrative aspect of true interdisciplinary work), and human rights fits all the criteria of a discipline.

The chapters in the second half of the book contain practical recommendations for designing courses and curricula. They are organized around the representation of HRE as education *about, through,* and *for* human rights, with a chapter devoted to each in order to create a transformative discipline founded in a critical pedagogy.

Betty Reardon, a scholar of peace education, writes of the distinction between human rights education (HRE) and human rights learning (HRL), defining the former as teaching the topic of human rights without having an agenda for action and the latter as involving political acts advocating change.[5] However, because the definition I propose here for HRE involves education *about, through,* and *for* human rights, it is roughly equivalent to Reardon's understanding of HRL. She also argues that HRL must be based in critical pedagogy to the extent that it is based on inquiry and analysis. So, following in the footsteps of another matriarch of human rights pedagogy, each of the following chapters makes specific recommendations for "doing" critical pedagogy.

In Chapter 1, I explain that the elements of critical pedagogy that define it for use here include question posing, critique, reflection, dialogue, and action—in other words, with less focus on trying to abolish social structures, which is a goal of some critical pedagogy theorists.[6] In Chapter 4, on education *through* human rights, teaching the skills of critical thinking and analysis is probably the single most productive approach to fostering critical pedagogy, especially if used alongside aspects of social justice education such as promoting equity and inclusion. When using class discussion meaningfully as an active-learning technique, it should also contribute to the dialogue and reflection aspects of critical pedagogy. In Chapter 5, on education *for* human rights, teaching strategic empathy, using problem-based learning, and teaching a critical advocacy can all contribute to a critical pedagogy. And, of course, education *about* human rights—the content we teach, which is covered in Chapter 6—should require all aspects of critical pedagogy through the readings we choose and the critiques we apply to them.

While *about, through,* and *for* are helpful organizing concepts, it is somewhat artificial to treat them as wholly distinct pedagogical practices. They are inextricably linked but separated here to highlight the pieces of each that must be incorporated to create a complete picture of best practice for HRE. We will begin with *through* and *for* because they inform the content of the curricula—that is, education *about* human rights.

I conclude this preface by acknowledging all of my colleagues who are working in human rights education. Faculty just starting out in the field of HRE owe a great debt to the pioneers who, in the last several decades, taught the lone human rights course in their institution or had the fortitude to initiate whole programs. You have bequeathed to those of us currently exploring postsecondary HRE an important legacy on which to build. We are able to talk about expansions and innovations to HRE only because you have created something substantive to build upon. Though what follows involves a measure of critique, I would like to communicate my profound respect for our joint endeavor to bring human rights into the lived experiences of students everywhere.

Chapter 1

The Arc of Human Rights
and Human Rights Education in History

I do not pretend to understand the moral universe; the arc is a long one,
my eye reaches but little ways; I cannot calculate the curve and complete
the figure by the experience of sight; I can divine it by conscience. And
from what I see I am sure it bends towards justice.
    —Theodore Parker, 1852

Owing in part to the mechanisms for the promotion and protection of human rights, most people are enjoying a longer life span and more stable food supplies than they did a century ago. The majority of the globe's children have been vaccinated, are literate, and experience fundamental freedoms. Enormous progress has been made for humanity, and that must be celebrated and communicated to our students. There is hope to build on, which is essential to keep in the forefront of our consciousness as we review some of the reasons why we need human rights education (HRE).

As of the end of 2015, there were in excess of 65 million refugees, asylum seekers, and internally displaced people around the world,[1] but a global rise in nationalism thwarts efforts to resolve the crisis. Despite the fact that the nineteenth-century antislavery campaign was one of the first international human rights efforts in history, there are more enslaved people now than during the Atlantic slave trade (12.5 million[2] Africans were shipped to the West between 1525 and 1866, and in 2016, 24.9 million[3] people were estimated to be in forced labor and another 15.4 million in forced marriage). Climate change is intensifying, and all evidence points to the poor and vulnerable suffering its dire effects exponentially more than the well-heeled. Here in the US, more of our citizens are imprisoned than in any Western country. Startlingly, more than ninety-five thousand minors were incarcerated in US adult jails in the year 2011 alone.[4] Economic inequality where upward of 42 million people go hungry every day is greater in the US than in most developed countries. More than half a million are unsheltered,[5] and thousands more suffer violence from the militarization of our police forces, poorly regulated guns in civilian hands, and all types of domestic abuse. If these, and other social problems, were viewed through a human rights lens, approaches to solving them would undoubtedly expand and improve. If the US government recognized Article 25 of the Universal Declaration of Human Rights[6] and the right to adequate housing, for instance, it would have to take more responsibility for ensuring shelter. Respecting Articles 5 (not being subject to degrading punishment) and 7 (nondiscrimination before the law) would force needed reform of the justice system—perhaps resulting in the promotion of rehabilitation instead of the continued rise of for-profit prisons and the disproportionately punitive sentencing of poor people and minorities. If the US promoted Article 14 (the right to seek asylum in other countries), immigration policies might refocus to center on a commitment to those whom the US has been party to displacing through various kinds of interventions, economic or violent.

General lack of awareness about the human rights regime is a huge impediment to progressing toward a more just and rights-promoting society. Though the modern concept of human rights emerged with the founding of the United Nations in 1945 as the first international organization to focus on cooperation for the protection of human rights, its Universal Declaration of Human Rights (UDHR) is not widely taught in US schools and universities despite its calls for universal promotion of HRE. The first sentence of the preamble to the declaration is a call for HRE: "The General Assembly proclaims this Universal Declaration of Human Rights as the common standard of achievement for all peoples and all nations, to the end that every individual and every organ of society, keeping this Declaration constantly in mind shall strive by teaching and education to promote respect for these rights and freedoms."

While HRE is not nearly as pervasive as it should be, the existing groundwork supports its widespread implementation in colleges and universities. Taking that next step to promote HRE in higher education will greatly influence other levels of education since, for example, teachers of younger students are college educated. What follows is a brief tour of the highlights in the history of the modern human rights movement that underpins this argument for codifying HRE at the university level. By examining the movement for human rights historically, understanding how the definition of HRE has evolved, and looking at the mandates outlined in the treaties and documents, this book demonstrates how the field is ripe to mature into a discipline.

Teaching/educating is a primary demand of the visionary UDHR, which was endorsed by the US government from its acceptance on December 10, 1948, when forty-eight countries voted in favor in the UN General Assembly. (Only those on the winning side of World War II were part of the General Assembly.) As of 2018, all nations on earth have accepted this declaration, indicating—at least in theory—that all have agreed with the rights set forth therein. The UDHR is mentioned in more than sixty countries' national constitutions, and every single country has signed at least one, if not all, of the nine major human rights treaties that followed the UDHR.[7]

History of Human Rights

The UDHR was drafted from 1946 to 1948; however, because of the Cold War the human rights movement became stagnant. Therefore, historians cite two periods for the birth of the modern movement: the 1940s, because of the advent of the UN and the UDHR, and the 1970s, with the beginning of the end of the Cold War, as discussed below. The 1970s also witnessed the birth of Amnesty International and Médecins Sans Frontières, the first international human rights classes in law and political science departments in the US, and an explosion of human rights nongovernmental organizations (NGOs).[8]

Even without the Cold War, Jim Crow laws meant the US was out of step with the UDHR. However, the Cold War had a significantly deleterious effect on the human rights movement in the US. The Soviets were part of the original Human Rights Commission (HRC) drafting group, consisting of representatives of eighteen member states.[9] They obstructed throughout the process employing delaying tactics such as changing their delegate frequently and voting against proposals. The start of the Cold War was on display in the HRC. Ultimately, they did not vote against the adoption of the UDHR; they abstained. Thus, it is no surprise that for the next several decades, human rights was not the lingua franca for international relations that it is today. The USSR claimed it was promoted as a tool of the West, and the universality of the UDHR was not acknowledged. But the Soviets were not solely to blame: at the height of McCarthyism in the US, human rights treaties were speciously associated with communism, especially because of economic rights. A conservative faction of lawyers and politicians in the US has always argued that ratifying international treaties threatens our national sovereignty. (For example, the US has still not ratified the International Covenant on Economic, Social, and Cultural Rights, calling them aspirational.)

Somewhat ironically, therefore, the West's wielding of human rights in the Helsinki Final Act was a key factor in the downfall of the Iron Curtain and therefore another event for human rights progress.[10] The 1970s Helsinki accords were the result of a Soviet proposal for a European security conference in the 1950s. Their goal was to prevent West Germany from joining the North Atlantic Treaty Organization. By the time Western Europe agreed to meet in the 1970s, the Soviets desired to be recognized as part of the international order.[11] Western Europe used the acceptance of human rights as part of the definition of what it meant to be a "normal" member of Europe. The USSR accepted insertion of a demand that they respect human rights in the Helsinki Final Act treaty. While they had no real intention of following through nor publicizing those provisions among their citizens, and Western analysts did not expect they would, civil society and NGOs in the West aided their counterparts in the East to demand the human rights provisions be enacted. In 1976 the Moscow Helsinki Watch Group was formed to monitor the agreements. (In 1981 America's Watch was formed, followed by Asia, Africa, and Middle East Watches, also in the 1980s. They eventually coalesced into one of our most formidable human rights NGOs, Human Rights Watch.)[12]

Civil society pressured US president Jimmy Carter and lobbied the US Congress to be more confrontational.[13] The former is credited with bringing the language of human rights into US foreign relations. Activists in the Warsaw Pact countries (former Soviet allies) were successful in using the human rights provisions against their respective governments. To distill a long, fascinating story, while not solely responsible for the dissolution of the USSR, the primarily nonviolent actions of civil society and its NGOs in numerous countries were crucial to the fall of the Soviet regime, beginning in 1989. And with the end of the Cold War, the number of human rights

NGOs exploded from just a few international human rights–focused NGOs to thousands. Currently, human rights NGOs number in the millions.

It is important to note another impact of the Cold War on HRE: most current educators were in school either during the Cold War or under its long shadow, and human rights was not even mentioned as part of our education. During that era, human rights went into a holding pattern. The Communist Bloc and the West seldom agreed on anything at the UN, especially at the Security Council, where far fewer resolutions were passed than during any other period because the Soviets and US so frequently wielded the veto. Human rights were not a common focus in newspapers, books, or academic works.[14] In contrast, there are currently more than fifty English-language journals with "human rights" in the title.

A great number of people attending the Vienna World Conference on Human Rights in 1993 hoped it was the dawn of a new era of possibility and that cooperation among nations would be more forthcoming. Many such hopes went unfulfilled, but the conference was, indeed, significant for the human rights movement. There the Office of the High Commissioner for Human Rights was established, and the 167 countries present agreed on the indivisibility of human rights—that is, economic, social, and cultural rights were declared as necessary as civil and political rights. And because the final Vienna Declaration and Programme of Action was adopted by consensus, the whole world was considered to have finally adopted the UDHR.

Foundations of Human Rights Education

The Vienna conference also initiated the Decade for Human Rights Education (1995–2004), which spawned the World Programme for Human Rights Education (WP). The WP is ongoing and consists of three phases: the first, 2005–2009, focused on primary and secondary education; the second, 2010–2014, concentrated on higher education, educators, civil servants, law enforcement, and military personnel; and the third, 2015–2019, centers on journalists and all who work in the media. For the first two phases, only seventy and thirty-six countries, respectively, sent an assessment of their achievements. Unsurprisingly, final reports for both phases highlight vast room for improvement.

Out of the WP came the UN Declaration on Human Rights Education and Training (UNDHRET) in 2011. The fourteen articles instruct governments to provide HRE in "all forms of education, training, and learning, whether in a public or private, formal, informal or non-formal setting. It includes, inter alia, vocational training (particularly the training of trainers, teachers and State officials), continuing education, popular education, and public information and awareness activities."[15] The document provides a definition of HRE that is discussed later in this chapter, but it is worth emphasizing that UNDHRET was published less than a decade ago. And though there have been numerous books, manuals, and guides published for teaching human rights for primary and secondary students, fewer than five focus on HRE in higher education. Perhaps the first important edited volume was George Andreopoulos and Richard Pierre Claude's *Human Rights Education for the Twenty-First Century* in 1997.[16] The book *Human Rights Education: Theory, Research, Praxis*, edited by Monisha Bajaj,[17] was published a decade later and heralded as the previous volume's "successor" by one reviewer. Also published in 2017, *Globalisation, Human Rights Education, and Reforms*[18] is another edited volume devoted to HRE. The inception of two new journals (in the US and Norway) further signals HRE's maturation. From the campus of the University of San Francisco, which offers the first Master of Arts degree in HRE, comes the *International Journal of Human Rights Education*, with Monisha Bajaj as editor in chief. The inaugural issue was published in October 2017. Audrey Osler edits a cooperative endeavor between Oslo and Akershus University of Applied Sciences and the University of South-Eastern Norway, *Human Rights Education Review*, which debuted in June 2018.

Two important organizations committed to HRE sprouted in the latter half of the twentieth century: Equitas's International Centre for Human Rights Education, in Montreal, and the Human Rights Education Association (HREA). Equitas began as the Canadian Human Rights Foundation in 1967. Founded by scholars and social activists—including the co-drafter of the Universal Declaration of Human Rights, John P. Humphrey; women's rights activist Thérèse Casgrain; and Dr. Gustave Gingras, an activist for people with disabilities—Equitas serves to promote HRE through conferences, workshops, and online resources. Founded by Felisa Tibbitts and Cristina Sganga in 1996, HREA offers educational tools and training programs in human rights topics for educators and practitioners. Thousands of people around the globe receive its email updates, and access information and course work on their comprehensive website. Another North American organization committed to supporting grades K–12 HRE is

Human Rights Educators USA (HRE USA).[19] None of the aforementioned groups focuses specifically on tertiary education, but a related organization, the University and College Consortium for Human Rights Education (UCCHRE) was born in 2016 to fill that gap. UCCHRE is working to establish an online resource for faculty in higher education. With these supports in place, HRE has the tools and momentum to fulfill its international mandate. In drawing from and building on this work, I provide recommendations for a systematic approach for teaching human rights in higher education in the latter half of this book.

Systemic Impact of Human Rights Education

A few years ago, a student who was in the Reserve Officer Training Corps took two of my human rights courses and, after graduating, emailed me from abroad. She shared a story about the effect the classes had on her work as an officer in the US Armed Forces. She was involved in creating an evacuation plan for the American military in-country in case of erupting conflict, and her fellow officers had decided that it would be expedient to leave American military prisoners behind in such an emergency. She wrote that her introduction to human rights conventions made her question her colleagues' decision. She became unpopular by challenging them but persevered, eventually escalating her concerns to the US Department of State, where it was ultimately determined that the evacuation plans had to include the prisoners. Literacy in human rights prompted her action to protect rights.

A biology student who studies a "neglected" tropical disease took a course I taught on health and human rights. She has carried her human rights knowledge into her graduate research on the disease and in her publications is now incorporating the human rights implications of ignoring the malady. Another former student is thinking of ways to introduce human rights into her population health graduate curriculum.

No doubt the thousands of faculty teaching human rights around the world could share such stories, as could the countless students who have taken human rights courses. We teach human rights to promote human rights. The UNDHRET explicitly enumerates such goals, including "empowerment"; "eradication of all forms of discrimination, racism, stereotyping, and incitement to hatred"; and "development of the individual as a responsible member of a free, peaceful, pluralist and inclusive society."[20] We want nothing less than to transform our society by educating and empowering our students.

An important reason we are often successful in this pursuit is that students bring their idealism into the classroom. Conversations with faculty teaching HRE offer anecdotal evidence that classes with "human rights" in the title consistently fill to capacity. Generally, students taking the courses have never heard of the UDHR and cannot accurately list the rights it enumerates, but they want to learn it, sensing it could be meaningful to their lives. This is a time in their psychological development and maturation when they are searching for meaning. What an opportunity for the human rights movement: to capitalize on the enthusiasm of intrinsically motivated young people to champion the cause of human rights!

Social justice education (SJE) would also benefit from incorporating HRE, because, while it does not necessarily involve teaching students human rights mechanisms, doing so would provide universal and normative tools. This is true for peace studies as well.[21] Because human rights are founded in laws that every nation on earth is to some extent party to, faculty can promote human rights as a mission of their respective governments, based on the commitment to the UDHR and subsequent human rights treaties. Students can use the language of human rights to frame issues of social justice.

We also need to increase awareness that human rights go beyond the civil and political. Each semester I begin courses with a brainstorming exercise that reveals students' preconceived notions of human rights. I tell them that there is a universal declaration that has thirty articles. I then group the students to discuss what rights they think everyone should have. Invariably, their lists mirror the US Bill of Rights and omit economic, social, and cultural rights. Indeed it is true that although most US states have a bureau of human rights, they really address only civil rights. For example, the US government does not promote either universal health care or fair and livable wages as human rights. A citizenry versed in human rights becomes enabled to demand their rights and to advocate for the rights of others.

The human abuses that currently plague the US reflect a more urgent need to provide society-wide education in human rights. In addition to the aforementioned examples, in the month after the election of Donald Trump, the Southern Poverty Law Center reported that in a survey of K–12 schools, "over 2,500 educators described specific incidents of bigotry and harassment that can be directly traced to election rhetoric. These incidents include graffiti (including swastikas), assaults on students and teachers, property damage, fights, and threats of violence."[22] It was no different on my university campus. The day after the election, students shared stories of intolerant language all around them. The dangerous climate of bigotry in the United States requires an institutionalized response. HRE provides the guidelines for living together. It is more than just a system for ameliorating abuses.

Religion and Human Rights

Mention of the 2016 US presidential election provides a useful segue for a comment on the relationship of human rights to religion. Much of the intolerance demonstrated since the Trump presidency began centers on religion. We have seen neo-Nazis parading anti-Semitism around Jewish synagogues. Anti-Muslim rhetoric has increased, and Trump's utterances fuel the flames. Religions can attract intolerance, and some religious factions preach intolerance for the "other." My background in religious studies inspires me to mention that for many people, the relationship between their religions, other religions, and the universality of human rights are completely compatible. Indeed, there is some debate about whether human rights have religious foundations, since the UDHR drafters were conscientious about making it a secular document. Although it contains no reference to a divine being or deity, scholars of the major world religions, including Hinduism, Confucianism, Buddhism, Judaism, Christianity, Islam, and indigenous religions, have either identified the principles underlying the UDHR within their sacred scriptures or teachings or generally agreed they were compatible. Most have a version of the Golden Rule in keeping with the principle of human dignity at the root of all human rights: "to wish for others as you wish for yourself," as in Islam; "what is hateful to you, do not do to your neighbor," in Judaism; and "whatever you wish that others do unto you, so do unto them," in Christianity. One can argue that "all the world's religions . . . are rooted in active non-violence. Islam means peace. Judaism upholds the vision of Shalom, . . . [and] Jesus was the most active practitioner of non-violence."[23]

In this vein, Rabbi Daniel F. Polish offers, "The phrase 'human rights' itself being of juridic coinage, is of course not employed by classical sources.

. . . But the system of values and ideas and practices which constitute the concept of 'human rights' is hardly absent from the Jewish worldview."[24] Haim Cohen's book *Human Rights in Jewish Law* provides hundreds of sources for Jewish civil, political, and economic rights.[25] Mohammed Abed Al-Jabri discusses rights whose sources can be found in ancient Islam. He writes, "Such are the rights of all human beings without exception or discrimination: the right to life, the right to enjoyment of life, freedom of belief, the right to knowledge, the right to disagree, the right to consultation, and the right to equality."[26] For Christians, "theological sources for [positive] Christian views of human rights are assertions that are based in an ontological understanding of humans, God, and the world."[27] So while religions and the vast conversation that has arisen about them and human rights is not a focus of this book, the essential role of religion in society, and that some have used religious doctrine to impinge on others' rights throughout recorded history, requires educators to understand that ignoring religions' compatibility is detrimental to the promotion of human rights.[28]

HRE Mandates

Having established the historical context for human rights education and identified many proximate reasons why we need standardized, systemic HRE (the US has treaty obligations to provide it; every sector of society has professionals involved in promoting and defending human rights, including employees in government, NGOs, and the business sector, and especially multinational corporations; the thousands of people involved in human rights work must be adequately supported with and informed by an education in human rights; and only in understanding one's rights is one prepared to advocate for them), let's explore the mandate coming from treaties and the three job sectors mentioned above in depth.

HRE Mandates in Treaties and Other UN-Related International Obligations

The international directive for HRE in several core human rights documents states that education is a human right and that education *about* human rights is essential for creating a world governed by rights. The UN's

Office of the High Commissioner for Human Rights compiled a list of 188 international instruments and documents that mention HRE directly or indirectly.[29] These include treaties, charters, declarations, guidelines, and recommendations, about 40 of which the US is party to.

As the primary document instructing governments to provide HRE, the UDHR was the first to expressly state that HRE is an international concern. The Convention on the Rights of the Child, which every country has ratified except for the US, also recommends HRE. Another nine human rights treaties support HRE, as do over a dozen general comments and recommendations attached to the treaties, including two that the US has ratified: the Convention on Civil and Political Rights, and the Convention Against Torture. And though they are nonbinding agreements, the US supports the previously mentioned World Programme for HRE and the UN Declaration on Human Rights Education and Training.

Specialized UN agencies such as United Nations Educational, Scientific, and Cultural Organization (UNESCO) and the International Labor Organization (ILO) have also authored documents to which the US is a party, including UNESCO's charter and the ILO's convention prohibiting child labor, both of which emphasize the need for HRE. In addition, the US has ratified the Geneva Conventions, which demand education about international humanitarian law for the military and "civil instruction" for the entire population.

Finally, the US participates in many of the United Nations' principal organs, offices, councils, and committees that monitor human rights and human rights education. Paula Gerber establishes that much of this monitoring neglects to focus on HRE, but it could and should be a place to hold governments responsible for its provision.[30] For example, the Human Rights Council has instituted a Universal Periodic Review (UPR), through which each of the 193 member nations of the UN must report on the state of its human rights obligations. Every three to four years, the UPR working group assesses each country's adherence to the human rights obligations established in the following documents: "(1) the UN Charter; (2) the Universal Declaration of Human Rights; (3) human rights instruments to which the State is party (human rights treaties ratified by the State concerned); (4) voluntary pledges and commitments made by the State (e.g., national human rights policies and/or programs implemented); and, (5) applicable international humanitarian law."[31] As previously explained, most of these documents demand HRE to some extent, so the Human Rights

Council could use the Universal Periodic Review to hold countries account-able to demonstrate compliance.

Human rights NGOs can likewise submit a report to the Human Rights Council in the attempt to compel change. In 2017, HRE USA and UCCHRE coauthored a report on HRE in the US for the 22nd Session of the UPR, focusing on "obligations by the US government in higher education institu-tions, specifically the training of teachers, military personnel, and social workers."[32] They found the US wanting in all areas and admonished, "There is currently no comprehensive national framework or action plan on human rights education. There is neither a government focal point for Human Rights Education or a National Human Rights Institute with a mandate to provide and ensure quality human rights education."[33] This contributes to one of their many conclusions that "across higher education institutions for professional training, curriculum standards related to human rights education are disparate and unregulated."[34] They also con-clude that the "vast majority" of teacher training programs, schools of social work, and military academies do not incorporate HRE in their curricula.

The US is a member of two regional organizations that emphasize HRE: (1) the Organization of American States (OAS) and (2) the Organization of Security and Cooperation in Europe (OSCE), which have nine and twenty documents, respectively, that discuss the necessity of HRE. While the United States has not signed most of the OAS treaties supporting HRE, the US did sign the charter, which mentions HRE, and also supports the 2005 Inter-American Program on Education for Democratic Values and Prac-tices. As a member of the OSCE, the US is party to all of its documents referencing human rights–related education, because all decisions and writ-ten documents are determined by consensus.

Thus, on paper at least, the US has committed to providing HRE. This trend can be considered universal because of all of the other regional orga-nizations with documents that cite the necessity for HRE, as the Association of Southeast Asian Nation (ASEAN), African, and Islamic organizations do. The Council of Europe has twenty-six documents that mention it, the European Union has nine, the League of Arab States has two, the Interna-tional Organisation of La Francophonie has four, and The Commonwealth (an association of 53 countries) has seven.

In summary, most of the documents the US has endorsed do not have the force of law but are nonetheless agreements the country has entered into. Consistent with the US's historical resistance to most human rights law (due to American exceptionalism), when the Human Rights Council drafted the UNDHRET, the US explicitly stated, "We are among a number of States that do not recognize such a right under international law, but are committed to 'promoting an individual's ability to know or seek out information regarding his or her human rights.'"[35] However, that the US is party to so many declarations and recommendations regarding HRE implies a greater commitment to and acceptance of the obligation to provide it than is reflected in that statement.

Governments and Human Rights

Because of the memberships and agreements, governments must then monitor and implement human rights at home and abroad. In fact, the UDHR was written primarily to instruct governments. The US Department of State explains on its web page: "A central goal of US foreign policy has been the promotion of respect for human rights, as embodied in the Universal Declaration of Human Rights. The United States understands that the existence of human rights helps secure the peace, deter aggression, promote the rule of law, combat crime and corruption, strengthen democracies, and prevent humanitarian crises."[36] Thus, there is a Bureau of Democracy, Human Rights, and Labor, which lists three main human rights efforts: (1) submitting an annual report to Congress about the state of human rights in almost every nation, (2) "promot[ing] early warning and preventative diplomacy" for human rights, and (3) partnering with and providing funds to human rights organizations.[37] The FBI has an International Human Rights Unit and works with the Immigration and Customs Enforcement's Human Rights Violators and War Crimes Unit. They both have the goal of investigating perpetrators of crimes against humanity especially when foreigners who have tortured or participated in genocide enter the US. Homeland Security and the Department of Justice also participate in this promotion of human rights.

Within the US there are "over 150 state and local agencies that enforce human and civil rights laws; governors; state attorneys general; mayors, legislators; and law enforcement. State and local actors have jurisdiction over a range of human rights issues, such as housing, education, and criminal justice."[38] Human rights oversight is not well coordinated or well organized among these entities; nonetheless, there are thousands of people responsible for human rights, even as the Human Rights Institute at Columbia Law School notes a general ignorance of human rights law among state and local officials. They suggest "education and training for state and local agencies and officials on their human rights obligations, including UN recommendations,"[39] though clearly a stronger HRE framework in all colleges and universities would provide a deeper foundation for a US commitment to human rights within the context of our governing structures.

A brief glance at the way US states interact with human rights is instructive. Every state has either a division, department, or commission that deals with human rights. Some use the phrase "civil rights" in their names, but most use "human rights": Idaho Human Rights Commission, Illinois Department of Human Rights, Kansas Human Rights Commission, Montana Human Rights Bureau, North Dakota Human Rights Division, South Dakota Division of Human Rights, and West Virginia Human Rights Commission, to list a few. A statement from Kansas's government website is typical because, like similar organizations, it monitors the implementation of antidiscrimination law, and citizens can file claims therein: "The mission of the Kansas Human Rights Commission is to prevent and eliminate discrimination and assure equal opportunities in all employment relations, to eliminate and prevent discrimination, segregation or separation, and assure equal opportunities in all places of public accommodations and in housing."[40] Most refer to ensuring adherence to the appropriate state and federal laws, though a few states, such as Illinois and New Mexico, have human rights acts. Citizens must be educated about their local human rights regimes to benefit from them.

NGOs and Human Rights

Perhaps the most visible institutions in terms of calling students' attention to human rights are the nongovernmental organizations (NGOs) and international nongovernmental organizations (INGOs). Students generally seem to be familiar with Amnesty International and Human Rights Watch, likely due to their size and their high social media profiles. They are likewise exposed to charity campaigns in times of disaster. Some even enroll in human rights degree or certificate programs with the goal of working for an NGO.

There are no comprehensive statistics on how many NGOs are focused on human rights. This is because they do not have to be registered, and small ones may come and go. However, there are many statistics about NGOs in general that illustrate the enormity of their work. Before World War I, maybe 30 new INGOs would appear each year. Between 1960 and 1984, INGOs increased from 1,268 to 12,686.[41] By the 1980s it was estimated that 100 new INGOs were created each year, and since 1996 that figure has soared to 500 new INGOs per year.[42] It's estimated that there are 10 million NGOs worldwide,[43] of which roughly 3.7 million are believed to focus on human rights.[44] A 2017 US Department of State report says there are approximately 1.5 million NGOs in the US,[45] working on everything from elections, climate change, needs of the disabled and the poor, and myriad other causes. How many of them could be considered human rights NGOs is an open question, but many of the estimated 11.4 million people employed by nonprofit organizations are, or could be, using the language of human rights.[46]

Some of the very largest INGOs, which work in numerous countries, have budgets that are bigger than those of some small nations and thus have a great deal of power to affect a problem situation. Four of the largest are World Vision, a religious organization with over 46,000 employees and an annual income of more than US$1 billion as of 2015;[47] CARE, with an income of US$530 million as of 2016;[48] Save the Children, with US$696 million in annual income in 2016,[49] and Médecins Sans Frontières (MSF) at €1.516 million in 2016.[50] The world's largest INGO is the Bangladesh Rural Advancement Committee (BRAC), which had an income of US$776 million in 2007.[51]

However, well-intentioned NGOs have also been responsible for increased suffering by prolonging conflict in Biafra (1967–1970), aiding killers in Rwandan refugee camps (1994), and abusing refugees in the former Yugoslavia (1994), among many other examples. In fact, MSF was founded by doctors volunteering with the International Committee of the Red Cross (ICRC), because they saw the "silent neutrality" of the ICRC as enabling the violent conflict between Nigeria and Biafra to continue. MSF "sought to put the interest of victims ahead of sovereignty considerations . . . determining to speak in public when faced with mass violations of human rights, including forced displacement or forced repatriation, war crimes, crimes against humanity, and genocide."[52] It is also the case that, too often, NGOs do not communicate with one another or UN agencies in crisis situations, resulting in duplicative efforts and resource competition. This is where HRE and NGO work become symbiotic: these experiences inform scholarship, and HRE supplies analysis and competent workers to improve upon and further the work.

On a smaller scale, but equally problematic, as Linda Polman documents in her book *The Crisis Caravan: What's Wrong with Humanitarian Aid?*, well-meaning individuals are apt to form NGOs and launch into disaster situations without consulting locals or those already providing aid, learning the political context, asking how or whether their help might harm, or even creating a methodology for their endeavors. Polman describes botched surgeries on children in Sierra Leone committed by incompetent and untrained or under-trained US do-gooders who believed their desire to "just do something, anything"[53] was sufficient to disregard any negative unintended consequences. Inexplicably, they didn't seem to remotely consider that their harmful actions would rise to the level of crimes if performed in their hometowns. From the largest to smallest, these organizations, and the people they are working to aid, would certainly benefit from a workforce and citizenry that are educated in human rights.

Business, Multinational Corporations, and Human Rights

Corporations are also highly visible in terms of human rights but often for different reasons than those of NGOs. While NGOs publicize violations, corporations—especially multinational corporations (MNCs)—often make the news for perpetrating violations. Multinational oil companies are regular targets of environmental and human rights NGOs. Royal Dutch Shell has a reputation for abuse of the Nigerian environment, where it is the largest extractor of oil. Spills and gas flares have polluted the land, air, and water, ruining people's livelihoods and compromising their living conditions. Local citizens campaigned against Shell until the government cracked down in 1995 when they tried and executed ten activists, including their leader, Ken Saro-Wiwa. Many blame Shell for their deaths, and Shell was sued for its role. US energy company UNOCAL was also taken to court, reaching a settlement in 2004, for supporting the Burmese military's use of slave labor on its pipelines. Chevron is accused of committing abuses in Ecuador by creating hundreds of polluting unlined oil pits and dumping millions of gallons of toxins into rivers. Multinationals in the extractive industries have also been blamed for violence perpetrated by the private security forces they contract with.

The garment industry has likewise experienced high-profile cases of human rights violations, such as the Rana Plaza fire in 2013 in Bangladesh, where five structurally unsound factory buildings collapsed and 1,135 workers were killed. The owner of the complex was cognizant of the danger and did nothing to prevent the disaster. This was the worst of many reported cases of labor abuses in the international clothing industry. In 2013, Apple, the maker of the iPhone, was in the news for its supply-chain factories in China, where people worked twelve-hour shifts, six days a week, with poor safety standards and were housed in substandard conditions.[54]

Since the 1950s, MNCs have begun to develop corporate social responsibility (CSR) policies. These express "a concern with the needs and goals of society, which goes beyond the merely economic."[55] Where once CSR was mainly concerned with corporate philanthropy, it is now often concerned with sustainability behaviors and human rights, or the "Triple Bottom Line": corporations are expected to be sustainable in terms of (1) the communities they affect, (2) the environment, and (3) their finances—or the three Ps: people, planet, profit. To this end, some MNCs have developed human rights policies, and some have established corporate divisions for human rights. While only about 360 corporations have publicly available human rights policies—a mere fraction of the 80,000 MNCs that exist—the number of MNCs doing some sort of responsibility reporting is thought to be higher because 81 percent of the MNCs listed on the S&P 500 Index filed sustainability or responsibility reports in 2016.[56]

Some of this reporting is due to the voluntary codes of conduct that offer a set of guidelines or standards that most often apply to multinational corporations. A sample of the higher-profile initiatives include the Kimberley Process for the certification of "conflict-free" diamonds (i.e., not being used to finance violent rebels); for the extractive industries there are the Voluntary Principles on Security and Human Rights, which "promotes implementation of a set of principles that guide oil, gas, and mining companies on providing security for their operations in a manner that respects human rights," and the Extractive Industries Transparency Initiative, which promotes "the open and accountable management of oil, gas and mineral resources."[57] Examples of more general codes include the International Organization for Standardization's ISO 26000 voluntary social responsibility standards, whose goal is to help businesses act "in an ethical and transparent way that contributes to the health and welfare of society,"[58] and the Fair Labor Association Code of Conduct, which "seeks to protect the workers who manufacture the clothing, footwear, agricultural products and other items enjoyed by consumers around the world."[59]

Because of the need for, and this emerging trend toward, addressing human rights in commerce, and the fact that so many graduates will end up working within or transacting business with corporations, it behooves the US education system to equip everyone with at least basic education in human rights. While the main focus of this book is on defining a discipline, it also champions the idea that human rights should infuse other fields of study.

Defining Human Rights Education

What kind of HRE will allow us to prepare people to work in the field of human rights, to champion their own and others' rights, and to be able to critique the human rights system? Despite a multitude of definitions that have been offered over the last thirty years or so, there is a surprising amount of consistency in what various authorities recommend. Generally, current HRE offerings highlight aspects of the human rights system that came out of the mid to late 1940s. Our definition of HRE must be expanded to include teaching about the UDHR and subsequent law, the UN human rights monitoring system, human rights violations or problems by topic or region, and human rights movements. I've spoken to many faculty who do not know about the human rights system and believe any social justice issue should be considered a human rights topic and course, without necessarily addressing the context of the human rights regime. To be considered HRE, a course must include a reference to human rights per se; thus, instructors of such courses must ensure that the language and literature of human rights underpins their syllabus. Social justice classes could make up part of a human rights degree but only when sequenced into a coherent curriculum that is primarily devoted to human rights. I argue for the expansion of HRE by following the consensus derived from the documents reviewed below. And I discuss the role of social justice education in Chapter 5, though first I want to be clear about the consensus on HRE from those who have delineated it.

Formal definitions include the following five points presented in 1991 by the H-Human-Rights Network of Amnesty International USA:

1. **HUMAN RIGHTS EDUCATION** declares a commitment to those human rights expressed in the Universal Declaration of Human Rights of 1948, the UN Covenants, and the United States Bill of Rights. It asserts the responsibility to respect, protect, and promote the rights of all people.

2. **HUMAN RIGHTS EDUCATION** promotes democratic principles. It examines human rights issues without bias and from diverse perspectives through a variety of educational practices.

3. **HUMAN RIGHTS EDUCATION** helps to develop the communication skills and informed critical thinking essential to a democracy. It provides multicultural and historical perspectives on the universal struggle for justice and dignity.

4. **HUMAN RIGHTS EDUCATION** engages the heart as well as the mind. It challenges students to ask what human rights mean to them personally and encourages them to translate caring into informed, nonviolent action.

5. **HUMAN RIGHTS EDUCATION** affirms the interdependence of the human family. It promotes understanding of the complex global forces that create abuses, as well as the ways in which abuses can be abolished and avoided.[60]

It is worth highlighting that HRE is recognized to be concerned with more than the simple acquisition of knowledge; it simultaneously entails teaching empathy and engagement as well as teaching for action. These three agendas appear repeatedly in definitions of HRE. In 1994 the Plan of Action for the UN Decade for Human Rights Education (1995–2004) defined the goal of HRE as

the building of a universal culture of human rights through the imparting of knowledge and skills and the moulding of attitudes which are directed to:

a) The strengthening of respect for human rights and fundamental freedoms;

b) The full development of the human personality and the sense of its dignity;

c) The promotion of understanding, tolerance, gender equality, and friendship among all nations, indigenous peoples and racial, national, ethnic, religious and linguistic groups;

d) The enabling of all persons to participate effectively in a free society;

e) The furtherance of the activities of the United Nations for the maintenance of peace.[61]

The decade produced the 2011 UNDHRET, which has the most widely cited definition.

Human rights education and training encompasses:

(a) Education *about* human rights, which includes providing knowledge and understanding of human rights norms and principles, the values that underpin them and the mechanisms for their protection;

(b) Education *through* human rights, which includes learning and teaching in a way that respects the rights of both educators and learners;

(c) Education *for* human rights, which includes empowering persons to enjoy and exercise their rights and to respect and uphold the rights of others.[62]

This list emphasizes knowledge, rights of the learners, and empowerment to exercise rights: education *about*, *through*, and *for* human rights. The World Programme document adds "reinforcing *attitudes* and *behavior* which uphold human rights."[63]

Lastly, it is helpful to review the academic scholarship on HRE definitions. Nancy Flowers interviewed more than fifty human rights practitioners worldwide about what HRE should consist of, and, interestingly, the "doers," as she calls them, came up with a parallel list of essentials for HRE as the two most important UN documents for defining HRE—namely, WP and UNDHRET. They agreed about the following:

• HRE must be explicitly grounded in human rights principles as expressed in the UN Charter, UDHR, and subsequent human rights documents. [*about* human rights]

• The methods used to teach human rights must be consistent with human rights values. [*through* human rights]

• HRE must be more than knowledge about human rights documents. It must involve the whole person and address skills and attitudes as well. [*for* human rights]

- HRE must lead to action, both in individual lives and in the local and global communities. [*for* human rights][64]

Felisa Tibbitts has written that most human rights faculty hope to teach "content, critical thinking, values, and social action,"[65] which is different phrasing for very similar key competencies.

Garth Meintjes argues that HRE is fundamentally different from what Paulo Freire calls "banking education" in his *Pedagogy of the Oppressed*.[66] Banking education is based on handing knowledge down from educator to student. The recipient is passive. But Meintjes believes HRE should have a different "psychological impact" that empowers learners to act.[67] Anja Mihr and Hans Peter Schmitz augment the definition with the need to teach emotional awareness of violations to elicit "personal and emotional re-action against human rights abuses."[68] This call for HRE to inform attitudes is aligned with the "57.8 percent of professors [who] believe it is important to encourage undergraduates to become agents of social change."[69] Moni-sha Bajaj, who reviews definitions of human rights, finds that scholars and practitioners "agree that HRE must include both content and process related to human rights." She further finds goals for "cognitive (content), attitudinal or emotive (values/skills), and action-oriented components."[70]

The definition of HRE as providing education *about*, *through*, and *for* human rights offers the analytic framework for both assessing and making recommendations for HRE in higher education for two reasons: First, we find a great deal of consistency among disparate groups thinking about essential components of HRE. A broad agreement for this definition can thus be inferred. Second, these three elements provide the framework for designing radical HRE curriculum with the potential for transformation. When we teach students the content of HRE—explicitly referencing the UN human rights system, including the laws and treaties underpinning it—run a classroom based on human rights principles, and teach skills for advocacy, we equip and empower them to become promoters and protectors of human rights.

Human Rights and Social Justice

We are now well positioned to distinguish between social justice and human rights, which will help illuminate what HRE offers over and above a non-rights-centered social justice education. In Chapter 4, I extol the virtue of bringing elements of social justice education into the human rights classroom, but here I want to elucidate the differences.

Human rights refers to something very specific. While the finer details may be up for debate, none would likely dispute that a set of norms, principles, and laws stemming from the UDHR comprise the core. Further, enforcement mechanisms and institutions devoted to defending and promoting human rights exist. The definition of social justice, by contrast, though a pervasive and widely accepted agenda for many, suffers more contestation. It is significantly more encompassing, leaving it open to meaning "everything and nothing."[71] Human rights can complement and support social justice, though. As Charles Beitz has written, the former has the potential to provide the necessary conditions for the latter. If social justice is about fighting oppression and striving for social equality, demanding that human rights be respected in all the detail given in the UDHR provides a map to get us there. The so-called human rights regime provides the tools and mechanisms for achieving social justice. In any event, the two phrases do not have identical meanings, so they must not be used interchangeably.

The Role of Critique: A Theory of HRE

Human rights education should be based on critical analysis and grounded in human rights. While it may be obvious to say that human rights is the basis of the knowledge, requiring that human rights be the basis of how we teach and the basis for affecting students requires more explanation. These ideas are fleshed out in the second part of the book, but here I offer a brief explanation of my theory and the relevant terms. Flowers has written about the need for a relevant theory,[72] and a few other scholars have made recommendations that a theory embed some element of critique that is explicated below. However, a complete theory of human rights education has not been established. Here I argue that human rights and critical analysis should not only be essential aspects of HRE, but they should also serve as its theoretical basis. This will inform our approach to the pedagogy of HRE: the knowledge we teach, the way we teach, and our goal of empowering people to transform themselves and society.

Academics have written about the need for a critical pedagogy,[73] critical consciousness,[74] thoughtful criticism,[75] critical compassion,[76] and critical reflection[77] in HRE. In Chapter 4, I add that explicitly teaching critical thinking will aid each of these agendas. Though each emphasizes a different aspect of HRE, they overlap. For example, for André Keet, the necessity of a critical pedagogy is a reaction to his conclusion that HRE was co-opted "into a conservative, 'declarationist' frame." He found that HRE is being defined by declarations of human rights rather than including a wider scope of what constitutes human rights. The correction, according to Keet, is to make it "anti-declarationist" and including "perspectivism, particularism and universalism."[78] It must involve "a radical decolonial critical theory."[79]

Henry Steiner calls us to critique the human rights movement. He writes, "The university should have a significant critical component. By 'critical,' I mean an approach that challenges and problematizes some fundamental aspects of the movement. . . . A critical approach should be open to rethinking norms and institutions."[80]

Michalinos Zembylas discusses the role of emotions and the need to teach students to have informed sentimentality and compassion as opposed to ineffective or "empty" emotional reactions. He explains, "Critical compassion is further cultivated if students begin to understand the conditions (structural inequalities, poverty, globalization, etc.). . . . But mere understanding is clearly not enough; students will become more susceptible to affective transformation when they enact compassionate action."[81]

Meintjes recommends that a goal of HRE be to teach a specific conscious approach to human rights. He says that instead of teaching statically about the history and content of human rights, for example, "we should accept the more difficult challenge of identifying and assessing the development of each student's own critical conscious, and creative thinking in which a strong respect for human rights is consistently reflected. In other words, . . . the development of a critical human rights consciousness."[82]

Ron Dudai insists on the need to reflect critically on human rights practices: "From the outside, the work of human rights activists can seem to have an absolutist quality. The public claims and demands of human rights organizations and movements appear coherent and uncompromising, clearly articulating the right and wrong of a given situation or policy, unambiguously demanding a remedy, showing little doubt, speaking truth to power; human rights may be the weapon of the weak, but they are claimed with confidence and certainty. Yet from the inside, the world of human rights practice is fraught with dilemmas."[83] He goes on to list numerous dilemmas requiring analysis, including the demand to determine the action for greater good among several choices without always having sufficient information or having to choose between two ills. And it is exactly the role of academia to be shouldering this mantle.[84] If universities play a role in empowering for action, then it is their job to be concomitantly analytical about such action.

Well-reasoned critique is an essential function of higher education, and critical analysis is inherent in the agenda of the human rights project to disrupt rights-disrespecting elements of the status quo. After all, human rights documents critique the actions of governments, NGOs must analyze the problems and events they aim to improve, and social movements must critique societal blind spots and norms that endanger human rights. Therefore, all education *about* human rights should have a strong element of critique and critical analysis, which are terms I use synonymously. This is not to say criticism isn't already being taught and written about. To teach human rights almost necessarily involves a critical analysis of history, current events, and the status quo.[85] Books such as *The Endtimes of Human Rights*,[86] *The Last Utopia*,[87] *Human Rights: A Political & Cultural Critique*,[88] and *Who Believes in Human Rights?*[89] are analyzing and questioning the very ideas and ideals of human rights. *A Bed for the Night: Humanitarianism in Crisis*[90] and *The Crisis Caravan: What's Wrong with Humanitarian Aid?*[91] are examples of books that both question and critique human rights practices. The needed elements are there, but a codified program of human rights education can ensure that human rights and critical analysis are baked into both the skills and the content we teach (education *about* human rights), as well as our approaches to teaching (education *through* human rights), while serving as a reminder that our goalpost includes teaching for attitudes and empowerment (educating *for* human rights).

In short, I am advocating for critical pedagogy. Critical pedagogy theorists exist on a continuum, though, and I locate myself at the moderate end of what is, admittedly, a radical scale. To the extent that pedagogy needs to promote democratic principles in the classroom in order to facilitate true democracy in society, I want to use it. To the extent to which critical pedagogy emphasizes "question-posing" and "reflection, dialogue, and action,"[92] I want to use it. However, I am not at the end of the critical pedagogy theory spectrum that demands that we completely decenter faculty authority in the classroom or overthrow economic and political structures with no plan for a viable alternative. My goals are, perhaps, more modest. Implementation of critical pedagogy is a consistent theme throughout the second half of this book. Because "there does not exist a homogeneous representation for the universal implementation of any form of critical theory or critical pedagogy,"[93] here is what I mean by a critical pedagogy for HRE: it must include the hallmark practices of questioning, critiquing, and analyzing all ideas; it critiques relationships of power in the world at large and in the classroom; and it includes a constant emphasis on critical thinking and empowerment.

It is appropriate to note that critical pedagogy is happening in human rights fieldwork. The idea of a top-down approach to helping others is increasingly understood as patronizing and less likely to offer the sufferers of violations the remedies they would seek. Participation by the targets of an intervention in its cocreation is now considered best practice, because it involves the empowerment, education, and support of the oppressed in identifying sustainable solutions. This participatory aspect is key to critical pedagogy, whether inside the classroom or out.

In summation, the explication of and mandates for HRE in human rights documents clearly lay the groundwork to support the argument that HRE is ready to be codified with its basis in critical pedagogy. We need universal HRE, and those of us at the fore must supply the working definition and a cohesive plan of action for how to implement it. Only then will it be possible to promote a comprehensive and coherent HRE curriculum for higher education. The next chapter surveys what is already taking place in HRE at the tertiary level, focusing mainly on the US, UK, and Canada with a brief global snapshot, and then proceeds to the heart of the argument for disciplining rights in the third chapter.

Chapter 2

The Current State of HRE in Higher Education: Confusion or Consensus?

> *Where, after all, do universal human rights begin? In small places, close*
> *to home—so close and so small that they cannot be seen on any maps of*
> *the world. Yet they are the world of the individual person; the*
> *neighborhood he lives in; the school or college [s]he attends.*
>   —Eleanor Roosevelt

Having reviewed the mandate for HRE, let's explore what is currently offered in higher education throughout the world. First we look at where such courses and degree programs are located, and then we analyze their content. This chapter demonstrates that certain human rights topics are almost universally taught. However, more often the content lacks consistency, thus highlighting discrepancies in what different faculty deem essential HRE for undergraduate students. That said, analyzing what is most often taught reveals a limited but undeniable consensus about many aspects of a curriculum for human rights, which can form the basis for more structured curricular components for HRE. The consensus is largely about knowledge—that is, education *about* human rights. Academia is not yet widely responding to the call for education *through* and *for* human rights. In what follows, I propose that if human rights programs consistently incorporate the knowledge content from the existing consensus, supplement with recommendations from the international documents, and root that in a critical pedagogy, HRE will mature into the more radical and effective academic program it should be. Likewise, it will then be structured in a way that makes it practical and sensible for colleges and universities to build more HRE into their institutions.

Surveying the Globe for HRE

The sources for the following research came from the few (not comprehensive) websites cataloging HRE programs, including the UN Office of the High Commissioner for Human Rights' (OHCHR's) Database on Human Rights Education and Training[1] and simple web searches. I also analyzed the websites of colleges and universities listed in *US News and World Report*'s top-ranked 150 institutions, relied on the US Department of Education database, and emailed colleagues to inquire about activity in their regions of the world. As it was not possible to be comprehensive, the goal was to survey the field thoroughly enough to recognize patterns in what is being taught and to harness that wisdom to forge the path for systemic HRE.

The accounting of existing HRE programs is sparse. Only a fraction of the estimated seventeen thousand universities in the world offer systematic HRE. On the other hand, one may simultaneously observe that HRE is pervasive because it has spread across the globe, especially through single course offerings. Hundreds, if not thousands, of courses with "human rights" in the title are offered in higher education around the world: several hundred were easily identified in Canada and the United States alone. In Europe our search yielded dozens, and there are still more in South Africa, Uganda, Ghana, and in India's numerous universities. In the Middle East we see undergraduate human rights courses in Egypt and Israel; and Argentina, Guatemala, Mexico, and Peru have offerings in South America.

As illustrated in Table 1, at least thirty-five universities are known to offer a Bachelor of Arts (or equivalent) program in human rights. Though most don't confer degrees in human rights, universities all over the world offer HRE. David Suárez and Patricia Bromley reported that as of 2000, over 140 universities in 59 countries have "academic chairs, research centers, and programs for human rights."[2] In addition to courses at the undergraduate level, one can pursue work at the master's and doctoral level. After law degrees, master's degrees in human rights are the most commonly offered, and BAs follow that. A few universities offer a PhD, a PhD minor, or a PhD with a concentration in human rights. For example, the University

Table 1. Countries with BA Programs in Human Rights

Region	Universities (by country)
Africa	Uganda: Martyrs University, Makerere University
Asia	Australia: Australian National University, Monash University, University of Adelaide
	India: Annamalie University, Dhanvantari Institute of Professional Education, Kurukshetra University, Loretto College, and the Universities of Mumbai and Mysore
Europe	England: Essex and Kingston Universities
	Ireland: National University of Ireland
	Italy: Universita Degli Studi Di Padova
Latin America	Argentina: Universidad de Lanus
	Columbia: Universidad de Alcalá
	Guatemala: Universidad de San Carlos de Guatemala
	Mexico: Universidad Autonoma de Chiapas, Universidad del Claustro de Sor Juana, Universidad del Sur
	Peru: Pontificia Universidad Católica del Perú
North America	Canada: Carleton University, St. Thomas University, York University, Wilfrid Laurier University, University of Ottawa, University of Winnipeg
	US: Bard College, Barnard College, Columbia University, University of Connecticut, University of Dayton, Southern Methodist University, Trinity College, Webster University

of Essex offers a PhD, the University of Minnesota and Indiana University both offer a PhD minor, and Columbia University offers a PhD with concentration.[3]

In the US as of 2010, more than 900 colleges and universities[4] allowed students to design their own majors. Because educational clearinghouses do not collect information on what courses of study are elected in self-designed majors, we cannot know how many students obtain human rights degrees this way but anecdotal evidence reveals that some do. An undergraduate can also get a minor or a certificate in human rights or have a concentration in human rights within another major. In looking at the top-ranked 150 institutions on the *US News and World Report* website,[5] we found that 35 of them offered a minor, certificate, concentration, or two of these. It is likely that dozens more colleges and universities offer one of these options, since teaching human rights is increasingly common in the more than 3,000 US universities.

Since the specific focus of this book is tertiary pedagogy, what follows is an examination of undergraduate curricula, including programs and individual courses.

Analyzing the Data

There is currently little uniformity across HRE programs or class offerings in higher education as revealed by degree titles, the content of undergraduate programs, and the content of introduction to human rights course syllabi. The information available, however, does offer clear indications of what faculty think are the essential topics and skills. Our data was gleaned from publicly available information on university websites, which are subject to change, and course offerings, which can fluctuate. Nonetheless, patterns are discernable.

The difference in the titles of the undergraduate degrees is illustrative of the variety of foci in them. In England, human rights is always attached to another subject, such as criminal studies, history, or political science. In Canada, BAs are available in Conflict Studies and Human Rights,[6] Human Rights and Social Justice,[7] Human Rights and Equity Studies,[8] Human Rights and Human Diversity,[9] or just Human Rights.[10] In Greece, Aristotle University of Thessaloniki has a human rights program called Contemporary World Problems and the Scientist's Responsibility.[11] Makerere University in Uganda offers a degree in Ethics and Human Rights.[12] Unlike some of the degree programs abroad, where the emphases are made clear by the degree titles, BA titles in the United States have very little variation, usually titled Human Rights or Human Rights Studies.

Though the names of the BA programs in the US are the same or similar, the content is not. For the last decade, not a single course has been common among them. At three of the eight universities (University of Connecticut, Barnard, and Bard), students choose courses for their degree from a limited set, but no one course is required of all who complete the degree. As of early 2019, at Connecticut students choose one course from three categories of courses: institutions and laws (five classes offered); history, philosophy, and theory (six classes offered); and applications and methods (twelve classes offered). The rest of the degree is made up of twelve credits from sets of forty-two electives. At Barnard students choose from either Introduction to Human Rights or Human Rights in Theory and Practice. And then they must take two courses from a list of about twenty-nine courses. Finally they choose three "related courses" from the entire course catalog. These three university programs are the least structured HRE programs in the US.

The other five US institutions have from three to ten required courses, and the most common is an introduction to human rights, though not all programs with set requirements offer it. For example, Southern Methodist University (SMU) has required courses, but an introductory course is not one of them. On the other hand, most have several courses from this set: an introduction to human rights, a history of human rights, a philosophy or theory course, a course focusing on human rights law, and a politics of human rights course. Less often, a methods course is required.[13]

In Canada there are also differences in undergraduate human rights degree programs. The number of courses required for each major varies from two to eight. York University and the University of Winnipeg each have at least five required courses, but it is not clear that they offer the three most common courses: an introduction, theory, or history of human rights. Winnipeg's course Concepts and Conventions in Human Rights is described as introductory, though it also requires two courses with "introduction" in the title: Introduction to Global Citizenship and Introduction to Women's and Gender Studies. York requires a course called Human Rights and Global Economy. These latter three courses indicate the different emphases in the two programs.

Universities in South America and England differ from North American institutions in that almost the entire undergraduate degree is made up of required courses. Essex offers six BAs in human rights, because students must pair it with one of the following: history, journalism, Latin American studies, philosophy, political science, or sociology. All the students take the same three year-long courses (or modules, as they are called in the UK): Foundations of Human Rights, Human Rights Organizations, and Special Issues in Human Rights. In the three-year program, only one to three optional courses are allowed—no long lists of electives here. This is also the case for the three Kingston programs, which are joint BAs of human rights

Table 2. BA in Human Rights Degrees in the US

University	Credits for major	Required Human Rights courses	Semi-required (from a list)	Electives (from a list or unspecified)	Other requirements
Bard College	36	0	4 (choose from a list of human rights core courses)	3 (human rights–related electives from a list)	5 courses (related to another disciplinary focus and a senior capstone)
Barnard College	33	0	3 (choose 1 of 2, and choose 2 from a list of 30 courses)	3	Senior thesis and another major
University of Connecticut	36	0	3 (choose 1 from courses under Institutions and Laws; History, Philosophy, Theory; Applications and Methods)	4 (from a list of about 50 courses)	1 capstone and 4 "approved" electives
Columbia University	31 "points"	3 (Intro, International Law, Senior Seminar)	3 (from 4 "categories" of topics)	0	4 courses focusing on another discipline

Table 2. (continued)

University	Credits for major	Required Human Rights courses	Semi-required (from a list)	Electives (from a list or unspecified)	Other requirements
University of Dayton	48	8 (including Intro, Capstone, Philosophy of, Politics of, Intl Law and Orgs, Faith Traditions and)	6 (from different fields, including economics, history, philosophy and political science, religious studies, and sociology courses)	0	3–6 experiential or research courses
Southern Methodist University	30	4 (America's Dilemma, Gender and, Politics and Legacies of Civil Rights, Ethics and	3 (from Gender and Human Rights track, Human Rights track, Public Policy and Human Rights track)	3 (from approved list)	2nd major or minor
Trinity College	33	3 (Intro, Philosophical Foundations of, Intl Law and)	2 "specialized electives"	5 "general electives"	Senior thesis or project
Webster University	42	7 (including Intro, Current Problems, Methods of Inquiry, Law, Theories of)	1 either: Social and Political Philosophy or Intro to Political Theory	6 (3 must have an HRTS prefix)	Senior overview

Table 3. Canadian BAs and Courses

University	Title of degree	Required courses	Other courses offered
Carleton University	BA Honours Human Rights and Social Justice	• Human Rights: Theories and Foundations • Power Relations and Human Rights	• Intro to Human Rights • Human Rights: Issues and Investigations • Selected Topics in Legal Studies • Social Justice and Human Rights • Philosophy of Human Rights • Politics of Human Rights
St. Thomas University	Human Rights	• Intro to Human Rights • Research Methods • Philosophy of Human Rights or Human Rights in Theory and Practice • The Rights Revolution or Discrimination and the Law in Canada • International Human Rights or Crimes Against Humanity • Capstone Seminar	• Human Rights and Literature • Non-Western Perspectives on Human Rights • Discrimination and the Law in Canada • Philosophy of Human Rights • Human Rights in Theory and Practice • Genocide, War Crimes, and Crimes Against Humanity • Human Rights Internship • The Rights Revolution in Canada • International Human Rights • Activism and Social Justice • Human Rights Advocacy through Social Media • Human Rights and Foreign Policy
University of Ottawa	Honours BSocSC in Conflict Studies and Human Rights	• Intro to the Study of Conflicts and Human Rights • Workshop in Essay Writing	• Lit and Composition • Intro to Macroeconomics • Micro Economics • Politics and Globalization • Canada and the Challenges of International Development • Intro to Human Rights Law • Quantitative Methods in Conflict Studies and Human Rights

Table 3. (continued)

University	Title of degree	Required courses	Other courses offered
Wilfrid Laurier University	Human Rights and Human Diversity	• Human Rights and Human Diversity • Intro to HRTS • Multiculturalism • Professional Seminar • Phil of Human Rights • Methods • Capstone	• Designing Digital and Social Media • Fundraising • Human Rights Education • Project Management • Roots, Race, Resistance: Post-Colonial Literature • Canadian Labour History • Indigenous Perspectives on Globalization
University of Winnipeg	3-year BA in Human Rights 4-year BA in Human Rights	• Intro to Global Citizenship • Intro to Women's and Gender Studies • Concepts and Conv. in HRTS • History of HRTS in Canada • Colonization and Aboriginal Peoples • HRTS Institutions • Models of Transitional Justice	• Practicum and Capstone in Human Rights required for 4-year BA students HRTS Electives: • Emerging Issues in Human Rights • Refugees, Resettlement, and Resilience • Global Human Rights Advocacy • Special Topics in Human Rights • Human Rights and Civil Liberties in Canada • Human Rights, Human Security, and the UN • Human Rights and Conflict Resolution • Chinese & East Asian Perspectives on Human Rights • Human and Indigenous Rights in Latin America • Post-Conflict Truth, Memory, and Reconciliation • Independent Study in Human Rights

Table 3. (continued)

University	Title of degree	Required courses	Other courses offered
York University	Human Rights and Equity Studies	• Intro to HRTS & Equity Studies • HRTS and Global Economy • Research Methods in Equity Studies • HRTS and the CA Charter of Rights and Freedoms • Social Theories and HRTS • Research Seminar	• Social Change in Canada • Women and Human Rights • Globalization and the Human Condition • Deviance, HRTS & Social Control • International Human Rights and Children • Equity and Human Rights in Schooling • Social Theories and Human Rights • Social Justice Theory and Practice

with either criminology, history, or sociology. None of the universities in South America allow more than a few electives, if any.

The variety in the list of semi-required courses—those courses where students choose one from a small list—is quite large in the North American universities. Further, the number of electives that can be applied to the human rights degrees is in the hundreds when the eight US BA programs are counted together. There are about forty different fields that students can take courses from as part of their electives for a BA in human rights. These range from African American studies, anthropology and art history, to economics, English, engineering, environmental studies, Jewish studies, political science, psychology, media communications, management and organizations, to urban studies. Almost none of the courses offered have "human rights" in the title. They include just the regular offerings in the departments. Some, like African American and environmental studies, might have more obvious connections to human rights, but others in art history or engineering might require more imagination to connect the dots, and none of the courses likely offers the context of human rights framing. The important point is that currently it is left up to the students to relate these outside courses to human rights. This is a weak educational strategy. Offering students guidance in making these leaps ensures that they will not neglect information that is useful or necessary—something a dedicated human rights discipline will provide.

The American Association for the Advancement of Science, for example, has a website with syllabi from various sciences that have a human rights, or related, focus. They have posted courses in Technology and Human Rights, Human Rights and the Environment, and Humanitarian Engineering, among others. It would not be difficult to include more disciplines in a human rights degree while at the same time making the role of human rights in them explicit. However, students in North American universities presently have a much less focused academic program than students in England and South America.

Undergraduate degrees in different countries require courses with topics specific to their own social and political environment. That they have regional differences makes sense. After all, to paraphrase Eleanor Roosevelt, human rights begin close to home. In Canada, both Winnipeg University and York University require Human Rights and the Canadian Charter of Rights and Freedoms. The Universidad Nacional de Lanús in Argentina requires Argentine History and Human Rights (Historia Argentina y Derechos Humanos) and Historical Configuration of Human Rights in Latin America (Configuracion Historica de los Derechos Humanos en America Latina). The Colombian Universidad Pedagogica Nacional requires Human Rights in Colombia (Derechos Humanos en Colombia). The Mexican Universidad del Claustro de Sor Juana requires Modern Mexican Problems (Problemas del México Actual) and Public Institutions of Mexico (Instituciones Públicas de México). In India, Kurukshetra University requires Human Rights and Duties in India and Societal Issues of Human Rights in India. Comparatively, the US is an oddity because, except for SMU, when surveying by course title, no other BA has a single required course about human rights issues that are particular to the US.[14] (The University of Connecticut offers Human Rights in the US, but it is not required.)

Patterns in the Introduction to Human Rights Course

Surveying over thirty introductory course syllabi from several countries (primarily the US), reveals more coherence than when comparing whole curricula. There are a few core topics that occur in nearly every syllabus, but perhaps because there is not a classic introductory textbook, the foci of the courses vary considerably. It is typical for a semester-long course to move from topic to topic with readings from a variety of sources. I found no course that relied on a single text, and some courses had reading selections from as many as twenty-five different sources over the semester. Many begin the course in a similar manner, but as the course progresses the faculty diverge widely in what they present from one course to another. Most commonly, the first week introduces origins of human rights or the Universal Declaration of Human Rights, followed by the theory or philosophies behind it. Syllabi list questions about the meaning of the term "human," the definition of "human rights," and "universality" versus "cultural relativism." Some provide readings about the history of human rights, and some spend time on civil and political, economic, and social and cultural rights. The similarities end there, and construction of the rest of the course is likely driven by individual faculty interest or expertise. The many subjects of introductory courses include Asia and human rights, business or corporations and human rights, children's and women's rights, food security, the Geneva Conventions or humanitarian intervention, genocide, globalization, health and human rights, human trafficking, nongovernmental organizations, poverty, refugees, social movements, torture, transitional justice, human rights law and regional instruments, and the United Nations. This wide interpretation of what counts as introductory material mirrors the diversity in faculty understanding of what should be considered human rights material.

Room for Debate

Thus far, what should be concluded from comparing the content of the BA degrees and the content of introduction to human rights syllabi? That degree titles and degree emphases differ would not necessarily indicate a weakness in HRE, but it could point to a lack of agreement on foundational content. Also, globally, there is little agreement about how focused and narrow a program of study should be. This is not unique to the HRE field.

For example, US colleges and universities have a long tradition of requiring a broad-based general education of undergraduates. Often US students are required to take a year or two of general education courses before they can pursue their major. In the UK and in South America, students study for their major immediately upon entering university. Their admission is based on their fitness for the particular degree. In the US, on the other hand, students are admitted on suitability to the university and are often free to enter undecided about what they want to study. The US has always placed an emphasis on the role of electives in undergraduate education. It is common for up to 70 percent of the courses in a 120-credit requirement to be outside one's major. The typical human rights BA has 32 credits of requirements, and for many of the BAs even many of those are based on student choice and not strict requirements in human rights.

It is illustrative to compare a degree in human rights to a degree in biology. In examining a dozen university biology degrees in the US—Ivy League and universities with human rights BAs—we find most BAs in biology require four or five standardized courses: Introductory Biology I, Introductory Biology II, genetics, ecology, and often evolution. In addition to the biology core, most of them require general chemistry, organic chemistry, physics, and statistics or biostatistics. A student majoring in biology is consumed with the field for the entirety of their undergraduate studies (after completing general education requirements) rather than being offered a superficial survey of information. It is also clear what they should know upon graduating, as up to a dozen courses may be required.

It is even more striking to compare a biology minor with many of the human rights minors and certificates that haven't a single required course. All of the biology minors require multiple foundational biology courses. Some human rights minors and concentrations allow students to choose from lists of courses rather than specifying any particular required courses. This permits some students to complete a minor without taking an introduction to human rights. The danger of this is egregious omissions. A graduate of an East Coast university mentioned to me that she learned nothing about the United Nations in her human rights minor, for example. To specialize in human rights at university, in any depth, should require at least a passing familiarity with the essential role of the UN in the regime of human rights, just as we would expect a student of biology to know something about DNA.

The lack of consistency in foundational topics in US human rights degrees is problematic and due partly to the fact that curricula are not always designed systematically (most likely because of resource constraints). Institutions rarely bless a new degree program with release time for faculty to do research for a new curriculum, much less offer them funds for new faculty to provide expertise in academic areas in which the institution may be lacking. And as has been mentioned, it is likely that most current faculty have not been academically trained with a doctorate in human rights. Degree programs are designed to take advantage of the local expertise and faculty resources already at hand. These factors help explain the variability in the BA programs, which can be overcome by employing the suggestions in the second half of this book.

Again, knowing that a student is working toward a human rights degree in the US reveals little about what they are actually studying. Defining human rights as an academic discipline would require standardizing offerings thereby ameliorating any vagaries in programs. Some academics defend the differences by arguing that human rights is particularly interdisciplinary, that it is wrong to expect uniformity in degrees, and that offering students a wide variety of courses to choose from is appropriate in an interdisciplinary field such as human rights. (I address the assertion of interdisciplinarity in the next chapter.) While some knowledge of human rights is fundamental to many other fields, it is to students' detriment that some universities confer human rights degrees in this way. Educational research explains that unfocused curricula "often permit naïve students broad choices among courses resulting in markedly different outcomes from those originally imagined."[15] This cited research does not include the field of human rights. So in how much more danger of graduating without the necessary knowledge and skills is a student in a lesser-codified field? In offering a degree, concentration, or certificate, universities are declaring the importance of the subject matter. And by teaching human rights, we are making a statement to our students that we want them to have knowledge and tools in that particular subject. Focused curricula do not have to negate introducing students to the breadth of the subject. A degree program can achieve specific learning objectives that include exposure to a big topic such as human rights. Without providing the parameters that a discipline provides, however, it becomes less certain that students have available a curricular map to guide them.

If the current degree programs are creating successful learning environments based on sound learning outcomes and educational practices, they are idiosyncratic and dependent on strong faculty particular to the institution. This is good for the students who attend their programs. If we want to embed human rights education more thoroughly in higher education, however, it needs to be built on transparent and transferable principles. Again, defining human rights as an academic discipline will provide the guidance.

Emergent Consensus

There is an emergent consensus around which we can design a discipline of human rights. Briefly stated, the discipline is rooted in a recognition that human rights is, first and foremost, defined by the human rights regime—that is, the declarations, laws, and main actors (governments, businesses, NGOs, and civil society). Most introductory courses contain a focus on some aspect(s) of these. The most common courses in the BAs also focus on the regime in courses on human rights history, human rights law, philosophy and theories related to human rights, politics and international relations and human rights, as well as international organizations and nongovernmental organizations. Another aspect of the consensus is that the language of human rights is applicable to many kinds of problems and abuses. Finally, there is a pattern of universities in different countries focusing on human rights issues that are particular to their nation.

It is illustrative to compare how degree programs define themselves with the call for education to be *about, through,* and *for* human rights.

Comparing Curricula to Definitions of HRE: Less Consensus

Remember that the UN definition of HRE emphasized education *about* human rights, *through* human rights, and *for* human rights. Education *about* human rights is teaching the knowledge of the human rights regime and the skills used in learning human rights. Education *through* human rights indicates an approach to the treatment of students and maintaining a classroom dynamic that is in accord with human rights values. Education *for* human rights means developing an attitude for living human rights or taking action for human rights.

Upon examining how US universities describe their BAs on their websites, one finds an emphasis almost solely on teaching the knowledge and academic skills they hope to impart. Not one of these sites mentions the objective to base their mode of relationship with their students on human rights principles. Surely it is hoped that human rights would be behind every course, but it is worth asking ourselves as faculty if we are taking all steps necessary to create an environment where everyone feels equal and everyone is heard. For example, when a group of students is discussing a controversy and is divided ideologically—surely more often the case than not—the faculty must have dexterity in navigating treacherous waters of discussion while modeling and teaching the skills of civility and tolerance. (Teaching best practices in these situations is reviewed in more detail in Chapter 5.)

Teaching attitudes or activism on behalf of human rights is rarely mentioned in published program literature. There are a few exceptions: University of Dayton, a Roman Catholic institution in Ohio, explains that one goal of their degree program is "intended to produce thoughtful and transformational servant-leaders who will apply the knowledge and skills obtained in the program to contemporary human rights issues and situations both domestically and internationally."[16] Another religiously affiliated institution, Southern Methodist University, has the mission of educating "students . . . to understand, promote, and defend human rights."[17] Trinity College explains that it "is committed to excellence in the study and practice of human rights."[18] Columbia University's human rights website states: "The Undergraduate Human Rights Program seeks to engage students in this dynamic and evolving field and to enhance their knowledge, skills, and commitment to human rights."[19]

In England, Essex University offers a detailed list of aims and learning outcomes for their various degrees in human rights. The website does not use the words "attitude" or "commitment," but it does state the aim of providing "a deep and critical knowledge of human rights and their practical application, and provide an unparalleled preparation for entering into or returning to human rights practice or further study."[20] They clearly intend to teach *for* human rights.

Carleton University in Canada lists five thematic areas but none mentions educating for attitudes or activism. The latter is at least mentioned, though: "The city and the university also play host to national and international visitors who offer insights into human rights activism."[21] Australian National University emphasizes understanding the practice of human rights—"Courses in this major address the human rights discipline in both theory and practice"—but their learning outcomes do not include teaching students how to be active for human rights.[22]

Again, most other university websites emphasize teaching knowledge, as Malmo University in Sweden does: "This three-year bachelor's programme provides you with an in-depth knowledge of human rights and how they are applied and affected by the world we live in."[23] Occasionally a university offers a course focused on advocacy and activism, which demonstrates that some faculty show intent to provide education *for* human rights. In general, however, ambiguity seems to exist in many institutions about the role of teaching attitudes and activism. Most faculty have received more training in knowledge acquisition than advocacy, so it is natural that teaching for direct advocacy is less common in academe. However, by offering a degree in human rights or teaching human rights courses in one's own department, one is making a statement that human rights is a topic of importance. It most likely implies a desire to create at least a human rights consciousness in students, which further implies developing an attitude in support of universal human rights. But the relationship of attitudes to advocacy requires further exploration, because to what extent does developing attitudes for human rights equal teaching students to advocate for them? (A more thorough discussion of this important issue in human rights pedagogy also occurs in Chapter 5.)

Recommendations in International Documents

A wealth of curricular advice for human rights has already been published in the international documents. Even though these documents are primarily focused on educational settings other than higher education, they offer many recommendations that are well suited for consideration here. A goal of this chapter has been to compare the mandate for HRE that exists internationally, for schools and fieldwork, with what is actually happening in higher education. The five publications with recommendations for HRE are (1) *The Human Rights Education Handbook: Effective Practices for Learning, Action, and Change* by Nancy Flowers, published by the Human Rights Resource Center at the University of Minnesota;[24] (2) *Human Rights Education in the School Systems of Europe, Central Asia and North America: A Compendium of Good Practice*, a publication of the OSCE, Council of Europe, and the UN;[25] (3) the *Council of Europe Charter on Education for Democratic Citizenship and Human Rights Education*;[26] (4) the OSCE's *Guidelines on Human Rights Education for Secondary School Systems*;[27] and (5) the Asia Pacific Forum's *Human Rights Education: A Manual for National Human Rights Institutions*.[28]

One finds a remarkable consensus that HRE consists of all three elements of education being *about* human rights, *through* human rights, and *for* human rights. Of the five documents listed above, the three that were published before 2011, when HRE was first defined by those three terms,

Table 4. What the Documents Recommend for Teaching About, *Through*, and For Human Rights

About *Through* <u>For</u>	Nancy Flowers: *HRE Handbook* (2000)	OSCE, CoE, and UN: *HRE in School Systems Compendium* (2009)*	CoE: "Charter on Education for Democratic Citizenship and HRE" (2010)*	OSCE: *Guidelines on HRE for Secondary School Systems* (2012)	Asia Pacific Forum: *Manual for NHRIs* (2017)
History of the Human Rights Movement	R	N/A	N/A	R	R
Human Rights Law	R	N/A	N/A	R	R
Current Human Rights Issues	R	N/A	N/A	R	R
Local mechanisms for redress	R	N/A	N/A	R	R
Education through human rights, i.e., activities or recommendations for teaching methods based on HRTS principles	R Provides numerous teaching activities, methods, and techniques	R 101 activities provided	R States the necessity of participatory teaching methods but doesn't provide specific recommendations	R Includes learning information literacy, participating in debates, networking, writing proposals, and organizing or joining campaigns	R 25 teaching "tools" provided

Table 4. (continued)

About *Through* For	Nancy Flowers: *HRE Handbook* (2000)	OSCE, CoE, and UN: *HRE in School Systems Compendium* (2009)*	CoE: "Charter on Education for Democratic Citizenship and HRE" (2010)*	OSCE: *Guidelines on HRE for Secondary School Systems* (2012)	Asia Pacific Forum: *Manual for NHRIs* (2017)
Educating for values, attitudes, & empowerment	R Provides recommendations for affecting learners	R Some recommended activities have these goals	R States the necessity of teaching to affect values and attitudes but is not a handbook with recommendations	R Includes goals of acceptance of and respect for persons of different race, color, gender, language, political or other opinion, religion; improving personal behaviors aligned with human rights principles; demonstrating compassion for and solidarity with those suffering human rights violations	R Includes reflections on their own actions and the consequences of their behaviors; identifying those human rights issues that are most pertinent to their group, community, or society; developing strategies to prevent and address human rights violations; strengthening individuals and communities to take action

Note. R indicates that the documents make recommendations for teaching this topic.
* These two documents did not make knowledge content recommendations.

do not lay out the agenda of HRE explicitly with those words. However, recommendations *about*, *through*, and *for* are contained in all. Both of the two post-2011 documents—the OSCE's *Guidelines* and the Asia Pacific Forum's publication—explicitly use the terminology of education being *about*, *through*, and *for* human rights. The greatest wealth of advice in all of these publications is providing recommendations for teaching *about* human rights.

It is instructive to combine these recommendations with the content of the BA degrees. As noted, the higher education programs emphasize knowledge and include the importance of education *through* and *for*. Ensuring that all three objectives were included would move the current offerings in universities toward transformative education.

Is the current state of HRE in higher education one of confusion or consensus? By now it's clear that there are elements of both. We can determine that there is consensus that we should be teaching specific knowledge *about* human rights. There is agreement about the fundamentals, yet some students might not be exposed to them. Also, there is consensus in documents and scholarship that we should be not only guiding our classrooms based on human rights principles but also teaching how to act for our own and others' human rights. However, there is not consistency among the US degree programs as far as what human rights degrees focus on or what content they teach. Students in different institutions may get vastly different educations. The extensive efforts already made on behalf of primary, secondary, and nonformal education settings have much to offer higher education.

This survey of extant HRE provides support for the argument that human rights must and can be disciplined. Speaking figuratively, more structure would aid students' education and, literally, the field should become an academic discipline. Human rights is an inherently multidisciplinary topic, but there is much that is specific to the field. There is a unique history and content that a graduate in human rights must know. The call to educate *through* and *for* is also somewhat unique to this field. Educators the world over agree that a human rights education must involve affecting students' values and attitudes to bring about change in society. Yet these are not specific demands of many academic degree programs. In the next chapter, I build on the reasons outlined here and make the argument for why human rights must, from here forward, be regarded as a discipline.

Chapter 3

Disciplining Human Rights

Discipline brings into play its power, which is one of analysis.
—Michel Foucault

Building on the mandate for HRE and the emergent consensus around human rights pedagogy for postsecondary students, we enter into the crux of the argument: Why must HRE be regarded and implemented as a discipline? As Chapter 2 demonstrated, the United Nations Declaration on Human Rights Education and Training and subsequent literature on HRE pedagogy offer consensus that human rights education should be both framed and delivered as education *about*, *through*, and *for* human rights. The literature also demonstrates considerable agreement on the foundational knowledge of human rights and argues that the curriculum must include an exploration of values, attitudes, and tools for action. No other field of study accomplishes this full agenda.

At the outset we must acknowledge that disciplines do not mirror reality;[1] thus, discussing disciplinarity is inherently fraught. Just as cartographers often impose artificial borders between places not separated by water or other environmental divides, natural barriers between academic disciplines don't necessarily exist. The confines of a discipline offer a way of categorizing and contextualizing knowledge within manageable, coherent parameters for study. The decision about where to demarcate the boundaries between convergent fields can be a bit arbitrary, involving an element of social construction, but lines must be drawn. Disciplines, like maps, change over time with new discoveries or through associations with other disciplines. For example, English language and literature was a discipline in the 1950s but "had within three decades grown roughly tenfold and differentiated internally into a multitude of specialties."[2] Computer science, once regarded as just a field, has grown into its own discipline. Some fields, such as women's studies or biophysics, have been contested as disciplines. (The distinction between fields and disciplines is the degree to which they encompass topics. A field, field of study, or study area is more open and inclusive of content. A discipline is defined as being narrower in focus. I offer a detailed examination of the parameters of disciplines in what follows.)

To further problematize our discussion, terms such as cross-, trans-, pluri-, post-, and de-disciplinarity do not have universally recognized definitions. Multidisciplinarity, discussed below, does have a widely accepted definition. Interdisciplinarity, also a clearly defined term in the scholarly literature, is often used colloquially to mean other things among faculty. This is somewhat tangential to the argument for codifying human rights as a discipline, but it's worth bearing in mind that the idea of a discipline once enjoyed far more stability, especially in the structure of the university, and that all of these terms rely on the existence of disciplines to begin with.

In the first half of this chapter, I review the definition of "interdisciplinarity," note how and when the term is used incorrectly, and recount some challenges for an undergraduate curriculum. I also define "multidisciplinarity" and enumerate reasons why it will fail to be sufficiently rigorous. Then, in the second half, I present how human rights fits the criteria of a discipline, upholding the conclusion that only as a discipline will HRE meet the demands set out by human rights documents. While human rights problems benefit from interdisciplinary research, only disciplining human rights will offer the needed structure to support such study.

Defining "Interdisciplinarity"

Many of the human rights BA programs in English-speaking countries herald their programs as "interdisciplinary."[3] A look at the definition of the term might lead us to conclude the word is often being incorrectly applied. Those researching and writing about interdisciplinarity base the interdisciplinary generation of knowledge squarely within disciplines. The National Academy of Science's definition is typical: "a mode of research by teams or individuals that integrates information, data, techniques, tools, perspectives, concepts, and/or theories from two or more disciplines or bodies of specialized knowledge to advance fundamental understanding or to solve problems whose solutions are beyond the scope of a single discipline or area of research practice."[4]

The National Institutes of Health further explains that the process requires faculty become familiar with the language of other disciplines, including knowing their assumptions, theories, and methods.[5] Thus, "interdisciplinarity" (1) refers to a method of knowledge creation using discipline-based knowledge and discipline-based methods from more than one discipline, and (2) necessarily requires integration. In fact, integration has been called the litmus test for determining whether or not a practice is interdisciplinary.[6] In looking at these explanations, it is clear that the argument that human rights cannot be a discipline because, as some faculty have told me, it's "too interdisciplinary" rests on the fallacy that interdisciplinarity can focus solely on a somewhat haphazard collection of disciplines, without also teaching integration.

In order to label human rights an interdiscipline, one would need to be explicit about which disciplines were foundational, teach their methodological approaches, and then integrate these disciplines and approaches. No human rights program, to date, seems to be applying the methodology of integration in their BA programs. It is more likely they are, in fact, multidisciplinary programs, and we will examine later in this chapter why that is a far less effective approach. Focusing on human rights becoming a strong discipline will fulfill those aims for HRE outlined in the previous two chapters.

Since interdisciplinarity is an approach to working with disciplines, interdisciplinary centers bring a number of disciplines under one roof to study a problem. One of the biggest literal examples of this is at Arizona State University, where the president, Michael Crow, dismantled disciplinary departments on an enormous scale. The university's School of Life Sciences was a reconstituting of the dismembered departments of "biology, microbiology, plant biology and the program of molecular and cellular biology."[7] They also have a School of Human Evolution and Social Change, School of Earth and Space Exploration, School of Politics and Global Studies, and others. However, the degrees granted are still disciplinary in nature, as are the courses taught. The great attempt at foregrounding interdisciplinarity in research has not affected that undergraduate curricula are taught disciplinarily. And it should be so. Interdisciplinary research depends on the disciplines involved, so undergraduate students must obtain their intellectual grounding within a discipline to have a hope of eventually embarking on interdisciplinary work.

The Oxford Handbook of Interdisciplinarity, which includes various chapters on the sciences and on the humanities, explains how interdisciplinarity "manifests itself differently in different disciplinary contexts."[8] The physical sciences approach differs from religious studies, for example. Jerry Jacobs, in his book *In Defense of Disciplines: Interdisciplinarity and Specialization in the Research University*, has further observed that interdisciplinary work has to be specialized.[9] He reviewed 789 peer-reviewed journals launched in 2008. About 25 percent of them used the terms "interdisciplinary" or "multidisciplinary" in their mission statements. He further categorized those into six kinds of interdisciplinary foci: from journals that are "disciplinary plus"—that is, they accept articles mainly from one discipline but also accept those from closely related fields (for example, the journal *Collaborative Anthropologies*)—to interdisciplinary journals focused on problem solving. The latter specialize in an area of problems such as those particular to health care—*Ethnicity and Inequalities in Health and Social Care*, for example. Knowledge is too vast for interdisciplinarity not to have to specialize.

Two main assumptions are clearly flawed: (1) that disciplines are just silos containing comprehensive knowledge that can be synthesized with other chunks of siloed knowledge, and (2) that disciplines are not already synthesizing knowledge. As previously described, disciplines are not perfectly discrete entities bound by permanent borders. Some academics patrol them more closely than others, some disciplines are more porous than others, but none are completely self-contained, stagnant entities. UK researchers Tony Becher and Paul Trowler argue that disciplines lie on a continuum of those that are "convergent, tightly knit disciplinary configurations and those which are divergent and loosely knit."[10] They cite economics as an example of the former and geography of the latter.[11] Indeed, faculty in one department often have more research interests in common with people from another department than they do with their own. The research of a medieval historian might be more closely related to a professor of medieval literature than a historian of the civil war. A scholar of speech and hearing may have more in common with the computer scientists with whom she analyzes speech patterns than with her colleague who specializes in swallowing disorders. The work of a sociologist studying food systems in Bolivia has more in common with her geographer colleagues than with her fellow sociologist researching educational disparities in low-income neighborhoods.

How many fields might fit the following evocative description of sociology? "The discipline is rather like a caravansary on the Silk Road, filled with all sorts and types of people and beset by bandit gangs of positivists, feminists, interactionists, and Marxists, and even by some larger, far-off states like Economics and the Humanities."[12]

Questions About and Failings of Interdisciplinary Approaches

Harvey Graff provides cognitive science as an example of an "interdiscipline" failing to be integrative that should be instructive to human rights. He writes, "It represents a particular pattern: defining interdisciplinarity by listing disciplines and not attending to their interrelationships."[13] He explicates the field's failure to bring the disciplines together by examining the hexagon commonly used to illustrate the cognitive sciences (see Figure 1).

Lines drawn through the center of the hexagon connect philosophy, linguistics, anthropology, neuroscience, artificial intelligence, and psychology, suggesting that the disciplines relate or interact with one another. After reviewing numerous histories of the field, Graff concludes that there has not been "a clear focus on relationships between and among disciplines and on specific problems and questions amenable to research that cross disciplinary lines and lead to the integration of diverse approaches and perspectives."[14] He agrees with the commentator who explains that some disciplines such as neuropsychology, linguistics, and psychology are doing cognitive science but each separately.[15] And another critic explains that you can be a cognitive scientist "if you are a cognitive psychologist and know a little bit about philosophy of mind, linguistics, and computer theory."[16] Cognitive science, therefore, is either considered to be something done within a discipline such as those mentioned above, or it's a multidisciplinary field in departments offering a degree in cognitive science.[17]

As indicated by the example of the cognitive psychologist familiar with other disciplines, disciplines already synthesize knowledge.[18] Traditional scholars and researchers housed within departments cross disciplinary

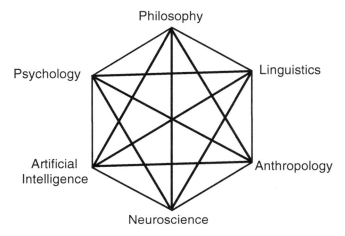

Figure 1. Hexagon of the Cognitive Sciences. The interrelated nature of the cognitive sciences is often represented with this hexagon, adapted from a similar one by George A. Miller. Adapted from "Cognitive science hexagon," by Charles Lowe, http://commons.wikimedia.irg/wiki/File:Cognitive_Science_Hesagon.svg, CC BY-SA 3.0; originally adapted from George A. Miller, "The Cognitive Revolution: A Historical Perspective," *TRENDS in Cognitive Sciences* 7, no. 3 (2003): 143.

boundaries all the time on topics of common interest through journals, conferences, and personal communications within home universities and beyond. Jerry Jacobs has conducted extensive analysis of how disciplinary faculty communicate with other fields. He effectively demolishes the idea of disciplines as silos via the citation data in the online *Web of Science*. He reports on research that found 69 percent of "references are cross-disciplinary, that is, the majority of references in a given journal are drawn from journals in other disciplinary fields."[19] Of course, most of us have found that literature searches are not usually restricted to fields. One researches a topic, which might be found in numerous journals with various foci. Who wouldn't agree with Becher and Trowler that "a considerable amount of poaching goes on across all disciplines."[20] We could not do our intellectual work without borrowing from and learning from each other.

Jacobs also reviews a variety of maps of knowledge and explains that their findings depend on variables such as terminology and whether the data come from individual papers or journal citations. And yet he concludes, "Every type of map of intellectual connections depicts a web of knowledge."[21] He reviews the data on the diffusion of ideas across disciplines, showing that a term can be found throughout the humanities or even the humanities and social sciences. Just two examples remind us how true this is: Jacobs sites the term "postmodern" as appearing over one thousand articles in at least nine disciplinary journals in the humanities, social sciences, and the applied fields of education, business, and law.[22] Julie Thompson Klein, a recognized authority on interdisciplinarity, notes how the term "organism" is a physical, chemical, biological, physiological, mental, social, and cultural object.[23] Methodologies invented by one discipline are borrowed and become embedded in others as well, be they statistical models used throughout the social sciences or laboratory techniques shared in the natural sciences.

When faculty read more general publications, such as *Science*, the *New York Times*, book reviews, and the *Chronicle of Higher Education*, they are exposing themselves to a wide array of knowledge. Jacobs also mentions National Public Radio and TED Talks as other disseminators of ideas.[24] And learning from colleagues outside our fields occurs by interacting in numerous ways at our universities, including secondary appointments, some kinds of committee work, attending talks, and teaching outside one's own narrow specialty.

Thus, Jacobs illustrates two points: First, disciplines do not have static boundaries, because ideas, concepts, methodologies, and problems do not respect them. And, second, academics themselves are constantly familiarizing themselves with related work in other fields, which sometimes impacts their disciplinary work as revealed in the *Web of Science* and other "maps" of scholarly activity.

We need empirical measures to define success and determine what leads to that success. Given the interest in interdisciplinary research by the government agencies funding science, one might conclude that the applied sciences especially need such measures. How do we know interdisciplinary is better? Is that true in every case or only in certain cases? Becher and Trowler explain that there is "considerable skepticism about benefits of collaborative research compared to the serendipitous scientific discoveries that come from basic science."[25] We know that narrow specialization also results in important discoveries, which is probably why the disciplinary system has retained its prominence in US higher education; it is a successful arrangement for producing world-class research. In fact, the expectation that disciplines would interact and influence one another was embedded in medieval thinking about the German university. Germans in that era believed in a unity of knowledge that was pursued through "ever-more simple but comprehensive theories" produced by specialization.[26] In his 1962 classic text on scientific paradigms (those individual theories and discoveries that dominate and define disciplines), Thomas Kuhn said, "By focusing attention upon a small range of relatively esoteric problems, the paradigm forces scientists to investigate some part of nature in detail and depth that would otherwise be unimaginable. . . . When the paradigm is successful, the profession will have solved problems that its members could scarcely have imagined and would never have undertaken without commitment to the paradigm."[27] And a recent 2018 report investigating the importance of integration in undergraduate teaching also concluded, "The committee agrees that the disciplines remain essential, exceptionally valuable, and generative features of contemporary higher education."[28] Disciplinarity and integration are not thought to be anathema to each other, and it is unclear that interdisciplinarity has accomplished what it intended to.

Scholars commonly turn to interdisciplinarity because it is thought to provide a method for addressing problems through synthesizing disciplines when a single discipline fails. But sociologists Jerry Jacobs and Scott Frickel have found that the assumptions about the weaknesses of disciplines and strengths of interdisciplinarity are not empirically based. There is no data proving that disciplines prevent problem solving, are not as good as interdisciplinary attempts at producing new knowledge, or that less disciplinarity and more interdisciplinarity is better.[29] Most disciplinary naysayers write from personal perspectives without doing studies or referring to evidence. For example, Michael Crow and William Dabars assert that disciplinary entrenchment is restricting focus and preventing the ability to address "social and environmental challenges of unimaginable complexity" without providing any data.[30] Robert Frodeman, the director for a center for interdisciplinarity study, claims that knowledge should be "dedisciplined," which seems to mean tied to social problems as if they have not been before. He does not define the term in his book on the topic, but he offers dedisciplined philosophy as an example. He would name this new subject "field philosophy," which is a socially applied philosophy where philosophers would be trained to work in corporations.[31] Charles Murray, a conservative critic of higher education, goes the furthest when calling the BA "the work of the devil."[32] I will refrain from digressing into the history of the land grant university's goal of "Science as Service," as one book devoted to the topic is titled.[33] I will not review the list of discoveries in the sciences, social sciences, and humanities that have contributed to humankind that Jonathan Cole enumerates in the 150 pages of his book *The Great American University: Its Rise to Prominence, Its Indispensable Role, and Why It Must Be Protected*.[34] (He does not mention any problems with disciplinarity in his follow-on book *Toward a More Perfect University*,[35] which is about recommendations for improving higher education.)

Interdisciplinary Pedagogy

Some fields are called interdisciplines, including those with "studies" in the title, such as women's studies and African American studies. But labeling them with the noun "interdiscipline" is a category mistake. The approach to the topic that is central to such studies—for example, women or African Americans—may be interdisciplinary, but it would be clearer if we just termed them "fields of study" if faculty did not want to call them disciplines. As shown below, however, there are experts in these area studies who have been arguing for calling them disciplines.

If faculty want to adopt an interdisciplinary approach to a set of disciplines, they would do well to follow Klein's collected best practices. She recommends that an interdisciplinary program includes "a spine of core ID [interdisciplinary focused] courses, paying attention to interdisciplinary theory, concepts, and methods," "at least 20 credit hours of ID courses," "a clearly defined ID mission," and "proactive attention to integrative and collaborative processes."[36] Additionally, one should place "integration and ID outcomes at the heart of the program."[37] Again, there is no evidence that educational institutions in the US have implemented any of these measures with regard to human rights BAs. Also, most of the required courses come at the beginning of the programs in the US, so it is unlikely that integration is being required at the end of a sequence of disciplinary-focused courses. One must be schooled in the various disciplines before an effective blending can take place. Perhaps it is occurring in capstone courses, but very few of the programs require a capstone. And the lack of synthesis in so-called interdisciplinary programs is a common critique.[38] Klein also notes how often such programs are accused of superficiality.[39] Jacobs and Frickel write, "A concern voiced by many academic commentators is that interdisciplinary work is too often the product of "amateurism

and intellectual voyeurism"[40] and results in knowledge of "dubious quality."[41] Frodeman exclaims that "calls for interdisciplinarity often signify
sound and fury but little else. The term itself is in danger of becoming an
empty signifier."[42] Interdisciplinarity is not a guaranteed panacea for the
perceived shortcomings of disciplinarity.

Perhaps this is why recognized interdisciplinary programs such as wom-
en's and African American studies have donned the cloak of disciplinarity
rather than shunned it.[43] Frodeman includes the field of science and technology studies as moving toward disciplinarity along with applied ethics.[44]
This is presumably because, pragmatically, it provides the stability that the
organizational structure of a discipline tends to offer: having a physical
home, being able to make hiring decisions, and having budget lines. In fact,
Ethan Kleinberg, one reviewer of interdisciplinary programs, concluded in
2008, "The majority of these programs, departments, and centers are not
substantially different from the academic disciplines, departments, and
divisions they were originally designed to challenge."[45] They, too, have spe-
cializations and compete for students and resources. Unfortunately, they
can also become "a secluded, self-legitimizing and backward-looking field
that lacks the rigorous foundation, methodology, and autonomy of traditional departments"[46]—in other words, they are not immune to the same
dangers as disciplines face.

Another observation about multi- or interdisciplinarity is the practical
problem of their place within the university. Institutions of higher education are primarily centered on disciplines and majors. Though there are
calls to dismantle the university as we know it (e.g., Michael Crow at Arizona State University), twenty million undergraduates continue to be part
of disciplinary departments.[47] Andrew Abbott argues that problem-focused
interdisciplines should not replace the current structure of universities,
because there are "far more research problems than there are disciplines."[48]
He argues, therefore, that it makes more sense to keep the disciplinary
structure and recognize that problems are transportable to many fields.
Human rights consists of innumerable problems that need input from so
many disciplines, which may make it seem that Abbott's is an argument
against forming a new discipline. But he also explains that "problem-
portable knowledge is precisely what disciplines generate."[49] Categorizing
abuses as human rights problems has provided a framework for creating an
ethic, laws, and vocabulary for calling out abusers and ultimately creating
conditions for ameliorating them. There is a subject now called human

rights. It has a name, content, and problems. Those problems must be exported to the various disciplines. And as has been shown, disciplines share problems all the time. "Neglected" tropical diseases (labeled such because they afflict the poorest people in developing nations and pharmaceutical companies deem them too unprofitable to research) offer a suitable example of portable human rights problems. Preventable illness and death from these diseases is a human rights issue, so a discipline of human rights insists it be approached through the moral and legal lens of a human rights problem. Addressing it also requires the work of medical researchers, policy makers, and businesspeople, to list only a few. They each need to analyze it from their own area of expertise in order to contribute to a solution.

Is Multidisciplinarity a Viable Alternative?

As previously suggested, it is actually more likely that what are currently termed "interdisciplinary" degrees are actually, in most cases, multidisciplinary. The majority of extant HRE degree programs in the US consist of a range of disciplines taken alongside a few human rights courses. Klein defines and explains, "Multidisciplinary approaches juxtapose disciplinary perspectives, adding breadth and available knowledge, information, and methods. They speak as separate voices in encyclopedic alignment. The status quo is not interrogated, and disciplinary elements retain their original identity."[50] In other words, the element of integration is missing. Students simply take a series of courses, perhaps with the expectation that they will discover the links between the classes. Multidisciplinarity does not entail all the steps that integration requires. Jerry Jacobs concludes that it "is the slightest form of all cross-disciplinarity linkage; indeed, it is not really interdisciplinary at all."[51] The cafeteria-style multidisciplinary approach lacks rigor and cohesion. It would be difficult to undergird the knowledge and skills in courses offered across different departments. For a student to be well equipped to address human rights problems in any capacity upon graduation, at the very least they must be literate in the vocabulary and documents of human rights, questions central to the field, the fundamental problems, and the roles of the important actors. Multidisciplinary programs are less likely to ensure critical analysis of the important aspects of human rights. For example, do students understand the debate about universalism versus the cultural relativity of rights? Can they articulate reasons for the divide between the noble rhetoric of the Universal Declaration of Human Rights and the reality of human suffering rooted in ignorance, incapacity, and corruption? Can they explain the various methods used to address abuses by NGOs, UN special rapporteurs, and the US military? With no courses in common among all the US programs, we cannot know conclusively but it is dubious, because without the frame and guidance, students are largely left to view the proverbial elephant from where they stand in relationship to it.

In reviewing the literature, it's clear that most HRE programs at the tertiary level are not following the agenda of HRE to be education *about*, *through*, and *for* human rights. The schools that offer courses on human rights fulfill *about*, but there are very few courses focused on teaching *for* human rights, and no such course is required for the US degrees. In the next chapter, we will see that there are few courses on teaching for activism. Teaching *through* human rights would be made evident only if it were codified in the language describing the ethos of course pedagogy, since it primarily takes place in the classroom. No doubt most faculty are conscientious about how they teach, but whether they have training on how to run a rights-respecting classroom is a separate question, and teaching through human rights is not an explicitly stated goal of any program. Multidisciplinarity is thus not currently ensuring the UN recommendations for HRE are even aspired to.

A practical approach to evaluating the coherence of the multidisciplinary curriculum is by applying the elements of critical thinking. The Foundation for Critical Thinking outlines the eight elements of critical thought, no matter the topic: a *purpose* or a goal, which is guided by a *question*, requires *information*, involves *inferences*, has *concepts*, is based on *assumptions* and *points of view*, and has *implications*.[52] It is likely to be difficult for a student in a multidisciplinary human rights program to determine the field's purpose, assumptions, concepts, and relevant information if they are taking courses in different fields that do not involve the language and literature of human rights. Since some universities offering BAs in human rights do not offer an introduction to human rights course or a capstone course, it's very likely that students would be unable to reflect according to these eight categories as they pertain to the subject of human rights. For instance, since the human rights regime (including human rights law, governments, the UN, and NGOs) is fundamental for promoting and monitoring rights, it has to be required information.

Human Rights: The Case for a Discipline

If neither interdisciplinarity nor multidisciplinarity offer the required route for problem solving, and if one accepts that disciplinarity is already accomplishing, or capable of accomplishing, synthesis of knowledge, then the next step is to demonstrate that human rights has the elements of a discipline. Recognizing it as such does not negate that it is inherently intertwined with other fields; rather, it offers the opportunity to maximize these relationships.

Several scholars maintain that there are three criteria for a discipline: (1) an identifiable field of study, (2) a body of knowledge associated with the field of study, and (3) a community of scholars.[53] William H. Newell and William J. Green explain that disciplines have also been defined by their subject matter (e.g., the past), their method (e. g., participant-observer), their perspective (e.g., the economic man), or the questions they ask (e.g., philosophic).[54] They argue that a discipline is just a sociopolitical organization focusing on a common set of questions and that there is no definitive set of characteristics for all disciplines. With respect to some of the above perspectives, I employ the following definition of a discipline for human rights, because it allows for a more comprehensive presentation of the content compared to a simple definition that a discipline is merely a social construct: a discipline has (1) a shared narrative of identity and community, (2) a common vocabulary and set of concepts, (3) a set of questions that guide inquiry and a shared set of problems to examine/resolve, and (4) a set of methods or strategies of interpretation, which construct what counts as evidence.[55] What follows demonstrates how human rights fulfills the criteria to establish it as a discipline, thereby enabling much-needed critical analysis of the field.

Shared Narrative of Identity and Community

The common narrative of identity and community includes the promotion and maintenance of human rights. A strong motivation for many people involved in supporting HRE is to see rights promoted and abuses stopped. The academic community of human rights is made up of the faculty who, first and foremost, teach, research, and publish on human rights topics. Community activists sometimes have strong connections with faculty and students because they visit or teach classes and provide internships to the students. The line between scholar and practitioner is permeable, because some faculty are also activists. Target communities, as subjects of study, also constitute part of this group with a shared narrative, and with community-based participatory research and similar methods, members of target communities become part of the academic and research teams. Target communities include victims of rights abuses, those who commit abuses, human rights professionals, and the organizations they work for in the public sector (governments), the private sector (businesses), and civil society (NGOs and social movements).

Common characteristics of an academic community include professional associations and scholarly journals. An academic association just for HRE in higher education has not yet begun, but non-lawyers who are primarily focused on human rights are likely members of the two associations with large human rights subsection memberships: the International Studies Association, or ISA (with 550 human rights subsection members), and the American Political Science Association. For example, at the 2017 annual ISA conference, there were seventy panels presenting on human rights, involving over three hundred papers. Also, as noted, there is a new consortium for HRE in higher education: the University and College Consortium for Human Rights Education (UCCHRE). The American Society of International Law and the Law and Society Association include human rights as part of their purview as does the Scientific Responsibility, Human Rights, and Law Program of the American Association for the Advancement of Science.

Also mentioned previously, there are at least fifty English-language journals with "human rights" in the title, fewer than 25 percent of which are primarily law journals. A few have specific foci: *Business and Human Rights Journal*; *Health and Human Rights*; *Conflict, Politics, and Human Rights in Africa*; *Muslim World Journal of Human Rights*; *Religion and Human Rights*; and *Security and Human Rights*. About 30 percent describe themselves as inter- or multidisciplinary. For example, since 1974, *Human Rights Quarterly* has been publishing scholarship from a variety of disciplines such as law, philosophy, and social sciences. Taken together, these journals publish hundreds of human rights–focused papers annually.

Numerous book publishers, academic and not, also have lines devoted to human rights and publish dozens of books classified as such each year.

Vocabulary and Concepts

The Universal Declaration of Human Rights offers the basic vocabulary, and the human rights regime offers most of the concepts, for HRE. Other essentials include important historical events, religious and philosophical concepts, and the idea of advocacy. Core courses in a degree program should rely on the language and literature of human rights embodied in the UDHR, to include not only civil and political rights but economic, social, and cultural rights as well. Though it is a declaration, and unenforceable from a legal perspective, the document provided the foundation for the system of human rights law that followed. This includes the nine core treaties and the fifty international human rights laws that currently govern international affairs.[56]

The human rights regime consists of the United Nations and its associated bodies (the World Health Organization, the International Monetary Fund, the World Bank, etc.), its treaty monitoring bodies, and special rapporteurs. The International Criminal Court and the regional courts of the EU, the Organization of American States, and the African Union represent part of the regime as well. So do human rights–oriented NGOs.

Key historical events relating to human rights issues include various moments in British history acknowledged as important to the birth of democracy, the antislavery movement, and the American and French Revolutions. Some historians go much further back in history and to all corners of the globe for antecedents to today's human rights movement, but from wherever we begin, there is adequate historical foundation for the discipline.

Advocacy is also a necessary aspect of the human rights vocabulary because the "how" of fostering rights-promoting and -protecting change is rooted in human rights and HRE.

Central Questions/Problems

Every student of human rights must consider questions and controversies that are central to the study of human rights. As noted previously, an introductory or theories class often begins with an exploration of the concepts of rights and what it means to have rights. How are rights defined? Are they universal? Why are certain rights included or omitted?

Other questions permeating courses include the role cultural differences play in how human rights are defined and promoted. Also, why is there a gap between the rhetoric of human rights and the dismal reality of widespread human rights abuses? What role do governments play in abuses and remedies? How should governments balance national security with individual rights? Students and scholars study the effectiveness of international organizations and civil society in promoting human rights. The methods of NGOs must be scrutinized, and myriad questions about each event or system involving human rights abuses must be examined to interrupt abuses and prevent further iterations of similar abuses. Students must be equipped with the right questions for analyzing them. And, of course, prevention and solutions for human rights abuses require critical examination. The issues particular to human rights are gathered in the aforementioned journals and in encyclopedias, handbooks, and dictionaries of human rights, which are arranged according to topic and country.

Methods

To assess human rights promotion, abuses, and the effectiveness of attempts for amelioration requires measurement. The field already has methods courses on both sides of the Atlantic. Some programs offer a general social science methods course, but only a few offer courses geared specifically toward human rights. There are several texts on methods in human rights research.[57] Data collection is the focus of the Human Rights Data Analysis Group at both the American Association for the Advancement of Science and the Benetech Initiative in Palo Alto, California.

By having methods courses in a curriculum, the discipline additionally establishes its ability to be critical of how human rights work is done and provides additional rigor in the field. In the book *Methods of Human Rights Research*, the editors lament the quality of research they found in reviewing a large sample of articles in two scholarly journals. Too many academics relied on secondary rather than primary sources, and often there was not enough transparency in methodology.[58] Additionally, a methods course can teach the best practices for using critical pedagogy "on the ground." For example, we should teach about all aspects of community participation, including participatory interventions and legal empowerment (i.e., teaching people how to use the declarations, treaties, and national laws or local ordinances that address the human rights problem they are facing).[59] Kathryn Sikkink, professor of human rights policy at the Harvard Kennedy School, has written on the topic of human rights research and advises that we should remember to "look to our colleagues in other disciplines . . . for new means of research and analysis"[60]—in other words, we need to "poach" just as many other disciplines do.

Thus, having met our established criteria for a discipline, human rights should be treated as one in colleges and universities. Communities of scholars, field professionals, and activists are present around the world. Stemming from treaties and conventions, and from various human rights reference books and textbooks, human rights has its own distinct vocabulary and concepts. Texts are filled with the central questions and strategies for approaching the problems. The field has called upon an array of disciplinary research methods and is currently developing its own.

When colleges and universities treat human rights as a discipline, the seven critical thinking criteria become our students' objectives: they will be able to (1) state the discipline's purposes (to promote human rights and solve human rights abuses and to critically analyze the modes of protection and promotion of human rights); (2) define its guiding questions (including what human rights are, why abuses occur, and what must be done about them); (3) bring the appropriate understandings to discern salient information (critical information literacy); (4) understand the inferences and interpretations (for example, what can be inferred from how human rights has been defined and how this informs or limits the kinds of conclusions that are reached); (5) reveal the assumptions (for example, whether current human rights conventions/definitions offer the best ideology); (6) identify the central concepts (included in the categories of rights and the legal regimes); and, finally, (7) analyze the implications and consequences of human rights scholarship and activism.

The Discipline of Human Rights in Relationship to Other Disciplines

In addition to having all the components that define a discipline, the field of human rights is, of course, reliant on other disciplines and should influence other disciplines. So on Becher and Trowler's continuum, would it be considered a tighter or more "loosely knit" discipline?[61] Obviously the latter, because so many fields are relevant to the study of human rights, even in light of the fact that there is a specific literature with topics and concepts unique to HRE. Other disciplines contribute to human rights as an academic field, both directly and indirectly. In the first case, other fields contribute directly to books and courses specifically focused on human rights, as is often evidenced by their titles. For example, history is the main contributing discipline in Paul Gordon Lauren's *The Evolution of Human Rights* and Micheline Ishay's *The History of Human Rights*.[62] Interestingly, the publishers of these two titles do not use "human rights" for the subject description on the back of the book. The former, published by University of Pennsylvania Press, is categorized as political science, history, law, and philosophy. The latter, published by University of California Press, is identified as history, anthropology, and politics. Some publishers do use "human rights" as a subject heading, but these two do not. In any event, most books and courses using the phrase "human rights" rely on other disciplines.

Examples of other books with both the name of the discipline or field and "human rights" in the title are *Development and Human Rights*,[63] *Linguistic Human Rights*,[64] *Business and Human Rights*,[65] *Human Rights and Public Finance*,[66] *Human Rights and Social Work*,[67] *Human Rights and Sustainability*,[68] *Human Rights in International Relations*,[69] *The Sociology of Human Rights*,[70] *The Political Sociology of Human Rights*,[71] and *Religion and Human Rights*.[72] Each of these would be appropriate for either a human rights curriculum or for study within the other stated field.

Which other fields of study are essential and direct contributors to a degree in human rights? A necessary first is law. The founding document for modern human rights is the UDHR. The International Bill of Human Rights consists of it and the two covenants that formulated it in law: the International Covenant on Civil and Political Rights and the International Covenant on Economic, Social and Cultural Rights. Thus, the delineation of human rights as civil, political, economic, social, and cultural is understood and actionable only within the context of the laws. The United Nations, an essential promoter and defender of human rights, relies on the law to carry out its duties. One could not understand how the institution functions without knowledge of the law that drives its monitoring actions, for example. All governments must adopt international law or otherwise translate signed treaties into domestic law, so every government is involved with human rights law to some extent. NGOs often rely on the law to fight for rights. No education about human rights can occur without some familiarity with its legal framework. This is why legal scholars and the law dominated the academic field of human rights for much of the twentieth century. Law degrees with a focus on human rights are awarded more often than any other kind of human rights degree. Human rights journals in the 1970s and the 1980s were primarily law journals.[73]

As Michael Freeman, emeritus professor of the Human Rights Center at the University of Essex, has pointed out, the law alone is not sufficient and will not, by itself, help us understand, prevent, and stop abuses. In his book *Human Rights: An Interdisciplinary Approach*, he focuses on the role of the social sciences.[74] After pointing out how they ignored the subject of human rights for various reasons—realism and positivism, in particular, do not accommodate the subject easily—they have been forced to reckon with the relationship to rights, especially with the Helsinki Final Act and President Jimmy Carter's bringing the topic to international relations. Political science and international relations are also essential contributors to the study of human rights. Freeman credits Richard Claude's 1976 book, *Comparative Human Rights*, as "pioneering" for political science and human rights.[75] In it, Claude demonstrated the necessity of political freedom and political participation for achieving the concerns of human rights. Freeman mentions international relations' regime theory as significant to human rights, as are the concepts of sovereignty and, more recently, the responsibility to protect, to cite only a few.

Sociology contributes "the social nature of the struggle for human rights," and the role of social structures and the theory of social constructionism[76] are necessary for understanding the social forces underlying abuses, for example. Freeman cites psychology for the concepts of sympathy and cruelty as being important for our understanding of different facets of human rights. He also mentions scapegoat and frustration-aggression theories, as well as what experimental psychology has taught us about the power of group conformity over independent moral thinking.[77] It would be difficult to understand genocides without social psychology. And bringing the lens of anthropology to human rights helps us to understand the role of culture in rights violations and how it can contribute to rights protections. Though the American Anthropological Association expressed disagreement with the idea of universal rights in their 1947 statement, since 1999 they have officially endorsed them by adopting their own *Declaration of Anthropology and Human Rights*. In the 1940s the association proclaimed that universality did not make sense in light of the fact that "standards and values are relative to the culture from which they derive."[78] Today they bring to the table the requirement to understand how rights are apprehended in diverse cultures and the idea that we need to localize or vernacularize the language of human rights to make it useful to specific environments.

History and philosophy have already been cited as essential partners to human rights because of their contribution to understanding the origins of rights. History is further necessary for analyzing the roots of today's abuses. Philosophy helps us to be conscious of the assumptions we make when addressing how others are behaving. Taking the example of female genital mutilation, when Westerners criticize non-Westerners for the practice without being explicitly aware of the culturally based morality that we bring to bear, effectively advocating for change may not be possible. Assessing the validity of our own views, and locating ourselves within the cultural influences of those views, allows us to step away from perceived superiority and into a collaborative stance through which change might effectively be approached.

While discussing the contributions of the humanities, the role of arts and literature must also be highlighted for its essential contribution in educating the world about human rights problems. Whether through fiction or nonfiction, the literary or the theatrical, visual or performance, the arts invite us to inhabit the lives of others in an emotionally evocative way, appealing to our common humanity and viscerally impacting the audience. The case could be made for other disciplines as being germane to a degree in human rights, such as economics, some sciences (public health/epidemiology, agriculture, engineering, etc.), and applied degrees, such as business or medicine.

Many disciplines also contribute to human rights indirectly by addressing topics or problems without specific reference to human rights. That is, there are many courses within human rights degree programs that may not refer to problems with the term "human rights" per se, but they are necessary and appropriate for a student's HRE. Here is a sampling of course titles from a list of several hundred: Anthropology of Poverty; Conflicts in the Middle East; Current Issues in International Relations, Ethics, Gender and Applied Economics; Immigration and Refugees; Mass Violence; Modern Africa; Moral Theory and Philosophy of Law; Public Policy; Protest Literature; and World Politics.

In order to imagine how this new discipline of human rights will work, it might be useful to provide an analogy. I propose that we examine religious studies for the sake of comparison.[79] Not only do many of the same disciplines play a role in both religious studies and human rights (including history, literature, philosophy, political science, and sociology), but both also include the symbiotic components of practice and scholarship. Researchers not only study the phenomenon of the practice; they also influence the practice. In religious studies, for example, analysis of biblical texts has deeply informed the theology preached from the pulpit. Mainstream Christianity accepts the historical context of scripture and thus does not take it literally. Likewise, Kathryn Sikkink provides an example of human rights scholarship influencing activists in her book *Evidence for Hope*. She shows that the negative assessment of the future of human rights made by academics Samuel Moyn and Stephen Hopgood are "heard loud and clear in human rights movements affecting activists' sense of self-worth and the directions for future work."[80] Each of these examples is small, in some sense, but when extrapolated to imagine the available universe of interplay between scholarship and practice, the magnitude of the impact is clear.

Both disciplines also have to cover a vast variety of practices—for instance, from Christian systematics to Native American ritual, and from working with victims of disasters to policy campaigning and legal efforts. Additionally, both religion and the practice of human rights lend themselves to interdisciplinary study (once the disciplinary basis is in place). The practice of interreligious dialogue and ecumenism can require the study of history, language, ritual, and culture. Likewise, in the field, human rights workers can use anthropology, social psychology, and engineering to address problems. And, finally, academic faculties from both religious and human rights studies can be made up of those who practice and those who do not. Religious studies is sometimes taught by those of faith and even religious leaders, but many faculty are not religious, and participation is not required to be an observer and analyst of the phenomenon of religion. Human rights faculty are sometimes activists with great field experience but not in every case. Religious studies thus serves as a helpful model as we try to imagine advancing this new discipline.

Looking Ahead: Practical Considerations for the Discipline of Human Rights

Having argued for the structure of a discipline, we now examine the practical question of how one might build a human rights department and who will comprise its faculty. As has happened with the evolution of other fields and is likely happening in the schools with human rights BAs, one hires faculty with a variety of different PhDs to support the course requirements. Faculty currently teaching human rights come from political science, international relations, history, philosophy, and any one of the disciplines contributing to human rights. But they all rely on and use the language of human rights. When degree programs are adding faculty, they look to see where they have gaps and the hire appropriately. Eventually, as human rights in academia launches faculty with MAs and PhDs in human rights, it will populate the degree programs. But there will always be room for PhDs in other disciplines within a human rights program, just as there is in many departments. One study showed that there is a wide range between those disciplinary departments with PhDs restricted to only those with the exact PhD for that discipline: history boasts 92 percent historians nationally, while only 58 percent of the faculty teaching computer science have a PhD in the subject.

Turning the study of human rights into a discipline is more than doable—it is necessary. Only one new human rights BA was created within the last decade, perhaps because it is difficult to promote an academic program that is ill-defined. We must stop thwarting our own ambitions to promote HRE by refusing to submit to the structure most successful in delivering content and methods.

Inter- or multidisciplinary education strategies do not offer a structured, coherent, and comprehensive curriculum on the human rights regime, problems in human rights, the human rights actors, and human rights research methods, nor does any other discipline supply them. While there are overlaps in topics with political science and international studies, for instance, and peace studies programs may share the goal of changing society, they do not contain HRE's conscriptions for how one must approach meaningful, non-harming change. This is especially true considering that work outside the classroom, including doing projects and research in communities, involves empowering people by educating them about their own human rights.

Though human rights has been labeled "interdisciplinary" by many programs and faculty, there is no uniformity in what that signifies, and I have demonstrated here why the label is often a misnomer. It does not make sense to argue that human rights is an inherently interdisciplinary field, and I have argued in this chapter that it's a fool's errand to try to achieve interdisciplinarity because of the many untested assumptions those who advocate it have. There is little evidence that today's complex problems can be addressed successfully without disciplines, because bringing disciplinary expertise to a topic while at the same time interacting with people in other disciplines thinking about the same problem is already a norm. The university does not need to be reinvented. Somewhat paradoxically, a strong discipline of human rights could contribute to interdisciplinary problem solving by bringing a fully realized human rights frame to real-world problems. Thus, recognizing human rights as a discipline is the clear path to increasing its presence in higher education and for producing graduates who are prepared for further study and work in the field. In summary, this field must be regarded, supported, and taught as a discipline.

Chapter 4

Educating *Through* Human Rights: Living Rights in the Classroom

> *But [we] also believe that citizenship education embodies more abstract*
> *qualities: learning how to become more comfortable with ambiguity and*
> *complexity, how to disagree without being disagreeable, and, perhaps*
> *above all else, how to be more empathetic.*
> —Michael B. Smith, Rebecca S. Nowacek, and Jeffrey L. Bernstein

Education *through* human rights addresses how we teach and the content that supports students' explorations of rights as they pertain to the learning environment. UNDHRET defines education *through* human rights as "learning and teaching in a way that respects the rights of both educators and learners." The international documents in Table 5 each have suggestions for achieving this goal. They recommend "participatory pedagogies," "learner-centered methods," and "active engagement." I offer four categories of advice rooted in their recommendations: (1) teaching critical thinking, (2) centering students' rights, (3) living the values of equality and nondiscrimination in the classroom, and (4) encouraging active learning. In what follows, I take their suggestions and turn them into three specific methods: (1) explicitly teaching critical thinking, (2) teaching social justice education (SJE), and (3) promoting active learning through discussion.

I have come to conclude that developing critical thinking must be at the center of HRE. In addition to the nationally collected data, it is apparent that multicultural education, social justice education, citizenship education,

and some aspects of critical pedagogy include a call to teach critical thinking. Scholars who promote the teaching of critical thinking skills often do
not use the phrase, but the practices they endorse fall under its umbrella. If
demanding the skills of critical thinking were an aspect of every course, we
would be providing a radical critical education in human rights. I say "radical" because actually providing a deep education is becoming increasingly
scarce and because we would be making all the important moves the various critical pedagogies hope for: decentering authority, questioning hegemonic knowledge, becoming inclusive, and transforming people. Critical
thinking undergirds educating for social justice and is supported by discussion and active learning techniques.

Grounding our teaching strategies in the three methods listed above will
ensure that our teaching is more transformative. Most of us have been
taught that we will successfully impart knowledge to students if our syllabi
of readings are strong and our lectures have rich content. But the research
increasingly doubts that claim.[1] The scholarship of teaching and learning
suggests our classes will not have the hoped-for impact unless we make
substantial adjustments to the traditional practices still pervasive in higher
education. Thus, a discussion about HRE necessarily requires reflection on
general findings about the lack of undergraduate learning among students
in the US. Adopting recommendations about improving teaching from the
extant critique of university education will have a profound effect on
designing excellent human rights courses and degrees.

The data reveal the disappointing inefficacy of undergraduate education
in the US, evidenced by poor writing and superficial thinking. Each year I
begin a lesson on food and human rights by showing a one-sided and
poorly researched film about food production and watch students ingest
the fear of genetically modified organisms (GMOs) without questioning
why the filmmakers haven't presented any scientific findings to back the
claims. It is fascinating and slightly disturbing to see class after class absorb
the film's message uncritically. Of course, they may bring preconceived
notions. And they may even notice that the presentation is biased. But a
student's comment that she doubted anything could change her mind
about the evils of GMOs after seeing the film was not atypical. Once we
analyze the messages and review much more research on the subject, the
students learn to question aspects of what they see. For instance, they learn
to separate their suspicion of corporate motivation in producing GMOs

from the science behind it. But this relies on thinking and analysis that aren't widely being taught.

My experience is anecdotal but consistent with general findings by others who have studied the issue formally. There are numerous books documenting the enormity of the problem, including Richard Arum and Josipa Roksa's *Academically Adrift: Limited Learning on College Campuses*[2] and Derek Bok's *Our Underachieving Colleges: A Candid Look at How Much Students Learn and Why They Should Be Learning More*.[3] In the latter book, Bok, a former Harvard president and educational researcher, shares data on how little students retain from lectures; he then concludes: "The residue of knowledge and the habits of mind students take away from college are likely to be determined less by *which* courses they take than by *how* they are taught and *how well* they are taught."[4] He observes and laments that when faculty are reviewing curricula, the focus on content sometimes leads to additional required courses when instead they should be collecting data and analyzing how well and where critical reasoning is taking place.[5]

In a June 2017 article investigating critical thinking in higher education, the *Wall Street Journal* reported that US students rank very low on problem solving when compared to their international counterparts.[6] They found that "the test data show . . . that many students earn their degrees without improving their ability to think critically." Bok shared the finding that "only a small minority of seniors emerge convinced that ill-structured problems are susceptible to reasoned arguments based on evidence, and that some answers are sounder than others."[7] Students arrive at college as naïve relativists, thinking that people's opinions cannot be judged, he writes. All too often they do not develop the higher-order thinking skills to move beyond that into awareness that some problems are complex without easy answers, while at the same time understanding that some of those answers are better reasoned. Arum and Roksa share similarly discouraging findings: "An astounding proportion of students are progressing through higher education today without measurable gains in general skills. . . . . While they may be acquiring subject-specific knowledge or greater self-awareness on their journeys through college, many students are not improving their skills in critical thinking, complex reasoning, and writing."[8]

There are equally troubling findings for quantitative literacy and writing abilities upon graduation.[9] Pedagogy informed by such findings should be a defining trait of human rights education.

Table 5. International Documents' and Other Scholars' Guidance for HRE *Through* Human Rights

UNDHRET	• Human rights education and training . . . should be based on the principles of equality . . . human dignity, inclusion, and nondiscrimination
World Programme Phase 2	• Make use of participatory pedagogies that include knowledge, critical analysis, and skills for action furthering human rights • Foster teaching and learning environments free from want and fear that encourage participation, enjoyment of human rights, and the full development of the human personality
OSCE: Guidelines on HRE for Secondary School Systems	• Instruction and learning processes facilitate the inclusion of all students • Students are given the opportunity to propose and make choices that influence instruction and learning processes • Learner-centered methods and approaches that empower students and encourage their active participation, cooperative learning, and a sense of solidarity, creativity, dignity and self-esteem
Nancy Flowers: *HRE Handbook*	• Empowerment of participants to define what they want to know and to seek information for themselves • Active engagement of all participants in their own learning and a minimum of passive listening • Encouragement of nonhierarchical, democratic, collaborative learning environments • Respect for the experience of participants and recognition of a variety of points of view • Encouragement of reflection, analysis, and critical thinking; • Engagement of subjective and emotional responses as well as cognitive learning

Education *Through* Human Rights in the International Documents

Table 5 has a sample of recommendations from international documents, including UNDHRET, WP phases one and two, and the OSCE's *Guidelines on Human Rights Education for Secondary School Systems*. Nancy Flowers's review of recommendations are included also, as there is a great deal of consistency among them. (We will revisit these same texts in

Chapters 5 and 6 for guidance on education *for* and *about* human rights, respectively.)

Critical Thinking

In Table 5 the salient phrases include, "critical analysis," "reflection, analysis, and critical thinking," "critical evaluation," "create new responses," and being able to make a "judgment or decision." All of these are encompassed in critical thinking (CT) and necessary for a critical pedagogy. This chapter's opening quote about citizen education requiring students "to become more comfortable with ambiguity and complexity" also contains aspects of critical thinking. Clearly, the goals of social justice and multicultural education include building the skills of critical thinking. In fact, as discussed below, Heather Hackman lists CT as one of the five essential components for teaching social justice.[10]

More often than not, scholars cite the need for improvement in one or two aspects of higher-order thinking rather than arguing explicitly for teaching critical thinking. This is probably because "faculty's knowledge of perceptions and concepts [of critical thinking] is severely lacking."[11] But if CT is defined as a focus of HRE, we will be fulfilling the call to deep thinking that should be standard in all university education. HRE can lead the necessary shift in higher education by embedding CT into its mission and student learning outcomes. Moreover, it would be antithetical to our purpose to teach about the human rights movement through critical pedagogy without teaching students to question, analyze, and critique the subject.

Despite the fact that fully 99 percent of faculty believe that teaching CT is a central goal of higher education,[12] "few are prepared to teach critical thinking."[13] We wish we were teaching critical thinking, and often we assume that we are, but the research indicates that likely we are not.[14] Further, CT is a learned process, does not come naturally, and is difficult.[15] As Nobel Prize–winning psychologist Daniel Kahneman has demonstrated, we have many biases, which are not conducive to the habits of critical thinking.[16] For example, we are driven by confirmation bias to seek information from those who think as we do. The Internet greatly facilitates this bias by making it easier than ever to find sources that support rather than challenge our perspectives. Other biases that disincline us toward more critical thought include availability bias and the halo effect. The former causes us to believe information that confirms what we can see readily rather than possibly more accurate information that isn't as easily available. The halo effect clouds our judgment about others and their thinking when we have strong negative or positive feelings about them. If you really dislike a person, for example, it is hard to recognize anything they say as being sound when they may be speaking a clear truth. If human rights educators identify these human leanings in ourselves and recognize the potential effects, we are taking an important step toward transformative teaching. And then we can offer the power of our lived examples to our students.

There is no single widely accepted meaning of critical thinking, but many commonalities can be found among the oft-cited definitions. Two of these emphasize reflection: critical thinking scholar Robert Ennis wrote that CT is "reasonable, reflective thinking that is focused on what to believe or do."[17] And Richard Paul, former chair of the National Council for Excellence in Critical Thinking and founder of the Foundation for Critical Thinking, cleverly quipped that CT is "thinking about your thinking, while you're thinking, in order to make your thinking better."[18]

Cognitive scientist Daniel Willingham says CT consists of "seeing both sides of an issue, being open to new evidence that disconfirms your ideas, reasoning dispassionately, demanding claims be backed up by evidence, deducing and inferring conclusions from available facts, solving problems."[19] Bok's definition is similar, citing the abilities to "to ask pertinent questions, recognize and define problems, identify the arguments on all sides of an issue, search for and use relevant data, and arrive in the end at carefully reasoned judgments."[20] The latter two scholars include considering more than one perspective, but Hackman introduces more nuance to that requirement. She says critical thinking requires

(1) focusing on information from multiple, non-dominant perspectives, and seeing those as independently valid and not as an add-on to the dominant, hegemonic one;
(2) de-centering students' analytical frame and opening their minds to a broader range of experiences;
(3) analyzing the effects of power and oppression; and
(4) inquiring into what alternatives exist with respect to the current, dominant view of reality of this issue.[21]

It is not enough to expose students to more than one argument. We must invite them to consider non-dominant voices, especially the voices of people who are not like them. This definition is particularly germane to HRE's mission, because affecting systemic change necessitates deep listening; centering the experiences, needs, and desires of those we desire to empower and uplift; facilitating their voices being heard; and building capacity for creating change.

Thus, the definition that I endorse for CT is an amalgam of Willingham's and Hackman's. In addition to including the need to critically evaluate evidence and learning to problem-solve, Willingham demands that we teach students to see multiple sides of an issue, and Hackman rightly asserts that we must include non-dominant views and the willingness to disconfirm our own ideas.

Courses can be designed or revised to include activities and assignments that require higher-order thinking. In fact, critical thinking should be made an explicit goal for students in higher education. In one large meta-analysis, the authors found that CT had the strongest effect on student learning when critical thinking was spelled out as an objective within the context of disciplinary content. That is, it is better to teach critical thinking along with disciplinary content than to teach a stand-alone course whose only focus is teaching CT—with the caveat that the skills need to be taught explicitly. For example, students might be asked to enumerate its elements and then be provided a definition of critical thinking. Then they need to see when and how they are applying it. The evidence of the meta-review indicated that when a set of critical thinking skills was taught alongside, and then applied to disciplinary content, the effect was significant.[22]

The Foundation for Critical Thinking offers a basic but essential assignment requiring CT, and aspects of it can be reiterated throughout a course. As mentioned in Chapter 3, they suggest teaching eight elements of critical thinking (in italics below) and then having them form the elements into questions to ask of a topic or reading: what is its *purpose* or goal?; it is guided by what *questions*?; requires or is based on what *information*?; involves or leads to what *inferences*?; has which *concepts*?; is based on what *assumptions* and *points of view*?; and has what *implications*? Washington State University created a rubric for CT partially based on this method.[23] They asked faculty to design assignments that would teach students to identify and present or identify and assess eight aspects: (1) the *problem/question* at issue (and the source's position), (2) the *student's own perspectives* and positions (aka "positionality," which we discuss in the next chapter, as it is important to the analysis of the issue), (3) *other salient perspectives* and positions, (4) the quality of the supporting *data/evidence*, (5) the influence of the *context* on the issue (sociocultural, scientific, educational, economic, technological, ethical, political, and or personal experience), and, finally, the (6) *conclusions*, (7) *implications*, and (8) *consequences*. Their preliminary research indicated a significant difference in students' critical thinking ability pursuant to participating in courses where the rubric was implemented as compared to students in courses without it.[24] For a human rights education, the requirement that students identify their own perspectives is especially relevant if students are to connect to human rights personally, understanding its relevance to their lives and their role in promoting rights.

Not every homework assignment needs to require that students identify all seven or eight elements of CT. Requiring all questions be answered in one assignment can be less effective at first than breaking up the skills into successive assignments. For instance, perhaps you ask students to focus on identifying the author's point of view and assumptions for one assignment, and in another you ask students to state their own biases and opinions. When faculty spread out higher-order thinking requirements over many assignments, they are more likely to stimulate a disposition toward critical thinking in their students. Unsurprisingly, research has fortified the notion that repetition is important in teaching these skills.[25] Thus, we should ask students to respond to these kinds of prompts often, in both written work and discussion. Below we will see that the merits of in-class discussion include several precursors to and aspects of higher-order thinking, including exposure to diverse perspectives, tolerance for ambiguity and complexity, finding assumptions, and synthesizing and integrating ideas.[26] And yet L. Dee Fink's research demonstrates that in-depth, substantial discussions in the college classroom are "extremely rare."[27]

The most sophisticated approach to teaching CT involves structuring curriculum such that increasingly complex activities requiring critical thinking occur throughout a degree program. A curriculum map is a helpful planning tool for this kind of cumulative, longitudinal skill-building. Such a map (see Appendix II) is formatted as a table listing courses in the first column and the outcomes or skills enumerated along the top row. The boxes within the table indicate where each skill is introduced, reinforced, and then mastered and assessed. Every skill is taught in at least three courses, requiring increased ability with each subsequent repetition.

Hundreds of institutions rely on the Association of American Colleges and Universities (AAC&U) VALUE rubrics as guides for teaching and

Try This: An Assignment for Teaching Critical Thinking

University of New Mexico colleagues Drs. Sheri Williams and Martina Rosenberg and I developed a method for teaching critical thinking, "Using Performance Tasks," that can be applied to almost any topic. The method was so named because students have to perform tasks with the material. In this case, students were asked to read, analyze, and write coherently, synthesizing the material, and then repeat the process after receiving and assimilating feedback. After three or four of such assignments in a semester, students report a greater understanding of what qualities makes one source stronger than another, and many demonstrate improvement in critical thinking. Though they claim to know how to evaluate a text, many discover that only in reading vastly different sources side by side do they begin to grasp the danger of weak but effective rhetoric as compared to solid, evidence-based arguments.

Materials: Readings presenting different arguments on the same topic from sources of differing quality, including sloppy and inflammatory media articles, opinion pieces, peer-reviewed journal articles, book chapters of varying value, etc.

Rubric: See Table 6.

Assignment: Circulate the critical thinking rubric and discuss. Then provide three to five reading selections (often an excerpt is sufficient) on a single topic. Readings can be done in class or for homework. This exercise is most effective when arguments made in the readings contradict each other. Finally, have students answer the four questions below. After grading the assignments, return with marked-up rubrics and demonstrate to the students where they were more and less successful in their answers.

Sample topic: Whether purchasing industrial agricultural products or "buying local" will do more to address world hunger. Possible readings include (1) *Relocalization Not Globalization*, by Vandana Shiva; (2) *Just Food: Where Locavores Get It Wrong and How We Can Truly Eat Responsibly*, by James McWilliams; (3) *In Defense of Food: An Eater's Manifesto*, by Michael Pollan (pp. 157–61).

Students are asked to respond to these three questions for each reading selection:

(1) What is the, or a, main point of the reading?
(2) What evidence or data is offered in support of that point?
(3) Is the evidence adequate to support it? Illustrate your answer by including sentences/examples from the text.

Synthesis question after considering all readings:

(4) Based on the readings, which system offers more benefits to humanity? Buying local or industrial agricultural? Include references or quotations from the readings to support your response.

Adapted from UNM Biochemistry and Medical Education Researchers, September 2014, and H. G. Andrade (February 2000). "Using Rubrics to Promote Thinking and Learning." *Educational Leadership* 57, no. 5(2000): 13–18. Retrieved from http://www.ascd.org/publications/educational-leadership/feb00/vol57/num05/Using-Rubrics-to-Promote-Thinking-and-Learning.aspx, and Sarita Cargas, Sheri Williams, Martina Rosenberg, "An Approach to Teaching Critical Thinking Across Disciplines Using Performance Tasks with a Common Rubric," in *Thinking Skills and Creativity* 26 (2017) 24–37.

assessment.[28] The AAC&U "Critical Thinking VALUE Rubric" can be found at https://www.aacu.org/value/rubrics/critical-thinking. An example of scaffolding for critical thinking skills would be to design four years of writing assignments with increasingly demanding prompts. To begin, we might ask freshmen to analyze an argument for only its main point and evidence. Then they might be offered a prompt requiring them to deduce an author's assumptions and biases, evaluate the evidence, and state the implications of an argument. In subsequent years, when this method of active reading and analysis has become habituated, we can offer increasingly complex problems or more ambiguous or challenging texts to continue to build capacity.

Every core course proposed in Chapter 6 has student learning outcomes requiring critical analysis. An introductory human rights course recommends knowing the basic debates and controversies relevant to human rights. An analysis of the universality of rights, for example, requires evaluating differing arguments. An analytic approach to introducing the main actors in human rights could include critique of governments, multinational corporations, international organizations, NGOs, and even religions for, by turns, violating and promoting human rights. Investigating only the flaws or solely the virtues of any of these actors is contrary to our purpose.

A theory course provides a wonderful proving ground for critical analysis, because a text on the philosophy of human rights presents conflicting arguments. In an advocacy course, students might study efforts, failures, and achievements in order to investigate effective methods and discern the possible pitfalls (unintended consequences) of activism.[29] A course centered on current problems can require that all issues be evaluated from multiple

Table 6. Rubric for an Assignment for Teaching Critical Thinking

Criteria	Excellent 3	Competent 2	Needs Work 1
Claims Made	Student states the important claim(s) correctly.	Restatement of author's claim(s) is only partially correct. Or it could be correct but is not a central claim for the author's main argument.	Does not state the author's claim(s) correctly.
Evidence	Student cites and specifies the correct data or evidence to support the claim. Offers a quote from the text.	Some aspect of the answer is correct, but another aspect may be incorrect, vaguely stated, or otherwise insufficient.	Did not provide evidence or data from the text or provided the wrong evidence for the claim(s) cited.
Evaluation	Student cites what is strong or weak about the argument and data/evidence provided.	Notices what is adequate or problematic, but answer also has some aspect that is incorrect or incomplete.	Incorrect answer or overstates the results; does not address any strength or weakness.
Synthesis, Integration	Student draws accurate conclusions from the combined readings based on the strengths and weaknesses of the texts.	Conclusions are based on readings but only partially correct. Something incorrect might be included in the answer. (For example, putting words in the author's mouth.)	The conclusion drawn is not based on a synthesis of the texts. For example, it might be based on student opinion.

perspectives while requiring critique of explanations, justifications, and arguments offered to explain events. A research methods course might include a critique of data and studies on the ethics of using human subjects. And the capstone should demonstrate the ability to critique, as its whole purpose is to exhibit mastery of the field, or some aspect of it, through a sophisticated, critical work.

Thus, critical thinking provides us with an impeccable vehicle through which to approach HRE. It addresses many necessities, including teaching the essential skills of analysis, perspective, and problem solving, all of which will aid in the pursuit of social justice.

Learning from Social Justice Education

As noted, the written guidelines for HRE represented in Table 5 were not primarily intended for higher education. They were also sometimes written for a global or large regional audience such as Asia or the EU. Often they specifically refer to teaching children or training the police or military. It makes sense to instruct people teaching in post-conflict situations where intolerance has been rife to teach based on the principles of equality and nondiscrimination. However, though university faculty are not the primary audience, the recommendations are important for and applicable to us as well. As the various scholarship on teaching civic engagement, social justice, and multiculturalism in higher education argues, such pedagogy is as necessary on US college campuses as anywhere else in the world.[30]

Without entering into a lengthy digression on the debates about the terms and differences between civic engagement, social justice, and multicultural education, I propose that there is sufficient overlap in their goals and those of HRE to borrow liberally from these fields. This is illustrated by the AAC&U VALUE rubrics discussed above. They are intended to serve as a "basic framework of expectations" for educators on fifteen teaching goals, including quantitative literacy, ethics, and written and oral communication. Though AAC&U does not offer VALUE rubrics for social justice or multicultural knowledge, the association does have them for civic engagement and intercultural knowledge, including measures for learning about "diversity of communities and cultures" and "knowledge of cultural worldview frameworks," "civic action," and developing attitudes of "empathy" and "openness." These terms are also relevant for teaching social justice and multiculturalism within a critical pedagogy. And we will see in the discussion below that developing empathy can play an especially significant role on education *for* human rights.

UNDHRET uses the phrases "principles of equity" and "inclusion and non-discrimination" as guides for faculty. SJE also prescribes teaching based on principles of fairness and equality.[31] Lauren Bialystok describes it as "a disposition toward recognizing and eradicating all forms of oppression and differential treatment."[32] Nadine Dolby, professor of curriculum studies at Purdue University, writes that multicultural education and SJE are not the same, but she considers social justice the foundation for multicultural education.[33] In what follows, I have elected to use SJE as a guide for how HRE can operationalize the recommendations from the international documents because the pedagogy of the two types of education so often intersect. Social philosopher and activist Maxine Greene's description of the purpose of SJE could have been written about HRE: "It is to teach so that the young may be awakened to the joy of working for transformation in the smallest places, so that they may become healers and change their worlds."[34] We see the theme of transformation and social change in both pedagogies.

Heather Hackman suggests five ways of promoting social justice in the college classroom: we need to teach content mastery, tools for critical analysis, tools for social change, tools for personal reflection, and awareness of multicultural group dynamics.[35] (I review her suggestions for teaching action and personal reflection to students in Chapter 5, on teaching *for* human rights.) Here let's examine content mastery and critical analysis. Hackman's twist, if you will, that is especially relevant for HRE is that "factual information must not merely reproduce dominant, hegemonic ideologies but instead represent a range of ideas and information that go beyond those usually presented in mainstream media or educational materials. More specifically, the 'facts' necessary for effective social justice education must represent broad and deep levels of information so that students can critically examine content."[36]

To address the issue of didactic preparation, I suggest using primary sources and a variety of texts through which to frame rights, as well as contextual information. To build on Hackman's definition, we would add that in order to master content, students must help construct the knowledge together and locate themselves within it. In this way they develop an ownership of what they have learned and a sense of self-efficacy in the process. Thus, students must then locate their own positionality within that context (e.g., "I am a white woman talking about racism against young black men" or "I am a lesbian discussing homophobia"), because our positions belie some of our biases and remind us that our points of view are simply that: the view from where we now stand. As Robin DiAngelo and Özlem Sensoy explain, if we encourage "students to try-on positionality, rather than insulate and protect their current perspectives, their understanding of social power [can] be expanded."[37] Human rights are deeply personal. Awareness of social power structures and our perceived place within them—ways we benefit from the status quo and ways we pay for the status quo—is crucial to the task of learning rights. This segues into a call for critical analysis.

The practical implications for HRE are that we teach the multiple perspectives generated by human rights topics. Whether it is varying first-person accounts of an event or philosophic debates, we want to always promote multiple perspectives inherent in conflicts revealing the realm of a complex reality that goes far beyond the idea of who is good and bad or right and wrong. Becoming aware of and comfortable with complexity is part of cognitive maturity, as is the ability to hold the tension of uncertainty instead of rushing to judgment.

Other scholars who offer practical classroom advice combine Hackman's two foci of mastering content and applying critical analysis with Paolo Freire's education for liberation philosophy in their recommendations to promote a critical literacy classroom for SJE.[38] Jill Marshall and Ana Maria Klein explain it as one that "encourages readers to move beyond passively accepting the messages they read in texts, and fosters good question-posing."[39] This is accomplished, in part, by work on one's emotional intelligence. Students benefit from questions that inspire them to reflect on their own biases and positions related to the topic at hand prior to engaging with contrary points of view.

Two further classroom techniques offered by Marshall and Klein, which also offer a window into the experience of others, are role-playing and civic debates.[40] In debating, students learn that disagreements and difficult topics can be discussed civilly within the rules of debate. An excellent way to "flip the script" on debate for the purpose of upending the attachment to one's viewpoint is to have students prepare for one side of the debate, exchange notes with students who prepared for the other side, and then argue the opposing view. These methods for teaching social justice are equally applicable for promoting human rights in education *through* human rights. That is, in using the approaches of "decentering" content, promoting critical analysis, reading primary sources, and engaging in the dialogic activities of role-play and debate, we highlight a human rights approach as we teach.

Active Learning

Focusing on a social justice approach integrates with not only critical thinking but also the recommendation that HRE rely on active learning. The World Programme uses the phrase "participatory pedagogies" and the OSCE uses "learner-centered methodologies," which can be considered synonymous with active learning. One rather basic definition of active learning is that it involves engaging "students in the process of learning through activities and/or discussion in class. . . . It emphasizes higher-order thinking and often involves group work."[41] Another definition, which helps explain why the process is important, emphasizes that the mind must be engaged. Active learning happens when "students make information or a concept their own by connecting it to their existing knowledge and experience. . . . An engaged student actively examines, questions, and relates new ideas to old, thereby achieving a kind of deep learning that lasts."[42] When done well, these activities are engaging and, in addition to teaching useful transferable life skills, make learning personal. In the exercise outlined below, we see how students can be invited to cocreate their own agreement for how they wish to engage and the boundaries they want respected. This offers them more authority and more responsibility in the learning environment, both of which are crucial aspects for enacting a critical pedagogy.

According to Elizabeth Barkley, neuroscience describes the brain functions that occur when active learning is taking place.[43] When students are connecting new information and content with their own experience, neuronal networks are strengthened. Research demonstrates that this is less likely to occur in lectures than in active learning. In one study the authors concluded from the "largest and most comprehensive meta-analysis of undergraduate STEM education published to date" that "the results raise questions about the continued use of traditional lecturing as a control in research studies, and support active learning as the preferred, empirically validated teaching practice in regular classrooms."[44] Further, "active learning has been demonstrated to improve retention of content but it can also stimulate critical thinking."[45] Students might hear differing viewpoints in the context of active learning as opposed to the lone voice they encounter during lecture. As they engage with differing views, one might be supported by noticeably stronger evidence, thus leading them to the awareness of what constitutes a well-reasoned argument. Alternately, they may hear two different but equally strong points, which might challenge them to the higher-order-thinking level of analysis or even synthesis.

In addition to evidence to supporting its use, active learning is also an especially appropriate approach for education *through* human rights because of several characteristics. Participation in one's own learning has an affective impact: it increases a positive emotional response to learning. Students begin to care more about the material, which influences motivation that is essential for learning. Since one of the goals of HRE is to elicit an emotional response from students, this is an important tool. Also, active learning contributes to a sense of community in the classroom. At the very least, students come to know one another through the various activities even if community building is not the focus. Requiring all students to participate in both whole class and small group discussions contributes to this. One can do activities with the intent of increasing group connections as well. Using icebreakers at the beginning of and throughout the semester is one example. Perhaps the most relevant aspect of active learning for HRE is that it requires inclusion of everyone in the room. Creating activities with techniques for getting everyone to participate is one way of demonstrating respect for people's perspective, experience, and knowledge.

The key to getting desirable results is planning sound classroom techniques. Not just any participatory activity motivates students and requires higher-order thinking. Educational scholarship repeatedly talks about the importance of real-world or big and complex problems for motivating and increasing learning. HRE is perfectly suited to this requirement to teach with big and important problems, some of which will directly relate to our students' personal lives. This is one field where it will often be quite easy to demonstrate relevance, because the topics of human rights are almost all current issues. Having students bring a relevant news article to class each week helps them make the connection between their studies and the state of the world.

Since there are numerous books containing active learning techniques for every size class, here I focus only on discussion—whole class and small group—as one of the most common, and one that is especially appropriate for HRE in the promotion of educating *through* human rights. Most handbooks with exercises include discussion, but what follows is a brief review of the germane aspects of Stephen Brookfield and Stephen Preskill's book, *Discussion as a Way of Teaching: Tools and Techniques for Democratic Classrooms*.[46] As indicated by the title, the two authors argue that there are political implications in requiring discussion as an aspect of one's pedagogy. It should serve as a model for dialogue in civil society, allow students to experience "democratic conversation," and move authority away from the teacher.[47] All of these ambitions align perfectly with the goals of promoting a course based on rights.

However, it is not easy to have a meaningful discussion. In fact, the authors say, it is a "staggering challenge" to bring democratic conversation to an undemocratic environment.[48] The authors argue that we need to promote critical discussion involving "mutual and reciprocal critique."[49] The four goals of critical discussion are (1) informed understanding of the topic, (2) increased self-awareness, (3) recognition of diversity of opinion, and (4) "to act as a catalyst to helping people take informed action in the world."[50] Again, this is a seemingly tailor-made agenda for education *through* human rights! In order to achieve this, Brookfield and Preskill suggest it requires cultivating nine dispositions in faculty and students: (1) hospitality, (2) participation, (3) mindfulness, (4) humility, (5) mutuality, (6) deliberation, (7) appreciation, (8) hope (for gaining understanding, perspective, or clarification), and (9) autonomy (courage to hold an opinion).[51]

The authors offer fifteen benefits of sound discussion, all of which ally with the goals of HRE and are thus worth providing here:

1. It helps students explore a diversity of perspectives.
2. It increases students' awareness of and tolerance for ambiguity or complexity.
3. It helps students recognize and investigate their assumptions.
4. It encourages attentive, respectful listening.
5. It develops new appreciation for continuing differences.
6. It increases intellectual agility.
7. It helps students become connected to a topic.
8. It shows respect for students' voices and experiences.

9. It helps students learn the processes and habits of democratic discourse.
10. It affirms students as cocreators of knowledge.
11. It develops the capacity for the clear communication of ideas and meaning.
12. It develops the habits of collaborative learning.
13. It increases breadth and makes students more empathic.
14. It helps students develop skills of synthesis and integration.
15. It leads to transformation.[52]

It is interesting to note how many points in this list are similar to the goals of social justice education and the goals enumerated in Table 5. SJE promotes democratic discourse, diversity of perspective, connection, and empathy. The international documents recommend collaborative learning, the tolerance for ambiguity involved in critical thinking, and transformation.

How do faculty ensure quality discussion? Students will not necessarily be skilled at the dynamics of listening carefully and responding to what others have said. It can be easier for them to just make sure one talks and states an opinion without regard to previous points made. Brookfield and Preskill advise establishing ground rules, preparing students for the discussion through reading assignments, and justifying the need for discussion. For getting a discussion started, they make recommendations for asking relevant questions, and finally they discuss assessment.

Asking the class to participate in determining the rules for discussion encourages them to take ownership of the process. Because not all students are happy to participate, it is also useful to share the benefits listed above. It can be helpful to ask them what has and has not worked for them in past experiences. Having discussions based on reading assignments helps students to feel equally prepared to have thoughts and opinions about topics. This does not ensure that everyone will feel confident to speak, but it is an important step in doing so. Asking questions about the text will also help students form a perspective while keeping the conversation tied to the text. These include asking students to write down questions that surface as they complete assigned readings or asking students to share an image or something that stands out in the reading for them. Prompts or sentence completion exercises can get the ball rolling: "The idea I most take issue with in the text is . . . ; the part of the lecture (or text) that I felt made the most sense to me was . . . ; the part of the lecture (or text) that I felt was the most confusing was."[53] This encourages an accurate summation of a passage while allowing students to share and explore their own thoughts.

Tying grades to discussion also emphasizes its importance. If we say that discussion is essential for learning but grade only on written work, then we are not sending a consistent message. One method offered is to ask students to keep a log that reflects on each of the fifteen benefits of discussion. After each conversation, determine whether each item was achieved. Faculty could also ask fewer questions to check in with students. Interestingly, Brookfield and Preskill do not think speaking in each session should be required, nor should faculty just grade on simple participation. In the authors' judgment, quiet students should not be forced to speak, but they would still be able to do the assessment. The authors have found that quiet students are more likely to speak eventually when they do not feel pressured by a requirement. On the other hand, some introverts have reported to me that they found value in having been required to contribute.

There are valuable alternatives to whole class discussion that can be more effective for large classes and for encouraging introverts. Guided small group discussions can also achieve the benefits listed previously. Research has shown that five is a good number of students to organize.[54] Smaller groups can allow for more tensions to surface, and larger ones can prevent some from participating. What questions faculty ask small groups to discuss is equally important, and the authors make recommendations. Conversations can be open-ended, or we can ask students to respond to the person who spoke previously, ensuring that students are listening carefully. Other books on active learning cited in Appendix IV have further suggestions for dialogic activities to keep small groups focused.

Like any other teaching practice, not every discussion will be successful. Hopefully, in employing these best practices for discussion, HRE faculty can achieve some of the benefits some of the time, taking the community in our classes and departments one step further on the road to practicing pluralistic democracy.

In summary, this chapter has offered critical pedagogy techniques for educating *through* human rights. We can accomplish this aspect of HRE by placing the skill of critical thinking at the forefront, informing how we teach SJE. Both critical thinking and education for social justice will be facilitated by active learning methods. These teaching tools can, in turn, help us with education *for* human rights, the topic to which we turn next.

Try This: World Café and Imaginative Interview

Below are two activities shared by Dr. Shayna Plaut of the University of Winnipeg that could be used in a variety of human rights courses. Both are group activities, although the first she adapted from the organization called World Café and facilitates small group discussions followed by whole group conversation. (The description below is based on the World Café's website.) The second one was created by Plaut and is group work that results in presentations.

World Café (60 Minutes)

The world café is a method developed in 1995 by a group of folks who wanted to have a community discussion about "critical social issues." It has since been used to help large groups have meaningful conversations about important topics. People are split into groups of no more than five, and they have approximately twenty-minute conversations together at "café" tables. They then split up, and all but one are "travelers" to new tables, while one stays behind as a "table host" to share highlights of the previous conversations with the new group. The founders recommend having at least three rounds of conversation. For the last round, students may return to their original groups to synthesize their discussions. Faculty might pose one question that is discussed in every round. Students can then learn from exchanges with multiple classmates about the same topic. Or a different question on the same topic can be posed for each round, which may lead to deeper or different insights. For more information, go to the World Café website: http://www.theworldcafe.com.

Activity steps: Arrange tables in a café style (four or five students around each table). Alternatively, chairs could be grouped in fours or fives. If you have tables, use large sheets of paper for a tablecloth if possible so that groups can write down thoughts or make doodles on it that pertain to the discussion.

- Pose a question that does not have an easy answer or has multiple answers, perhaps based on an assigned reading.
- Discuss for 15–20 minutes.
- Rotate to a new group. The table host relays some of the highlights of the previous conversation. Repeat.
- Have a whole class discussion. Can have people list a few main points on the board so that the highlights of the conversation are available for everyone to see.

*Imaginative Interview (Several Weeks, Mostly Done Outside
of Class as Homework)*

Plaut had students in the class read different books. Some groups read fiction, others narrative nonfiction, and some journalism. The imaginative interview assignment required they imagined interviewing the author, a character in the book, or someone related to it, and making a 10–12 minute presentation to the class. She wrote in an article that the "results were phenomenal in creativity, application, depth and ingenuity." She shared three examples. One was a video interviewing several journalists on the topic of the book written by Linda Polman (*The Crisis Caravan*). The second was a two-person play about an aspect of the graphic novel (Amir Soltani's *Zahra's Paradise*). They imagined interviewing someone who was not in the book (President Mahmoud Ahmadinejad) but was relevant to it. And, third, students made an audio podcast after reading the Thomas King book *The Truth about Stories*. They interviewed indigenous storytellers about themes the author wrote about.

Hopefully, it is now clear that making a decision to use pedagogical techniques of critical thinking, social justice, and active learning will inform what content one chooses to teach as well as how one will teach that content. These choices will determine the readings and the syllabus, helping to ensure diversity of perspective. They will make the classroom a lively place of fervent thought critique.

Chapter 5

Educating *For* Human Rights: Affecting Values and Teaching Advocacy

> *Presentation of information as truth devoid of critique runs the risk of creating a dogmatic and prescriptive classroom environment. In a social justice classroom all content is subject to debate and critique.*
> —Heather Hackman

Having established the importance of rooting course content in critique and the value of providing different voices and multiple perspectives on problems, we turn our attention to elements of education that center on values, attitudes, and empowerment. Educating *for* human rights is intended to shape, clarify, and mature a person's value system and inspire them to action through critical pedagogy techniques.

The UN Declaration on Human Rights Education and Training prescribes "empowering persons to enjoy and exercise their rights and to respect and uphold the rights of others" (Article 2c). The World Programme suggests we must be "developing values and reinforcing attitudes and behavior which uphold human rights."[1] The human rights practitioners that Flowers interviewed added, "HRE must be more than knowledge about human rights documents. It must involve the whole person and address skills and attitudes as well." And, "HRE must lead to action, both in individual lives and in the local and global communities."[2] An analysis of HRE educators' online discussions on the HREA website revealed "they highlight the ultimate goal of creating citizens who enact human rights, not

just students who know that they have human rights."[3] Using critical pedagogy to develop a critical consciousness will help achieve these goals of
changing students and society.

Numerous scholars advocate for change in endorsing *transformational*
human rights education. Felisa Tibbitts and Peter G. Kirchschläger explain
that HRE is "attempting to distinguish itself on the basis of its potential to
'empower' and 'transform.' "[4] Anne Becker, Annamagriet de Wet, and Willie van Vollenhoven also argue that rights-based education "should tran-
scend knowledge about human rights, moving towards transformative
action."[5] Monisha Bajaj echoes this in her survey of various HRE models in
several countries, finding that many aim for "transformative action."[6] The
University of Dayton's website conveys the hope that their HRE program
will "produce thoughtful and transformational servant-leaders."[7]

How exactly do we operationalize "transforming" students' values and
preparing them for action to "transform" society? Can it be done without
pushing a particular ideology but rather allowing them to maintain their
agency? It is important for us as a community of scholars to answer this
clearly. We have to begin by acknowledging that teaching human rights is
political because it is an inherently political topic. Also, teaching is always
done with some bias. Decisions about what and how to teach are based on
choice influenced by many factors. But there are ways of teaching human
rights—just as there are ways of teaching social justice or any topic—
without pushing a subjective ideology.

We must prioritize teaching students how to think, providing them with
adequate source material, and steering clear of teaching them what to think.
There is consensus that a human rights education should affect attitudes
and values, and promoting normative values is not antithetical to critical
thinking and a critical pedagogy of human rights. However, insisting on
dogmatic adherence to any views runs the risk that we may inspire aversion
to rights work in our students by short-circuiting their process of discovery.
Research has shown that professors who push partisan ideas undermine
their credibility with students.[8] And for those students with strong opinions, we risk encouraging ideologues who can argue passionately but aren't
able to meet others in the space of uncertainty to process a way forward
through contentious dialogue. We need to move students away from polar-
ity and encourage an exploration of ideas they disagree with.

A safeguard against pushing one's ideology is to base one's teaching on
normative principles. That which is backed by custom and law can provide

Table 7. International Documents' and Other Scholars' Guidance for HRE *For Human Rights*

UNDHRET	• Providing persons with knowledge, skills and understanding and developing their attitudes and behaviors, to empower them to contribute to the building and promotion of a universal culture of human rights (Article 2) • Pursuing the effective realization of all human rights and promoting tolerance, nondiscrimination, and equality • Contributing to the prevention of human rights violations and abuses and to the combating and eradication of all forms of discrimination, racism, stereotyping and incitement to hatred, and the harmful attitudes and prejudices that underlie them (Article 4)
World Programme Phase 2	• Empower communities and individuals to identify their human rights needs and to claim them effectively • Foster knowledge of and skills to use local, national, regional, and international human rights instruments and mechanisms for the protection of human rights
Claudia Lohrenscheit	*Emphasis on Respect, Responsibility, Solidarity* • Empowerment • Participation in the transformation of community life and society
Nancy Flowers: *HRE Handbook*	• Promotion of personal enrichment, self-esteem, and respect for the individual • Empowerment of participants to define what they want to know and to seek information for themselves • Encouragement of behavioral and attitudinal change • Emphasis on skill building and practical application of learning
OSCE: Guidelines on HRE for Secondary School Systems	• Respect for oneself and for others based on the recognition of the dignity of all persons and of their human rights • Acceptance of and respect for persons of different race, color, gender, language, political or other opinion, religion, national or social origin, property, birth, age or other status, with awareness of one's own inherent prejudices and biases, and commitment to overcoming these • Openness to reflecting and learning so as to improve personal behaviors aligned with human rights principles

Table 7. (continued)

OSCE: Guidelines on HRE for Secondary School Systems (continued)	• An active interest in human rights and justice-related themes • Appreciation of the link among rights, responsibilities, equality, diversity, nondiscrimination, social cohesion and intercultural and interreligious dialogue • Confidence in claiming human rights and an expectation of duty bearers to protect, respect, and fulfill human rights • Compassion for and solidarity with those suffering human rights violations and those who are the targets of attacks resulting from injustice and discrimination (especially vulnerable groups) • A belief that one person working collaboratively with others can make a difference in promoting human rights locally and globally, and motivation to doing so • Commitment to sustaining and safeguarding human rights and to not being a bystander when the dignity and rights of others are violated • Motivation and flexibility in carrying out collaborative efforts for human rights (e.g., as leaders, mediators, or activists)
Tibbitts quoting Meintjes (Meintjes, "Human Rights Education," 68.)	Critical human rights consciousness might have the following criteria: • the ability of students to recognize the human rights dimensions of, and their relationship to, a given conflict- or problem-oriented exercise; • an expression of awareness and concern about their role in the protection or promotion of these rights; • a critical evaluation of the potential responses that may be offered; • an attempt to identify or create new responses; • a judgment or decision about which choice is most appropriate; • an expression of confidence and a recognition of responsibility and influence in both the decision and its impact.

the justification for promoting specific values. This is not to say that all laws are rights-respecting and that none should be argued; slavery was once legal. But the US does take a stand on many social and political issues. Encouraging students to appreciate the importance of the rights the US has stood for across many generations is a defensible political agenda for the classroom, as is discussing the rights the country has yet to acknowledge.

This is easier to do with civil and political rights, which have an enormous body of law supporting them. However, the US government publicly promotes the UDHR on the State Department's website. On the homepage of the Bureau of Democracy, Human Rights, and Labor it is written: "The values captured in the UDHR and in other global and regional commitments are consistent with the values upon which the United States was founded centuries ago."[9] And on the web page pertaining to human rights in particular, it says: "The protection of fundamental human rights was a foundation stone in the establishment of the United States over 200 years ago. Since then, a central goal of U.S. foreign policy has been the promotion of respect for human rights, as embodied in the Universal Declaration of Human Rights."[10] This implies an endorsement of economic, social, and cultural rights as well.

Those rights surrounded by more controversy can be taught by exploring how Americans have debated them, especially since my theory of HRE requires the analysis of debates as an aspect of critique. We do have a long tradition of workers' rights, unions, and welfare, for example. President Franklin D. Roosevelt wanted to add a bill of economic rights to the Constitution. The key is to introduce students to the conversation in all of its nuance and depth. While the data also show that there are more leftists and progressives working in academe than there are in the general population, they also demonstrate that students do not report suffering from this imbalance. Conservative students are not normally persecuted for their ideology,[11] though a large segment of society fears the effects of the liberal professoriate.[12]

Human rights advocate and professor Henry Steiner argues, "The university . . . must study the human rights movement. But it is not the movement's advocate." He explains that precisely because students may be bringing a deep commitment to the moral vision, and because human rights offers an "idealism and hope for a better world," excessive veneration of the movement is a risk.[13] We must therefore train future leaders by educating them about problems within the movement as well as human rights abuses. We should problematize and illustrate the challenges and contradictions in human rights. Law professor Peter Rosenblum wrote that he tries to teach his students to be "ambivalent advocates." That is, he wants to encourage committed activism but not an uncritical one.[14]

Lauren Bialystok, a professor of social justice, offers five recommendations for teaching social justice in Canada that are applicable in any liberal democracy. The first is to teach principles that have legislative backing, including teaching human rights codes (for the US that can be the Constitution, Bill of Rights, UDHR, and the signed human rights treaties). Discussing the inconsistencies in the government's support of such principles is also a necessary facet of a critical pedagogy. For example, a good topic to explore is that the government says it stands for the UDHR but will not sign most of the human rights treaties turning the principles of the UDHR into law. Also on the topic of controversial principles, Bialystok's second suggestion is to teach those that are "compatible with a reasonable pluralism" while acknowledging the objections. She raises the example of abortion as something that is legal but opposed by some segments of society. Same-sex marriage is another contemporary example. Faculty cannot teach that these actions are unacceptable simply because a religion teaches that. Rather they have to present the law and can make students aware of the relevant objections.

The third suggestion is to "not engage in partisan politics or political activism that students do not choose." This is a crucial instruction for HRE faculty. While controversies and debates should be explored, "signing students up for rallies or marching them down to city hall inhibits students from forming their own conclusions autonomously." We cannot force them to take up any particular issue. Thus, I would argue that one should not offer credit for taking part in a particular event.[15]

However, Bialystok's recommendation number 4 is to teach the skills of democratic engagement. Courses can teach and promote civic engagement but only through teaching the principles behind it and the skills for doing it, not by requiring any particular action of students.

Because, as Bialystok's fifth recommendation instructs, we must "respect students' freedom to refrain from activities that contravene their own (emerging or tentative) comprehensive doctrines. . . . students should be exposed to SJE but entitled to hold their own opinions."[16] We can teach with the agenda of promoting human rights, but we cannot demand students think a specific way about human rights. We must follow best practices in teaching and allow them to be critical of any position.

With these guidelines in mind, let's return to the topic of how to teach for transformation. I propose three kinds of classes: (1) courses on arts and literature to cultivate empathy, (2) courses on advocacy, and (3) the capstone. Together they can provide the affective dimension of HRE and teach practical skills for action, which are aspects of critical pedagogy.

Art and Literature Courses

Literature has always served the function of introducing readers to new worlds and perspectives far from their own. Perhaps this is because, as Richard Rorty has written in an essay about the role of emotion in human rights: "these [last] two centuries are most easily understood not as a period of deepening understanding of the nature of rationality or of morality, but rather as one in which there occurred an astonishingly rapid progress of sentiments, in which it has become much easier for us to be moved to action by sad and sentimental stories."[17] When we hear stories of others, we can imagine what their reality is like. Such stories have had a profound effect on our sentimentality. As was recently written, "Literature isn't just for book lovers. Ever since it emerged four thousand years ago, it has shaped the lives of most humans on the planet."[18] This shaping has not always been for good, but we will explore the positive ways it has.

Other reasons for using literature cited in Alexandra Schultheis Moore and Elizabeth Swanson Goldberg's volume *Teaching Human Rights in Literary and Cultural Studies* include to defamiliarize and disorient students from their original opinions; to question what it means to "speak effectively, to define truth, and to address power;" to develop students' reading and writing abilities and to "foster students' sense of global citizenship"; and "to teach students to acknowledge other readers' perspectives and to begin to build for themselves a 'rickety bridge' to the world beyond the classroom."[19] Below I focus on the role of emotion—namely, empathy—in HRE.

Cultivating Strategic Empathy

Michalinos Zembylas has written about the crucial role of emotion in human rights education in conflict-ridden societies[20] as well as its importance for the critical pedagogy of HRE.[21] He argues for infusing our approaches with "pedagogic discomfort," "mutual vulnerability," and "compassion and strategic empathy." Pedagogic discomfort is created when students and teachers interrogate closely held values and beliefs. This is an act of mutual vulnerability. We must also encourage positionality—the act of making explicit our unique positions and relationships to the issues we raise—in order to allow us to notice our biases, the unawareness of which precludes real learning. It likewise prompts the admission that none of us has a complete view of what we are discussing, allowing us to become more curious.

Zembylas urges faculty to listen closely to students holding beliefs that may cause harm. This little instruction will be quite radical for the faculty who have argued that their job is to *tell* students who have wrong or bad beliefs (racism is usually the example) that they are wrong. And herein lies the role of empathy that Nadine Dolby argues for in her book on multiculturalism. We need to teach with the empathy that Zembylas promotes and to provide opportunities for our students to empathize—to give them practice with empathy in order to cultivate it.

We can become frustrated by what our students think or by the well-documented ignorance of the millennials.[22] They are not always well informed about current events, and at that age, Dolby reminds us, they might not be very experienced. Many will have not traveled beyond their comfort zones, literally or figuratively.

Most definitions of empathy incorporate the ability to feel what another is feeling. (Sympathy is alternatively defined as having pity or feeling sorry for another rather than feeling the same emotion.) Neuroscience has confirmed the fact that the secondhand experience of seeing someone else's pain is similar in the brain to firsthand experience.[23] Dolby is surely right in concluding that "much of this new discourse suggests that reason cannot be separated from emotion."[24] If we want to affect students' thinking about human rights, we must also affect their emotions. Science supports the scholarship, which argues that learning about human rights requires the skills of reason and emotion.

Teaching Empathy Through the Arts

Scholars such as Zembylas and Lynn Hunt write about the relationship of emotion—specifically empathy—and rationality in the realm of human rights. The latter has famously argued that human rights was invented alongside the rise and popularity of the epistolary novel in the eighteenth century. She quotes Denis Diderot, the cofounder of one of the greatest documents of Enlightenment rationality, the *Encyclopédie*, writing about the effect of one of these novels, "despite all precautions . . . you are thrown into conversations, you approve, you blame, you admire, you become irritated, you feel indignant."[25] These common experiences led to increased

Try This: Susan Katz's Use of Voice of Witness

Dr. Susan Katz at the University of San Francisco uses oral history as a peda-gogical tool to make the human rights content come alive in her course Human Rights Education: Pedagogy and Praxis. She uses the Voice of Witness (VOW) book series in her course. VOW is also the name of the organization founded by novelist Dave Eggers. Its mission is the production of educational resources for using oral histories in the classroom. The organi-zation has produced several theme-based book collections of oral histories on topics ranging from being a refugee to testimonies from victims of wrongful justice in the United States. They also have a compilation called *The Voice of Witness Reader*. There is a teacher's guide with twenty-three lessons as well as guides for each of their other books. Though the target audience is K–12, Dr. Katz has found the books and some lessons very useful in her graduate course. VOW is often able to put faculty in touch with oral history narrators who can speak to the class via Skype.

Description: Creating an oral history
Materials: Students, One or more of the VOW books of oral histories, a recording device
Assignment:

- Read a selection of histories from VOW books.
- Select a human rights issue of special interest that you want to research and develop for your final project.
- Choose someone with life experience related to this issue who agrees to an interview and will be your "narrator."
- Conduct and audiotape an interview of approximately 30–45 minutes with your narrator. Make sure to have consent form signed beforehand. (A sample form can be found in *The Power of the Story: The Voice of Witness Teacher's Guide to Oral History*, available to faculty who purchase a book.)
- Transcribe this interview and bring to class for editing workshop.
- Edit and submit to narrator for approval.
- Add introductory description of one paragraph.
- Submit final revised version

To learn more about Voice of Witness, visit http://voiceofwitness.org.

awareness of autonomy and empathy, which were required for the idea of individual rights to take hold, according to Hunt.

For many faculty, the easiest way to teach empathy through the arts within the confines of the classroom is through reading, showing videos, and sharing pictures. These are often the techniques used by psychologists and neuroscientists who perform studies on empathy. The participants in experiments are shown or asked to read scenes in which someone is experiencing pain. And the response of the participant is studied, be it the hemodynamic activity in the brain via fMRI (functional magnetic resonance imaging)[26] or neuropeptides.[27]

However, research also demonstrates that feeling empathy does not necessitate doing anything about the other's suffering. Or worse, empathetic reactions can be unjust. Anneke E. K. Buffone and Michael J. Poulin[28] researched the role of neurohormones in empathetic violence. They tell the story of a father walking in on his five-year-old daughter being raped and proceeding to beat the perpetrator to death then and there. The father was not found guilty of homicide, because he successfully convinced a court that killing the man was not his intent, as evidenced by his calling 911 upon realizing what he had done and expressing remorse. They conclude their article counseling caution about "empathy training."[29] Simply teaching people to feel more empathetic will not guarantee a just response. Expanded definitions of empathy in relation to teaching take this fact into account.

Zembylas writes of teaching strategic empathy (being both critical and strategic about empathy[30]), and Dolby discusses informed empathy ("empathy that carries with it the potential for change, not charity"[31]). Others, including Tania Singer and Olga Klimecki,[32] note the role of compassion in empathy and argue that aspect should be contemplated more than feeling others' pain, in order to prevent compassion fatigue. Marketers and torturers can be good at getting inside people's feelings but without compassion. They do it to manipulate (albeit for very different reasons).

The scholarship makes evident that our capacity for empathy, like the ability to think critically, is part of a biological process that can be cultivated. We can choose to not teach it and not help our students become more empathetic, or we can teach it carefully, through storytelling, by introducing students to the physical and psychological experiences of those who suffer human rights abuses. Literature and human rights courses that are already being taught include novels and memoirs from all over the world, as well as poetry and films. Theater and human rights courses use plays to teach human rights themes. Some faculty are teaching music and human rights courses, revealing how music has been used to tell stories and protest injustices.

Of course, we can include literature and other arts on nearly any human rights syllabus. In the quest to educate *for* human rights throughout the curriculum, even when literature is not the focus of a course, stories can be included. Numerous genres tell stories in fiction or nonfiction; therefore, a lot of avenues are open to faculty. One can have students read selections from an autobiography, a memoir, an interview, or novels and poetry. Documentaries and films, too, can bring many topics to life with images and sound.

Experiential Learning

But how do we facilitate translating empathy into action? It is well established that feelings do not necessarily lead to action. Part of the problem is that all of us, students especially, can feel overwhelmed by the hugeness of injustice. We can experience what Jack Donnelly calls the "possession paradox,"[33] when we possess rights but don't enjoy them. Also, as Dolby reports, students of this generation "do not feel adequately informed or able to make a difference as individuals."[34] Thus, in addition to educating students about abuses and their causes, we need to provide them with the tools for addressing them. This includes educating them about the long haul. Sometimes changes take decades or longer. Four out of the six sources in Table 7 recommend that we need to "empower" our students. UNDHRET Article 2 states that we should "empower them to contribute to the building and promotion of a universal culture of human rights."[35] The World Programme, Section 8d says we need to "empower communities and individuals to identify their human rights needs and to ensure that they are met."[36] Flowers finds that we need to promote "empowerment of participants to define what they want to know and to seek information for themselves."[37] We might term her added requirement as teaching information literacy.

"Empower" implies enabling someone to do something, and the *New Oxford American Dictionary* provides a definition that is perfectly suited to this context, defining it as to "make (someone) stronger and more confident, esp. in controlling their life and claiming their rights." Those are exactly outcomes we wish for with HRE: building strength, confidence,

Try This: Whole Class Debate (Activity for Exploring Empathy in a Play)

Dr. Maria Szasz at the University of New Mexico has created this activity for her Theatre and Human Rights course to explore the role of empathy in a play. This leads to a discussion of whether or not the students felt empathy. Though it may seem a bit formulaic, students are consistently enthusiastic about this debate. It forces them to analyze how writers do (or do not) engender emotion in an audience. (This debate works particularly well with Bertolt Brecht's *Mother Courage and Her Children* (1939), as Brecht wrote the play in his "epic theatre" style, which deliberately alienates the audience, yet the audience still feels empathy for the character of Kattrin, Mother Courage's youngest, mute child.)

Time: About 30 minutes.

Activity Steps: After reading a play a small class is divided in half. A bigger class can pick about 18–20 students to debate in front of the class (9 or 10 students on each side). While the teams are meeting, other students can discuss in pairs arguments and evidence, which can be presented after the debate. Provide the students with a debatable statement: (Name of playwright) successfully causes the audience to feel empathy with (name of character). Everyone participating in the debate must speak at least once.

- Team A are the affirmatives: they agree with the statement. They must provide supporting evidence from the play and cite passages.
- Team B are the negatives: they disagree with the statement. They must provide supporting evidence from the play and cite passages.

Format for Debate

Allow the teams to meet for 15 minutes to discuss their strategy, including finding passages and determining points to make in the speaking roles of each person.

Round 1:

- Team A member makes an opening statement. (About one minute)
- Team B member makes an opening statement. (About one minute)
- Team A/Affirmatives: five team members each make a single-topic argument supporting their team's opening statement. (About five minutes)
- Team B/Negatives: five team members each make a single-topic argument supporting their team's opening statement. (About five minutes)

Give the two groups another ten minutes to meet for preparation before the next round.

Round 2:

- Team A/Affirmatives: members respond, by turn, to Team B's claims from Round 1. (About five minutes)
- Team B/Negatives: members respond, by turn, to Team A's claims from Round 1. (About five minutes)

After the debate, have a whole class discussion. The following questions can be asked: Which arguments were strong on each side? Did the rest of the class have arguments and evidence not presented during the debate? Did anyone personally change his or her mind because of the debate? If so, what supporting evidence from the play helped change their minds? How so?

control, and claims to rights. To achieve these outcomes, two other under-graduate courses are helpful for education for human rights: an advocacy course and a capstone course. The first includes teaching the knowledge and skills necessary for advocacy, and the capstone is the culmination of the degree program. They should be project based and involve critique. The advocacy course would include creating an advocacy project while learning about tools and strategies for effectiveness. And the capstone has the primary objective of a student's exhibiting a thorough grasp of the program outcomes with an emphasis on demonstrating critical thinking via a research paper or project. Discussing these two courses requires a slight digression from the role of experiential learning in an HRE program, because projects that require students to interact with current issues or real-world problems in some active way are experiential. And experiential learning is essential for a human rights education that aims to produce advocates.

Many pedagogical activities exist that fall under the heading of experiential learning. They range from certain types of active learning to problem- and project-based inquiry to service learning.[38] Many people think experiential learning consists of learning that takes place outside the classroom. But not all extracurricular activities achieve the goals of experiential learning; it can take place in the classroom as well. Specific conditions

Try This: Human Rights Role-Play

Cece Shantzek, a doctoral student at Fielding Graduate University, designed this role-playing activity to encourage empathy while also exposing students to current issues in human rights and the institutions that must address human rights violations.

Description: Pairs of students present a human rights violation by role-playing the individual suffering as a result of a human rights abuse and an advocate working on their behalf.

Assignment: Pair up and research the circumstances of the individual's violation and from whom that person would seek redress or amelioration for the individual situation or the class of violations it represents (individual may be deceased). In a 6–8 minute presentation, one student plays the individual whose rights have been abused and introduces him or herself and the circumstances of the violation to the class. The other student acts as though making a presentation to an organization as an advocate for his or her partner, imploring something be done to stop the problem. Thus, students need to address a government body, NGO, or civil society entity (e.g., multinational corporation or religious body).

Materials needed: Faculty need to supply the appropriate number of names of individuals representing a wide range of topics and regions of the world, including local and national issues (or students can determine a person to research with faculty input). Individuals can be selected from Google searches on specific topics, the daily news, and Amnesty International or Human Rights Watch websites. Examples of such individuals and topics include:

- Shaker Aamer, tortured while imprisoned at the US Naval Base in Guantanamo Bay, Cuba
- Lilly Ledbetter, underpaid (as compared to male counterparts) for her whole career as plant manager for Goodyear Tire Company
- John Crawford III, shot to death by police while shopping at Walmart (Could substitute or add Sandra Bland, Philando Castile, Tamir Rice, Eric Garner – all citizens killed by police)
- Leyla Hussein of the UK, who underwent FGM (female genital mutilation)
- Jana, a 19-year-old Yazidi woman taken hostage and enslaved by ISIS
- Matthew Shepard, a 21-year-old gay man who was a political science major at the University of Wyoming, who was beaten and left for dead on October 6, 1998
- Malala Yousafzai, a Pakistani education activist who was shot by the Taliban at age 15

- Emmanuel Jal, a South Sudanese man who was coerced into becoming a child soldier at 7 years of age
- Shi Tao, a journalist in China who was arrested and jailed in 2005
- Aly Diabate, unwittingly recruited by a slave trader as a child of not quite 12
- Hillary Transue, sentenced to three months in juvenile detention for building a spoof MySpace page about her assistant principal
- Dilorom Abdukadirova of Uzbekistan, jailed for 10 years at a peaceful protest against the country's economy
- Nolanda, a single mother in Albuquerque, New Mexico, who was homeless with her children and found shelter through CLNkids (Cuidando Los Niños).

have to be met for something to be considered experiential learning. The definition provided by the Association for Experiential Education provides some of those criteria: "Experiential education is a philosophy that informs many methodologies in which educators purposefully engage with learners in direct experience and focused reflection in order to increase knowledge, develop skills, clarify values, and develop people's capacity to contribute to their communities."[39]

Direct experience with material or people and focused reflection are key to this kind of educational experience. In the classroom, debates and role-plays can be examples of experiential learning, though one might want to argue that those are instances of interaction with material more than they are "direct" experiences. The point is that students engage with material differently than they do in a lecture setting, and it is an empowering experience when they interact with their world.

Extracurricular activities will not fulfill the goals of experiential learning if they are done poorly. That is, if they do not involve a lot of student engagement with the process of posing questions, designing a project, making decisions, and doing guided reflection all along the way, an experience might not lead to deep learning. Faculty cannot simply leave students alone during experiential learning—our involvement is key. We need to provide mentorship and require that students reflect on each step of the process. We need to ensure that they become self-aware and able to critique their own attitudes, biases, strengths, and weaknesses. Research supports the concept that when done successfully, experiential learning counts as a "high impact practice."[40] And since a fundamental outcome of this type of learning is to "develop people's capacity to contribute to their communities," as defined above, experiential learning should be woven throughout core human rights courses and highlighted in the advocacy and capstone ones. Let's review what the design of each of these two types of courses might look like.

Advocacy Courses

Five student learning outcomes are suggested in Chapter 6 for an advocacy course. Upon completion of the course, students will be able to:

- critically evaluate human rights campaigns;
- demonstrate knowledge of methods for using the various UN entities for addressing human rights abuses including the UPR, treaty monitoring committees, special rapporteurs;
- demonstrate knowledge of the complaint procedures that are available in one's own city and at the country level;
- identify the role of NGOs and the private sector/business in the promotion and maintenance of human rights;
- develop an effective advocacy strategy employing participatory methods whenever possible.

A course with these outcomes will provide students with both the knowledge and the opportunity to create an advocacy project while practicing critique of human rights campaigns. Such classes could be the space for introducing students to and critiquing the methods of society's great dissenters.

An example of an advocacy course is one being taught at Columbia University by Jo Becker. She is also a longtime human rights campaigner and currently is the advocacy director of the Children's Rights Division at Human Rights Watch. Her Human Rights Skills and Advocacy course walks students through different advocacy assignments, including writing an op-ed, composing an advocacy letter to a policy maker, developing a role-play where students present their case to a policy maker, writing a submission to a treaty-monitoring body, and drafting a strategy paper addressing a specific human rights issue. Along the way, students examine international human rights campaigns described in a book of case studies she wrote, *Campaigning for Justice: Human Rights Advocacy in Practice* (2012).[41] They also discuss a local campaign to end the use of "stop and frisk" by the New York City Police Department. They learn about mechanisms for addressing abuses in the US from advocacy with local councils to Congress and the UN's mechanisms. Becker also introduces the class to historic individual dissenters by having them read the autobiography *My Name Is Jody Williams: A Vermont Girl's Winding Path to the Nobel Peace Prize.*[42] Her class appears to be a perfect example of an experiential course that takes place primarily in the classroom. Note that it does not dictate students take a particular stand on a specific topic.

Capstone Courses

The capstone course is a fundamental part of a comprehensive degree program. This final experiential course or set of courses is commonly at the end of a disciplinary degree program. The course(s) most often consists of a major paper, scholarly research, and an internship or service learning. If a main goal of HRE is to empower students to act, then a requirement to complete a major project provides experience that will be important in their professional development. If designed correctly, students not only prove their learning publicly, but they also demonstrate to themselves that they have the know-how to do something important for human rights. Recall Dolby's findings that students feel overwhelmed and powerless in the face of the world's problems. The capstone can address that sense of inefficacy. In focusing for a semester or more on a real-world problem in a practical application of skills and methods learned and then creating a presentation of their work, they are acting on behalf of human rights.

A considerable amount of research supports the effectiveness of the capstone course for undergraduates. The AAC&U lists both senior research capstones as well as internships and service- or community-based learning projects as being high-impact practices. And capstones across the country are usually of these several types. High-impact practices are characterized by "more engaging educational practices [in which] faculty members help students to make connections and take on big questions."[43]

Try This: Advocacy Assignments

Here are six writing assignments that Jo Becker of Columbia University and Human Rights Watch uses in her Human Rights Skills and Advocacy course.

1. Initial Advocacy Strategy Paper: Length 3–4 pages

Write your strategy paper as if you are representing a medium-size NGO with resources to carry out your plan.

Suggested format:

- Issue/problem statement: Explain the human rights problem you want to address; refer to other sources if you can, using footnotes (not longer than one page);
- Why? Explain briefly (one paragraph) why this issue should be addressed now;
- The change you are trying to achieve: Identify your long-term (i.e., your ultimate vision) and your short-term goals (e.g., what you hope to achieve over a 3–5 year time frame);
- Advocacy strategies/activities for an 18–24-month time period;
- Your partners/allies and how they can help you.

2. Op-Ed (Opinion Piece for a Newspaper or Magazine):
Length 700–750 Words

Choose a topic or a problem and solution that you want to inform the public about.

- Grab a reader's attention, make them want to continue reading to learn more.
- Have an advocacy angle, outlining who you would like to do what.
- Include evidence to back up your claims: statistics, personal experience, testimony/stories of people affected by the abuse you are describing and references to reports or scholarship.

3. Advocacy Letter: Length 2–3 Pages

Write a letter to a person of influence requesting that they address a situation/problem. The target of your letter should be a real person who is a policy maker or person of influence (e.g., a foreign minister, minister of justice, head of a UN agency, UN ambassador or member of Security Council, etc.).

Although formats vary, a good advocacy letter will do the following: state in the first paragraph the reason you are writing; explain who you represent (particularly important if the letter's recipient is not likely to know you or your organization); acknowledge positive steps they may have already taken to address your issue; give background information with supporting evidence to outline the problem you are asking them to address; refer to previous commitments they may have made on the issue or relevant national or international law/standards that apply; clearly outline what action you want them to take.

4. Advocacy Role-Play: 6–7 Minutes

Your assignment is to participate in a role-play with the policy maker you are writing to in your advocacy letter. The role-play will consist of an initial presentation of around 3 minutes, followed by questions and discussion with the official, and then feedback from the class. You should plan to introduce yourself, explain why you wanted to meet, give relevant background on your issue/why it's important, and outline what steps you hope the official will take to address it. Since we hope to simulate "real-life" situations, you should be prepared for variations, including interruptions, possible indifference, hostility, etc. Do background research on the individual you are meeting.

5. Submission to a Treaty Body: Suggested Length 6–8 Pages

Write a report to a human rights treaty body from the perspective of a particular country.
Background research:

- Pick a treaty with one or more articles related to your issue; you can check which countries have ratified a particular treaty at the UN treaty website: http://treaties.un.org/pages/Treaties.aspx?id = 4&subid = A& lang = en.
- Research what the relevant committee has already said (in its concluding observations) on this issue during the country's last review.*
- Research what the government has said about this issue in its last report to the committee.*
- Compile information about violations or noncompliance under the treaty for your issue and country, corresponding to the relevant treaty article(s). This can include examples of violations and/or problems with the government's laws or policies.

*Find this info by using the UN treaty body database (http://tb.ohchr.org/ default.aspx) on the OHCHR website, where you can enter in the treaty, the country, and what documents you are looking for. In this case, you want the concluding observations and the state party reports. Most of these documents are available in multiple languages—choose the one you want from the letters on the right side, e.g., E = English; S = Spanish; F = French, etc.

6. Final Revised Advocacy Strategy

Your final paper (up to 10 pages) will be an expanded and revised version of your first assignment—your advocacy strategy for your issue. Your long-term goal should be the same as in your initial paper; however, you may revise your medium- and short-term goals and objectives as you see fit. The main challenge of this assignment is to add and elaborate activities and strategies on how you are going to achieve your goals, based on what we've discussed in the class over the semester. For example, these might include:

- Use of media: outline upcoming hooks that you anticipate that you could use for press releases or op-eds and specific news outlets you might target;
- Use of social media: ideas for incorporating social media into your advocacy;
- Use of UN mechanisms: identify the special rapporteurs, working groups, and treaty bodies to whom you could submit information on your issue (including your "asks"). (In this case, indicate only those treaty bodies where the country has actually ratified, and research when the country is coming up for review as a state party. You might also include advocacy related to the Universal Periodic Review by the Human Rights Council, if the timing is right.);
- Use of US or third-party governments: ideas for engaging Congress/Parliament through legislation, resolutions, sign-on letters, etc.; strategies for engaging influential government officials and the change in policies that you hope to achieve;
- Use of coalitions and campaigning: ideas for building broader coalitions and/or engaging the public on your issue, including around upcoming events or hooks that relate to your issue.

Time Frame: The time frame for your strategy is flexible, but 3–5 years for your medium- and short-term goals and 18–24 months for your initial plan of activities are recommended.

They are effective because of several key elements, including independent writing and research; integration, synthesis, and application of learning to real-world settings; engagement with people different from themselves; and interaction with faculty and students on substantive matters. Further, capstones "greatly improve students' attainment of institutional learning goals through deeper learning and immersion in their discipline."[44] In addition to serving as a "cap" or integration of students' course work, capstones should be a bridge to their next stage, be it professional work or graduate school.[45]

Again, capstones come in different types—writing and research focused or having an outside-the-classroom experience. Which kind to choose for a degree program depends on several factors, including the mission of the academic program, the courses it is going to cap, and faculty and community resources. In any event, the capstone should be a continuation of the degree program. That is, skills expected of students during the capstone should be introduced and practiced in earlier courses. Those that we associate with critical pedagogy, including critical thinking, strategic empathy, or participatory research, could be demonstrated in the capstone. Robert C. Hauhart and Jon E. Grahe found that there is a huge difference between poorly designed capstones and well-designed ones.[46] The latter are either recognized as being longer than a semester, such as a yearlong capstone, or if the lead-up courses are not named as part of the capstone per se, there are prerequisites for it, such as writing-intensive and research methods courses. The point is that the most important skills need to be scaffolded throughout a curriculum, and the most successful capstones consist of a sequence of courses.

It is also the case that more highly structured capstones prove to be more effective in terms of student learning.[47] Even though capstones are characterized by independent work, students benefit from being given detailed guidelines. These include timelines and deadlines for each stage of the project; contracts with community supervisors when doing work away from the classroom; paper requirements, including page length and style; and a schedule of meetings with faculty and the agenda for those meetings. An example of the University of Connecticut's capstone course can be found in Appendix I.

In summary, through taking part in courses on or using literature and the arts, advocacy courses, and capstones, students will be provided paths for affecting their attitudes and values and tools for empowerment. In implementing these courses with critical pedagogy, we will be fulfilling the call to education *for* human rights. Currently, however, all three of these types of courses are not required in any human rights program in the US or Canada.

Perhaps there is some hesitancy to teach those agendas to which we know conservative critics of higher education would object. They might accuse us of indoctrinating students and pushing a radical activist agenda.

We, faculty, must be confident that there is a correct way for approaching values and teaching advocacy in the classroom. We need not be at odds with our country's lofty agenda for education to promote civic engagement for living in our democracy. This necessarily includes caring about and advocating for our rights.

Chapter 6

Educating *About* Human Rights: Designing a Human Rights Curriculum and Courses

> *If human rights education is to become a genuine field, then we are challenged to become more coherent (even among our diversity of models), to be unique (offering value and outcomes that other educational programs cannot), and to be able to replicate ourselves.*
> —Felisa Tibbitts

Having discussed the importance of, and some critical approaches for, creating a rights-respecting classroom, including methods of exploring values, attitudes, and empowerment, we can establish the curriculum for a discipline of human rights: a major, a minor, a concentration, and a certificate. We can also establish the elements of individual course design. As Felisa Tibbitts observes in the chapter's opening, it is time for us to establish a coherent field of study. She continues:

> In order for human rights education to become more qualified as a field, there are several criteria that we can begin to explore and document:
> a) a core body of knowledge;
> b) clear goals for learners;
> c) pedagogy built on sound knowledge of learner, learning theory . . . ;
> d) documentation of success, and sharing of best practice—with sensitivity to culture;

 e) preparation of trainers;

 f) recognition and integration of the field within educating organizations.[1]

This chapter's agenda is to provide a description of an HRE model and, through explicating the core knowledge and offering clear outcomes, demonstrate that it is both unique and replicable. Thus, here I integrate the findings of the first half of the book and the pedagogical mandates of the previous two chapters to propose the knowledge content: education *about* human rights. As defined by the UN Declaration on Human Rights Education and Training, education *about* human rights is "providing knowledge and understanding of human rights norms and principles, the values that underpin them and the mechanisms for their protection."[2]

Educating *about* human rights is what formal institutions that provide HRE do. Transmitting content to students is what universities were created for. Further, there is more guidance for what such content should consist of in the HRE literature than any other aspect of HRE.

All guidance related to HRE includes learning about the documents (some mentions are implicit) and the mechanisms and skills for promoting and protecting human rights. The documents reviewed in Table 8 reveal commonalities such as the requirement to teach issues, violations, and emerging problems. Two mention teaching values, the debates, and history of human rights. The most comprehensive content list comes from the OSCE's *Guidelines for Human Rights Education for Secondary School Systems*. It includes everything in the above list and much more. Though written for secondary schools, this list is easily translatable to higher education. Each item can be appropriately framed for a variety of developmental levels. The "root causes of human rights violations," for example, might be presented to younger students in a factual manner but explored with university students with less certainty and more room to grapple and expand awareness.

In Table 9 I have noted in brackets the courses for which HRE content is well suited. Often material is appropriate for several courses; for instance, introductory courses might offer a glimpse of a topic that is explored in more depth in another course.

Turning these content recommendations into a curriculum could take numerous forms. Many of the guidelines listed in the table already appear in different courses. For example, the OSCE guideline to teach "arguments

Table 8. International Documents' and Other Scholars' Guidance
for HRE *About* Human Rights

UNDHRET	• Providing knowledge and understanding of human rights norms and principles • Values that underpin them • Mechanisms for their protection
World Programme Phase 2	• Indivisibility and universality of human rights, including civil, political, and economic, social and cultural rights and the right to development • Analysis of chronic and emerging human rights problems (including poverty, violent conflicts, and discrimination) • Knowledge of and skills to use local, national, regional, and international human rights instruments and mechanisms for the protection of human rights research about HRE
Claudia Lohrenscheit	• History and content of human rights documents • Combination of human rights and human duties that emerge out of them as well as the responsibility of the individual • Controversies of human rights in the international debate • Realisation (instruments) and practice of human rights (including national and international actors) • Knowledge about human rights violations (including all forms of inequality and discrimination) • Various forms of resistance, key events, and important persons or organizations in the worldwide struggle for human rights
Nancy Flowers: *HRE Handbook*	• Human rights history and documents • Human rights issues • Human rights values and skills • Debates over content

for the universality, indivisibility, and interdependence of human rights and common challenges to each of these perspectives" is taught in introductory and theories courses. The history of the human rights movement is also currently taught in introductory courses, courses focused on history, and sociology courses. Thus, what follows in this chapter are suggestions based on a curriculum consisting of a particular set of core courses. Together they cover all the content recommended in the tables in this chapter and are not inconsistent with syllabi I have surveyed.

Table 9. OSCE's *Guidelines for Human Rights Education for Secondary School Systems*

OSCE: Guidelines on HRE for Secondary School Systems	• The history and philosophy of human rights, including the Universal Declaration of Human Rights [Intro, theories] • Human rights as a values framework and its close relationship with other ethical, religious and moral value frameworks, as well as other social goals and developments, such as democracy, peace and security, economic and human development, and globalization [Intro, theories, history, literature] • Human rights . . . principles: participation and inclusion, equality and nondiscrimination, accountability, freedom from all forms of violence . . . [Intro, theories] • International human rights standards elaborated in international and regional instruments [Intro, law, advocacy] • The evolving nature of the human rights framework and the ongoing development of human rights in all regions of the world, linked to the human struggle for freedom, equality, justice and dignity [Intro, theories, history] • State obligations in relation to human rights, including review of domestic legal frameworks, treaties and mechanisms of protection at the national, regional and international levels [Intro, law, methods] • Arguments for the universality, indivisibility and interdependence of human rights and common challenges to each of these perspectives [Intro, theories, law, literature] • Rights in conflict with one another and the need not to establish hierarchy among rights but to maximize respect for all rights in such circumstances [Intro, theories] • Human rights and international humanitarian law and protection during armed conflict, efforts to secure justice on the international level (i.e., the International Criminal Court) and the prevention of crimes against humanity [law] • The root causes of human rights violations, including the role of stereotypes and prejudice in processes that lead to human rights abuses [Intro, history] • Critical human rights challenges in our communities and societies and factors contributing to supporting or undermining human rights in one's own environment (e.g., political, legal, cultural/social, religious and economic) [Intro, advocacy] • Complaint procedures that are available in one's own environment when human rights have been violated [methods, advocacy] • Current or historical human rights issues or movements—in one's own country, on one's own continent or in the world—and individuals and groups that contributed to the upholding and defense of human rights, such as women and persons belonging to minority groups [current issues]

Table 10. Table of Suggested Program-Level Student Learning Outcomes

	Upon completion of the program, students will have:
Education *about* human rights	• Knowledge of the human rights regime (law, United Nations and appropriate entities therein, international and regional courts) • Knowledge of the main human rights actors (role of government, civil society and nongovernmental organizations, and business) • Knowledge of the events (past and current) and philosophies germane to human rights
Education *through* human rights	• Ability to critically evaluate all of the above • Actively engaged in their own education through participatory learning • Become more empathetic
Education *for* human rights	• Ability to perform research on human rights problems • Formulated and expressed own values and views on human rights orally and in writing • Ability to take action on behalf of human rights issues important to him/her

But first, program-level learning outcomes must be established. These indicate what a student should have achieved by the time they finish the program, and from these the required courses are determined. Courses in turn have student learning outcomes (SLOs), which tie in to the program-level outcomes.

A thirty-six-credit major might equal twelve three-credit courses with eight of the twelve being required of everyone and the remaining four courses chosen from a short list of offerings. The core could consist of Introduction to Human Rights, History of Human Rights, Theories of Human Rights, Introduction to Human Rights and Humanitarian Law, Current Issues in Human Rights, Human Rights in Literature or Theater, and Methods in Human Rights Research. The first six courses correspond to the content contained in the previous tables and are commonly found in undergraduate degree programs. In the literature cited in Tables 8, 9, and 10, only the World Programme's Second Phase document mentions research: "Higher education institutions develop new knowledge and advance critical reflection in the area of human rights, which in turn inform policies and practices in human rights and in human rights education. Through an assessment of existing experiences and comparative studies, research can support the identification and dissemination of good practices as well as the development of innovative methodologies and tools based on those practices; research can also guide lesson-learning and evaluation exercises."[3] Only a few BA degree programs include a research course, but because research is fundamental to human rights work and critically thinking about them, it should be required for all students of human rights.

In what follows, I take the content from the previous tables and a compilation of what I have gleaned from a decade of reading syllabi to create SLOs for nine required courses. The general practice is to write no less than three and no more than six SLOs per course; if there are too many, the course might lack focus or be unachievable. Also, this set of SLOs should be more or less constant no matter who teaches the course; therefore, there is still capacity for faculty to add an additional SLO or two that are particular to their individual course. Each SLO should be assessed as, again, too many would be burdensome. It must be remembered that SLOs will not capture everything one wants to accomplish in a course. They provide clear guidelines to students and external viewers but are not meant to provide a description of a faculty's every goal. However, because we want students to incorporate elements of critical pedagogy, skills such as critical reading, analysis of arguments, critical assessments of advocacy projects, or variations of these skills should be reflected in the SLOs.

In addition to these nine required courses, a student needs to take four more. These could come from a limited list with an emphasis on political science, international relations, and the other social sciences—anthropology, economics, psychology, and sociology—as they are particularly germane to human rights. A chart of elective offerings might look like what you see in Table 12.

Within these categories a nearly limitless variety of courses could be offered, because under each title in the table many courses with different foci could be provided, depending on the interest and expertise at the university. For example, courses already being taught having to do with economics include Human Rights and Global Economy, Human Rights and Business, Corporations and Human Rights, Contesting Development: Global/Local Impacts and Human Rights, and Globalization and Human

Table 11. SLOs for Nine Required Courses

	Upon completion of the course, students will be able to:
Introduction to Human Rights	• Identify the components of the human rights regime • Articulate important events in the history of human rights • Critically reflect on the philosophical and religious contributions to human rights • Describe debates and controversies in human rights, including their universality, indivisibility, and a hierarchy of rights • Critically examine current problems in human rights facing the US, other countries, the world
Theories of Human Rights	• Demonstrate a clear understanding of the key disputes surrounding the validity, content, and legitimacy of human rights • Articulate different theories about the foundations for human rights • Demonstrate knowledge of human rights as a values framework and its close relationship with other ethical, religious, and moral frameworks • Explain how rights can be in conflict with one another • Know the arguments about the universality, indivisibility, and interdependence of human rights
History of Human Rights	• Demonstrate knowledge of events in world history spanning generations and continents that could be considered precursors to today's understanding of human rights • Demonstrate knowledge of individual rights advocates • Assess how different world religions contributed to and are (are not) compatible with human rights • Analyze debates about the history of human rights • Describe the evolving nature of the human rights framework
Current Issues in Human Rights	• Identify current human rights events • Analyze causes of human rights problems • Identify and critically assess the main actors in human rights, including governments, civil society and nongovernmental organizations, and businesses, and their strategies for addressing abuses

Table 11. (continued)

	Upon completion of the course, students will be able to:
Human Rights in Literature, Theatre, Music and or Film	• Examine how literature moves readers to engage issues of human rights • Critically assess how authors evoke your empathy, sympathy, outrage, and complicate your perspective • Appreciate these complexities from a cross-cultural, global perspective • Explain visual representation of rights violations in film, musical representation, and compare visual and textual modes of storytelling
Human Rights Law	• Demonstrate knowledge of the International Bill of Human Rights and core human rights treaties and other human rights law • Explicate efforts to secure justice on the international level (i.e., the International Criminal Court) and the prevention of crimes against humanity • Identify state obligations in relation to human rights, including review of domestic legal frameworks, treaties, and mechanisms of protection at the national, regional, and international levels
Research Methods for Human Rights	• Demonstrate knowledge of key research methods, including qualitative (interviewing) and quantitative (collecting and using data) • Be familiar with human rights databases • Design research projects • Demonstrate understanding of ethical standards in research
Advocacy for Human Rights	• Critically evaluate human rights campaigns • Demonstrate knowledge of methods for using the various UN entities for addressing human rights abuses, including the UPR, treaty monitoring committees, special rapporteurs • Demonstrate knowledge of the complaint procedures that are available in one's own city and at the country level • Identify the role of NGOs and the private sector/business in the promotion and maintenance of human rights • Develop an effective advocacy strategy

Table 12. Proposed Elective Courses

Group 1 Choose one:	• Anthropology and Human Rights • Psychology and Human Rights • Sociology and Human Rights
Group 2 Choose one:	• Political Economy • Economic Globalization
Group 3 Choose one:	• Political Science and Human Rights • International Relations and Human Rights
Group 4 Choose one:	• Women's/Gender Studies and Human Rights • Human Rights in the US • Human Rights in Africa • Human Rights in the Middle East • Human Rights in Asia • Human Rights in Latin America • Human Rights in Europe

Rights. Courses about women and gender include Issues in Women's International Human Rights and International Violence Against Women, Transgender Human Rights, and Women's Rights. Courses specific to human rights in Latin America include Testimony and Human Rights in Latin American Literature, The Culture and Politics of Human Rights in the Américas, and Human Rights in Latin America and the Caribbean. For every single category in Table 12, numerous courses are already being offered that pertain to it.

Also, if faculty find requiring nine courses to be too much, then several could be collapsed into one. A curriculum could assure that current issues are woven into every course and thereby skip offering a dedicated course to it. The introduction and history course could be combined easily; the introduction and theories courses would likely work well together too. An introduction to human rights law could be incorporated into an introductory course or with a course in current issues. It is more important to design the curriculum around learning outcomes than around topics—but more on design later.

Minors, Certificates, and Concentrations in Human Rights

Most universities currently offering a minor in human rights require students take five or six courses for a total of fifteen or eighteen credits. Often all minors have only two or three courses in common. That is, two or three courses are absolutely required of every student in the minor while the rest of the requirements tend to be choices from a limited list. And it is often a list of courses with "human rights" in the title (indicating that the courses are directly related to human rights). However, some HRE programs allow student choice from beginning to end, requiring that at least a few come from a limited list. Capstones are often included in the minor. Stanford University's human rights minor offers a sound example of a curriculum that has a foundational required course, requires a choice of "practical" (perhaps experiential) course, and has a capstone. The two courses absolutely required of all students are taken at the beginning and end of the program: Perspectives on Human Rights Theory and Practice and the Human Rights Capstone, consisting of either "a 25-page research paper on a human rights topic . . . or some alternative culminating work requiring equivalent effort approved in advance by the supervising faculty." In addition:

> Students must complete at least one course across each of three streams to ensure breadth and depth. . . .
>
> Foundations: courses from disciplines including History, Law, Philosophy, Political Science and others that introduce theoretical or historical foundations of human rights
> Contemporary issues: courses that focus on particular human rights issues such as poverty, gender equality, public health, or the environment.
> Practice: courses dedicated to practical application of human rights principles through skills development, advocacy training, and experiential or community engaged learning.[4]

This is a stronger model than the minors with no required courses.

Interestingly, the existing certificates and concentrations in human rights also hover around a requirement of eighteen hours. Theoretically, there is a difference between a minor, concentration, and certificate. However, in practice there is a lot of overlap as to what universities require for these three kinds of programs, suggesting that one cannot conclude there is a serious difference in the types of programs. A concentration is traditionally defined as a specialization within a major, while a minor does not necessarily have any content entailed in one's major. For example, at the

University of Minnesota, the BA in global studies has a concentration in human rights and justice, which requires five courses related to human rights as part of the major. Students can choose the five from a select list of courses, some of which have "human rights" in the title, though most do not. But at Columbia University the human rights concentration is not associated with a major. The one course absolutely required by all is Introduction to Human Rights; students chose another seven from a list of about fourteen courses, almost all of which have "human rights" in the title. I would suggest the latter is a stronger program for educating students in the discipline of human rights.

A certificate should indicate that the student has undertaken a body of work that reflects specialized knowledge. Some say it should be a professional degree that includes and prepares one for real-world experience, which is what seems to differentiate it from the minor, except that some minors require an experiential capstone. The University of Iowa's eighteen-credit undergraduate human rights certificate is an admirable example of a certificate including a professional aspect. It consists of completely required courses except at the end, when students can choose between two final human rights courses. In addition to the three required courses—Introduction to Human Rights, History of Human Rights, and Philosophy of Human Rights—the university's website lists four courses under the heading "human rights practice," and students must take three of them.[5] The two required are (1) Human Rights Systems: Institutions and Mechanisms Enforcing and Implementing Human Rights and (2) Human Rights Advocacy. Then students choose between (1) Seminar in Human Rights Praxis: Supervised Internship and (2) Topics in Human Rights. Iowa's program is strong because of its required foundational courses and emphasis on practice or educating *for* human rights.

As just demonstrated, minors, concentrations, and certificates can be, are, and should be focused on those areas in human rights that mark it as a discipline. Two other ways human rights has been infused in university curricula that have potential for spreading HRE are general education requirements in the US (breadth requirements in Canada) and within other disciplines. As mentioned in the first chapter, numerous disciplines already have books written on human rights and their field, so a wealth of resources exists in terms of texts. The sciences have strong backing from the American Association for the Advancement of Science. The organization has a collection of syllabi on science courses with a human rights focus.[6]

Currently they include these subject areas: bioethics, demography, earth science, engineering, geography, health, and medicine. AAAS also has syllabi for some social sciences: anthropology, political science, psychology, and sociology. The nascent University and College Consortium for Human Rights Education's website will continue to be a resource for faculty with its syllabi collector for any discipline's human rights course.

Many universities also offer human rights courses as a general education, breadth, or freshmen learning community course. Not only do these courses introduce students to human rights issues, but many faculty report that they are also a great recruitment tool for their human rights programs and that the classes fill to capacity. At the University of Winnipeg, Kristi Kenyon offers History of Human Rights in Canada as a humanities requirement. Columbia University has infused human rights into sections of the undergraduate writing course. Two courses I teach at the University of New Mexico—a history of human rights class and Globalization and Human Rights—fulfill a humanities and social science core requirement respectively. University of Dayton has designed its Introduction to Human Rights course to fulfill two general education requirements: (1) Diversity and Social Justice and (2) Practical Ethical Action. What is essential to all of these courses is that they rely on texts using a human rights lens and often introduce the basic elements of the human rights regime.

Designing Courses

Examining education *about*, *through*, and *for* has yielded guidance for the establishment of the discipline of human rights. Now let's look at incorporating each of those elements into designing individual courses. As discussed in Chapter 4, how courses are taught turns out to be more important than course content. For example, research has found that knowledge retention after a lecture is brief. Active learning and engaging the affective dimension are critical to integration, so we must take care to design courses that are geared toward deep learning.

Scholarship on creating and implementing great classes abound. One widely used approach was created by L. Dee Fink in his book *Creating Significant Learning Experiences*. In it, he expands on Bloom's taxonomy for cognitive learning, adding affective components with the goal of creating change in students. He concisely concludes "no change, no learning."[7] He

Try This: Introduction to Human Rights, Two Exercises

Dr. Sandra Sirota, a postdoctoral research fellow at the University of Connecticut and former director of an NGO dedicated to human rights education, has developed these two activities for introducing students to human rights, which she has used successfully for many years.

Ideal Community Activity: Time 15–30 minutes

Objectives: For participants to be able to identify human rights and human rights violations in their own neighborhood as well as strategies to create change. This lesson can be used on the first day of any number of human rights classes. It serves as an icebreaker, demonstrates to students that they have prior knowledge about human rights and advocacy, and provides opportunities for critical thinking about human rights from day one of class. The goal is to have students design an ideal community.

Materials: Large paper and markers.

Instructions for Students: In groups of 5 (approx.), have students think about a community they all have in common—it can be as small as the college or town they live in or as large as their country or even the world. They should write the name of their community on the center of the paper.

Using words, pictures, or symbols, around the community name, write your answers to the following questions:

(1) What do you like about the community? What are its strengths?
(2) What would you like to change about your community? What are some problems and shortcomings?
(3) What strategies can you use to change one or two of these negative aspects of the community?

Have a few or all (depending on time and size of class) groups present their community to the class, responding to all three questions.

Use the group presentations as a launching point to discuss human rights and human rights violations in our daily lives. Rather than asking participants to share human rights violations or telling participants about them, let the discussion come about on its own. Note to the participants the issues they raise that are human rights and human rights violations; for example, air quality, crime, electricity issues, access to health care, trash, etc.

Whole Class Discussion:

- What human rights does the community enjoy? Ensure students recognize the rights they identified (e.g., healthy food, adequate housing).
- What human rights violations have been identified? For example, is there an issue with discrimination? Is health care a problem?

• What advocacy strategies have been identified? Do students suggest meeting with their representatives? Do they want to raise awareness among their peers? Do they wish to advocate to any authorities?

Debrief: How are human rights and human rights violations relevant to our lives? What issues have the participants identified that they care about?

Human Rights Country Activity: Time 20–30 minutes

Materials: UDHR.
Objectives:

• To introduce students to the Universal Declaration of Human Rights (UDHR).
• To demonstrate that based on the country people live in and their identity, they are able to enjoy and are denied certain rights.
• To explore the challenging process that was involved in creating the UDHR.
• To provide students with the opportunity to critique the UDHR.

Activity: Participants are split into groups of 5 (approx.). Have the numbers 3, 23, 8, and 7 written on folded pieces of paper. Different and/or additional numbers can be used as needed. Each group picks a number. Tell the participants the number they picked is the number of rights their group's country has. Participants take out their UDHR copies (you can use a plain language version if appropriate) and, in their groups, work together to choose which of the rights (choosing from articles #3 to 27 of the UDHR, as the other articles are general statements) their country will have and why. Each group should name their country.
Optional: Groups can share one right that they would add to the UDHR. Participants can create a flag, motto, and description of their country as well.
Each group presents their country to the larger group—state the name of the country, the number of rights they have, and which rights they chose.
Optional: Each student can now choose to move to another country if they like. Have participants share why they are moving to that country or why they are staying in their own country.
Debrief: Ask participants what it felt like to be in a country with more or fewer rights than the other countries. What does it feel like to have to choose only a certain number of rights? How does this relate to the real world? In the real world, is it that easy to move to another country where they could have more rights? Remind the participants that people often do not choose where they live (for example, which country they are born into or where their parents take them), but based on where they live and their identity (race, gender, sexuality, religion, etc.), certain rights are secured or denied.

outlines six areas through which students learn and change, and they map nicely onto our tripartite definition of HRE rooted in critical pedagogy.

Fink's six categories are (1) foundational knowledge, (2) application, (3) integration, (4) the human dimension, (5) caring, and (6) learning how to learn. *Foundational knowledge* meets the requirement to teach *about* human rights. *Integration*, defined as getting students to see connections between ideas, people, or between realms such as school and work, is described as giving "learners a new form of *power*, especially intellectual power."[8] Therefore, integration fits with education *for* human rights, as does *application* of skills, as both are important for empowering students to act. Inciting students to *care* (develop "new feelings, interests, and values") about the subject also aligns with education *for* rights. Fink's *human dimension* ("discover personal and social implications of what they've learned" and how to "interact more effectively with others") and *learning how to learn* fit with education *through* human rights.

With the taxonomy in hand, Fink guides faculty through a "backward" three-phase course design. The initial phase is where one establishes the primary components such as the learning goals for the some or all of the six areas. That is, you begin by establishing the end goals, hence it is a backward design. In the intermediate phase, one connects those goals with the topics and activities needed to achieve them. The final phase is where, among other steps, assessment is coordinated. As an example of how designing a course based on Fink's taxonomy could be approached, I'll share an abbreviated attempt for a course I created called Solutions to Human Right Problems. This is an upper-division course, not part of a human rights program, and it does not have prerequisites, so it includes some content from an introduction to human rights course. In a BA program it could count as a current issues course. The focus is on exposing students to current issues in human rights through learning about the rights promotion and rights violations of some of the major actors in human rights: the US government, the UN, human rights and humanitarian NGOs, and multinational corporations. Students do readings about how each of these have helped and harmed human rights, and in the process they learn about what is occurring now.

The course design that follows includes the fulfillment of phase one, which is to answer questions to formulate significant learning goals; then writing the actual learning goals and determining the activities to reach them, as part of accomplishing phase two, and the assessments go with them, fulfilling some requirements of phase three. The big assignment for this course is project-based learning steeped in the principles of using an open-ended, real-world problem requiring students to research information on solutions, propose solutions, and share their findings.

Foundational Knowledge

This accomplishes education *about* human rights.

Phase One: Student Learning Objectives

"What key information (e.g., facts, terms, formulae, concepts, principles, relationships) is/are important for students to understand and remember in the future?"

- The key ideas for them to remember years from now are that there is an extensive body of human rights declarations and laws, and that the various "actors"—namely, the US government, the UN, NGOs, and multination corporations—all have a history of promoting and monitoring human rights and sometimes abusing rights. All of these entities need to be subject to critical evaluation, because they each do well and err.

Phase Two: Student Learning Outcomes and Accompanying Course Activities

- Upon completion of the course, students will be able to name key elements of international human rights law. The activity for accomplishing this is reading and discussing the human rights regime.
- Upon completion of the course, students will understand how each main entity has both promoted and monitored human rights and committed violations. This is accomplished through readings about each entity doing good and doing wrong, reading a national newspaper and bringing in an article that illustrates or is related to an article in the UDHR each class period. For example, they will compare and contrast the writings and documentaries of Johan Norberg, *Progress* and *Globalization Is Good*, a defender of globalization as a source of human progress, with John Perkins, an "economic hit man" hired

by multinational corporations involved in assassinations of presidents who resisted forced economic liberalization for their country, in *Confessions of an Economic Hitman* and *The Big Sellout*.

Phase Three: Assessment

- Learning/knowledge integration is assessed through writing assignments of varying lengths.
- Short weekly assignments about the reading are graded before the next class period. (Essays are graded within a week of being turned in.)
- The grading rubric is explained, and the results of assignments are discussed in class.

Application Goals

This accomplishes education *for* human rights.

Phase One: Student Learning Objectives

"What kinds of thinking are important for students to learn? Critical thinking, creative thinking, and/or practical thinking? What other skills do you want them to develop?"

- competency in writing and presenting
- critical and practical thinking
- information literacy

Phase Two: Student Learning Outcomes and Accompanying Course Activities

- Upon completion of the course, students will be able to define critical thinking and have practiced it in writing.
- Upon completion of the course, students will have demonstrated the ability to engage in problem-based learning.
- Upon completion of the course, students will be information literate. This is achieved through repeated exposure and evaluation of both peer-reviewed articles and lesser quality texts.

- The central assignment for this course is to choose a local human rights problem (past projects have included examining food insecurity on campus, analyzing the city's flagging human rights board, working with a lobbyist on passing a health care for all bill) and research an example of each main actor in this course—an MNC [multinational corporation], UN, US government agency, and an NGO's approach to addressing the problem. Analyze their approaches and design an intervention in which they all contribute to your solution. The final product is to present findings and recommendations to the relevant recipients, which in the above example were a college dean, the city's civil rights lawyer overseeing the human rights board, and a legislative committee.

Phase Three: Assessment

- Critical thinking and writing are assessed in written assignments.
- Both weak and strong examples of student writing are shared with the class when papers are returned for feedback.
- Presentations are assessed with a rubric.

Integration Goals

Phase One: Student Learning Objectives

"What connections (similarities and interactions) should students recognize and make . . . ?"

- Students are exposed to the ways various entities interact through their readings and problem-based learning project.

Phase Two: Student Learning Outcomes and Accompanying Course Activities

- Upon completion of the course, students will have analyzed the connections between institutional missions and approaches to problem solving. This is achieved with texts in a course reader with excerpts about the US government, the UN, MNCs, and NGOs, the class reads *A Path Appears* by Nicholas Kristof and Sheryl WuDunn,[9] *The Idealist*

by Nina Munk,[10] and watches the documentary *Poverty Inc.*,[11] in addition to completing the research for their own problem-based project.
- Upon completion of the course, students will understand their own connection to global human rights problems. This is accomplished with their work on a local problem.

Phase Three: Assessment

- Peer assessments are made for short research essays and presentations via a rubric the class helps write.

Human Dimensions Goals

This accomplishes education *through* human rights.

Phase One: Student Learning Objectives

"What could or should students learn about themselves?" and "What could or should students learn about understanding others and/or interacting with them?"

- Students choose which project to work on (making this a learner centered course).
- They also learn the importance of recipient participation in any and all human rights work.

Phase Two: Student Learning Outcomes and Accompanying Course Activities

- Upon completion of the course, students should have developed well-informed opinions about what makes sound charitable and humanitarian work.
- Upon completion of the course, students will have experienced empowerment working to address a human rights related issue. Reflection questions are used to aid students' awareness.

Phase Three: Assessment

- Responses are graded based on completion rather than students' opinions.
- Another assessment is done at the end of course, asking them what personal beliefs have been affected. (Students are offered supportive feedback rather than graded on this assignment.)

Caring Goals

Accomplishes education *for* human rights.

Phase One: Student Learning Objectives

"What changes/values do you hope students will adopt? Feelings? Interests? Ideas?"

- They will recognize that change is possible and that there have been constant improvements to human well-being.
- They will develop or change attitudes and values about their own ability to work for human rights.

Phase Two: Student Learning Outcomes and Accompanying Course Activities

- Upon completion of the course, students will have a deeper understanding about what they care about in terms of human rights topics.
- Upon completion of the course, students will have a deeper understanding of what motivates actors to address human rights problems, especially businesses. This is partly accomplished by hosting a local businessman on the importance of corporate philanthropy in our community, which is often students' first exposure to the idea of corporate benevolence.

Phase Three: Assessment

- I determine whether some change in students' thinking has been achieved in written reflections, including two-minute papers immediately following a discussion or guest speaker.

Goals for Learning How to Learn

Phase One: Student Learning Objectives

"What would you like for students to learn about: How to learn about this particular subject? How to become a self-directed learner of this subject?"

- Students will learn how to stay informed of current issues (because most are not in the habit of reading a national news source, including international newspapers and magazines).
- Information literacy will be increased.

Phase Two: Student Learning Outcomes and Accompanying Course Activities

- Upon completion of the course, students will have practiced the habit of reading the daily news.
- Upon completion of the course, students will have practiced the component skills of critical thinking.

Phase Three: Assessment

- Students earn points toward their final grade for bringing in an article or opinion piece and discussing its main point and point of view.

The demonstration above only hints at the efficacy of Fink's course design model (multiple guides for which can be found by Internet searching "creating significant learning experiences"). But hopefully it's clear that it can help us achieve education *about, through,* and *for* human rights in a single course by making our objectives clear, offering due consideration to what activities can help us to fulfill them, and then assessing at the end to gauge the curriculum's success. Assessment is key to the process.

Assessment and HRE

A fitting conclusion to this book, therefore, is a brief discussion on the necessity of assessment and suggestions for doing it meaningfully. The most

Try This: Scavenger Hunt for Human Rights

Dr. William Simmons at the University of Arizona designed this human rights scavenger hunt. It introduces students to current issues and teaches information literacy while also providing them the opportunity to contribute their research to Global Human Rights Direct (GHRD). The website founded by Simmons "is a place to make connections and hear from human rights experts from around the globe. GHRD is 1) a videoconference speakers bureau, 2) a social media site, and 3) a living archive for human rights."[12] The assignment below encourages students to use the website as an information resource and contribute content. (Simmons welcomes having students contribute content.) However, the assignment could be adapted for a research paper or a creative presentation as well.

Pairs of students will conduct a scavenger hunt to gather as wide of a variety of resources on a human rights issue and collate their information onto the Global Human Rights Direct website (www.globalhumanrightsdirect.com). Most of the information will be placed on GHRD under Human Rights Issues, but you will see that there are links from the Issues pages to NGOs, videos, groups, profiles, testimonials, and media files. It is best to first upload items to the other pages (videos, testimonials, etc.) and then create NGO pages where you can link to videos and testimonials. Then finally you can create an issue page.

First, you need to choose a human rights issue. You can get a sense of a general range of issues by randomly clicking on the map on the GHRD website, and Amnesty International's and Human Rights Watch's websites. Be sure to pick an issue that is not already on the issues page on GHRD.

Then, gather a wide variety of sources related to your issue. You should aim for 20–25 interesting sources from at least 10 of the categories listed below. You should annotate at least 10 of your sources. An annotation is just 2–3 sentences that describe the source, explain why it would be important to someone and then offer a bit of commentary.

Be sure to check out the Suggest an Issue link on GHRD (under Contribute Content) to get a sense of what you will need to have. You will need a brief background, key facts, etc.

Categories of Sources to Gather

(1) Academic: academic Articles (From Academic Search Premier or other Library Databases); academic books (Great if you can find the books and book reviews (i.e., from Amazon, Academic Search Premier, or the Human Rights and Human Welfare Website); Conference Papers Archives: American Political Science Association, International Studies Association, American Sociological Association, others; Working Papers on the Social Science Research

Network (SSRN) Website; List of Leading Scholars in the Field. Find
through: Google Search—include the word "Vita," Scholar Google,
Academia.edu; University Course Syllabi on this or Related Issues

(2) The Arts: Literary/Fictional Sources, Poetry, Artwork (sculpture,
public art, etc.), Photography

(3) Videos: YouTube, DVDs, Netflix, Other web videos, Filmmaker's
Library and Films on Demand on the Library website, Witness.org

(4) Working on the issue: NGOs; Leading Activists; Leading Politicians
or Other Policy Entrepreneurs (someone who has made this their pet
issue) in the U.S. or elsewhere; Court/Tribunal Cases

(5) Government and IGO Reports: International (UN, WHO, etc.),
Regional (OAS, AU, EU), National, U.S.—the U.S. State Department
Report, Other Country Development Agencies (DFID, USAID,
CIDA, SIDA, etc.)

(6) Media Sources: newspapers and magazines; social Media Sources:
Facebook, Twitter, etc., Podcasts—check out ITunes U., webinars,
blogs. Are there any listservs on the topic? You could join one or
two; leading websites devoted to the Issue

(7) Other Types of Resources: images, maps, events about the issue

important reason for evaluation and assessment is to determine if we are
succeeding in accomplishing the objectives we've set forth. Some of us
would go so far as to say that good design, including assessment, could do
a lot to help us reach our teaching dreams[13] or ideal goals,[14] including con-
veying the skills we intend to impart with a critical pedagogy.

There is a lot of good literature on how to conduct effective and meaningful assessment (though it is likely we have all endured the burden of
useless measures). We owe it to our students and to our subject matter to
consistently evaluate and improve our courses. We do not hesitate to have
our research peer-reviewed. We recognize the value for human progress
that comes from critiquing each other's scholarship. Likewise, we should
not hesitate to have our teaching assessed, especially since faculty have
autonomy within the process. Generally, we establish learning outcomes,
thereby identifying the targets for and means of assessment. Maybe at the
program level you coordinate assessments with colleagues, but the onus is
on each of us to make use of this tool to ensure the highest possible quality
of education for our students.

David Suárez reviewed a discussion board on HRE and found a surprising resistance toward assessment.[15] Commenters, made up of people from

NGOs and those involved in formal education, suggested it was unnecessary, saying it was a waste of resources (time) and that it couldn't be done. One may not find the negative attitudes entirely surprising, because assessment done poorly does indeed waste people's time, but the assertion that HRE cannot be evaluated is unfortunate and untrue. We absolutely have the know-how and tools to assess our educational efforts. Even HRE's ambition to affect people's values can be measured to some degree (with self-report questionnaires and reflections). Based on Fink's work on how to do meaningful assessment, what follows are suggestions for evaluating student work and learning that provide both them and faculty with useful feedback. Then we turn to a brief discussion of assessing whole programs.

Fink suggests four features of each assessment in order to make them educative assessments instead of auditive assessments (which serve only as an audit of student learning at the end of a section or whole class). Educative assessment additionally offers timely feedback to students in order to reinforce their learning. According to Fink, the first of the required elements is that assessment should be forward-looking rather than a review of what should have been learned. The assessment tool (assignment) should ask students to engage with and apply what has been learned. Second, faculty should provide the students with clear criteria and standards for success. Often this is conveyed in the form of a rubric, which is used to both inform students of the requirements and to grade their work. Third, self-assessment is also essential in order for students to recognize what is required for change to take place. One example offered is to ask students to participate in creating the rubric by having them suggest the criteria for success and failure on an assignment. Ask them what the qualities of an excellent, mediocre, and poor performance would be. Another effective method is to have them apply the rubric to their own work before you do as a tool for self-reflection. Fink's fourth suggestion is that feedback must be provided to students frequently throughout the semester, immediately after students have done the assignment, discriminatingly using the previously established criteria and standards, and should be given kindly and respectfully. Students are less able to hear critiques if it makes them feel defeated or demeaned. My applications of Fink's recommendations are included in the above presentation of my Solutions to Human Rights course.

Fink's model is for student and course-level evaluation primarily, though it could be adapted to the program level. A program's faculty should state what the expected learning outcomes are, reach agreement about which courses will focus on each outcome, decide on assignments and assessments for those courses, and use the data at the end of the year to review progress on the program outcomes. Therefore, all work collected as data can be anonymous, because what is being evaluated is the success of the program and not an individual faculty member or student. A key aspect of program-level assessment is a discussion of how the results will be used to make changes if necessary. Everyone teaching in the program needs to be part of the program evaluation, including part-time faculty, in order for the process to be effective.

As a community of scholars of HRE, we have everything necessary to create a unique, academically sound discipline of human rights based in critical pedagogy. We have the need, the right historical moment, and a solid foundation in extant programs, courses, books, and journals indicating that we meet disciplinary criteria requiring a strong community of scholars and a common vocabulary and set of concepts. We have all the tools and know-how for educating *about*, *through*, and *for* human rights.

The second half of this book is a handbook intended to help faculty design curricula based in critique. This chapter has enumerated the consensus on the content that is required to produce knowledgeable graduates. This can be considered minimum content for those who may argue that I have neglected essential topics. There are ways to incorporate all the topics I outline consensus about in a series of human rights courses, while also including those that others might deem paramount. Or the major and minor I presented earlier in this chapter could be considered complete content for what can be accomplished within the credits allotted. While there may be room to argue when it comes to necessary content, there is no room to argue about the necessity of good curriculum design. Faculty of HRE must implement the recommendations from the latest research on teaching and learning if we are to declare our new discipline to be on the cutting edge in every way.

Chapters 4 and 5 included the evidence-based methods and argued that for HRE to be transformational, faculty have to teach based on human rights principles and must work toward affecting student attitudes and values while offering the tools for empowerment. At this moment in time, therefore, we have all the necessary arguments and information for building a discipline of human rights.

Afterword

A Vision for Future Directions

On some topics, this book has set out to articulate what has been hiding in plain sight: scholars are largely in agreement on what the phrase "human rights" points to (the UDHR, human rights treaties, the regime, human rights NGOs, the debates about universality and primacy of rights, the abuses committed by state and non-state actors, etc.), and there is an emergent consensus among scholars on HRE. I hope I have elucidated that if codified as a discipline, HRE would not only address a dereliction in our educational system by teaching rights as our treaties require but also that in following the best practices in teaching and learning scholarship, we will improve the university system on the whole by creating a rights-aware and rights-respecting environment. We stand ready to empower a generation of young people, through building their awareness of human rights (theirs and others') and giving them the space and guidance to cultivate within themselves the capacities for thoughtful debate, empathy, and critical analysis. In so doing we will graduate human rights workers and human beings who are more prepared to meet the overwhelming problems of our time.

If you see any measure of hyperbole in this vision, it isn't mine. The preamble of the UDHR enjoins nothing less than this. Have another look: "The General Assembly Proclaims this Universal Declaration of Human Rights as the common standard of achievement for all peoples and all nations, to the end that every individual and every organ of society, keeping this Declaration constantly in mind, shall strive by teaching and education to promote respect for these rights and freedoms, and by progressive measures, national and international, to secure their universal and effective recognition and observance."[1]

Here I conclude my campaign on behalf of disciplining human rights with two additional observations: (1) we need more HRE for faculty and future educators, and (2) we need new books and materials for specific courses. We must encourage our colleagues to learn about human rights and to incorporate it into their curricula. Whatever their field, HRE belongs in their classroom. Active learning, critical thinking, and student-centered, rights-respecting classrooms should henceforth become the norm. The movement toward universal HRE will require every one of us and all the creativity and commitment we can muster.

There are many steps along the path to universal implementation of HRE. In order to grow the number of faculty teaching human rights, those of us with experience can mentor those without. We could begin with campaigns on our campuses to seek inclusion from all faculty of any small measure of human rights education in their existing courses. Even if it's only one class session per semester that teaches precepts or stances consistent with HRE, we will be assured to never graduate an entire college class who has never heard of the UDHR and has no idea that we are beholden to fulfill its promises. Seeding rights in this way is only a beginning, but begin we must. I list books and suggestions for learning more about the human rights system and movement in Appendix V. But we could also hold reading seminars and workshops in our institutions where texts and debates could be discussed and methods of teaching could be shared.

Another step forward is creating additional HRE resources. In researching this book, I have come to see the gaps in the literature as opportunities to invite more voices to the conversation. There are a few pioneering texts for the history of human rights (Paul Gordon Lauren [1998] and Micheline Ishay [2007, 2008]), and for theory and human rights (Patrick Hayden, David Boursema),[2] but beyond that, instructors are putting together syllabi with a large mix of texts (often including Jack Donnelly's *International Human Rights*). There are good reasons for having different kinds of materials, and Appendix III has lists of suggestions for each core course. But we can grow the discipline as the international documents intend if we have more texts created specifically for the courses we are looking to teach. For example, we need an introduction to human rights text that systematically presents the elements of the human rights regime, framed to fulfill the goals of the chapters on education *through* and *for* human rights (first-person accounts, art, activities, etc.). While there are good edited volumes being used in introductory courses, they inevitably miss essential material because of their reliance on multiple authors. The field needs books for a semester-long introductory course on human rights law for non–law students that include active-learning content, such as first-person accounts of using the law to ameliorate human rights problems. It would be wonderful if there were also a *Norton Anthology*-esque book for literature and human rights. It could include all manner of stories, from testimonials, memoirs, fiction, poetry, and art from numerous cultures and perspectives. Also, there is currently no textbook centered on teaching human rights advocacy. There are many books that can be included for some aspect of such a course, but there is not yet a dedicated text.

I close with an appeal to readers: participate in cocreating this new discipline. Join the conversations by sharing information on human rights topics on the Global Human Rights Direct website. Share syllabi, assignments, and classroom activities on the University and College Consortium for Human Rights Education website. Contribute to this burgeoning discipline by discerning your contribution. Campaign in your faculty senate and with administrators for HRE on your campus. Coordinate distribution of copies of the UDHR to every incoming freshman, and use the language of human rights in the orientation when talking about consent or other rights-related topics already in the program. Talk to people already incorporating the principles described in this book into their curricula, and begin. Don't doubt that this is the time, and this is ours to do. As Eleanor Roosevelt wrote, "Nothing has ever been achieved by the person who says 'it can't be done.'"[3]

Appendix I

The University of Connecticut Capstone

At the University of Connecticut, human rights majors and minors have a required capstone. The majors can choose to write a thesis or take the service learning/internship course. The minors only take the latter. This capstone is highlighted here because it is a fine example of one meeting the requirements of a high-impact experiential practice that requires a significant reflection component. The university describes its capstone as providing the "opportunity to apply the knowledge gained through coursework into practice. The seminar component of the internship helps students to reflect upon the connections between theory and practice." The aim is for the experience to "cap" the curriculum in the major and the minor.

Each student has a "learning work plan" in which they have to describe their work at the organization and how it relates to human rights. The student, supervisor at the agency they are working for, and the faculty mentor sign it. Students are mentored at the organization they work with and by the seminar facilitator for the course described below.[1]

Excerpts from Service Learning/Internship Syllabus

Course Overview

In addition to completing 120 hours of internship work, you will attend the seminar class, and complete a blog on your experiences at your internship site. The seminar class will provide you with an opportunity to meet with other HR interns and learn some additional skills applicable to work in the HR field. The blog should act as an online journal for you to reflect on your internship experience. You will also be required to read and comment on the blogs designed by your classmates.

Final grades are based on the completion of 120 hours at your internship, attendance at the six seminar classes, completion of your reflection blog posts, and on the comments posted on your classmates' blogs.

Course readings include selections from

- *Changing People's Lives While Transforming Your Own: Paths to Social Justice & Global Human Rights,* by Kottler and Marriner (2009)
- *The Impossible Will Take a Little While,* by Loeb (2004)
- *Practical Idealists,* by Wilson, Barham, and Hammock (2008)

Reflective blog posts example questions:

- "Reflect on this quotation by Paul Loeb: 'The difficult I'll do right now. The impossible will take a little while.' How does it apply to your current internship work?" OR "Reflect on this quotation, 'To feel the affection that comes from those whom we do not know,' Neruda writes, 'widens out the boundaries of our being, and unites all living things.' How do we develop a sense of human solidarity with those we've never met?"
- "Reflecting on our passions and values can help to identify the purpose we would like to pursue. How has your internship experience broadened or clarified your passions and values?"
- "Consider job options available to you. What are your thoughts on human rights work after having your internship experience? Describe a job opportunity that you would love to find."
- "As you begin to piece together your different passions, experiences, and skills that make you uniquely you, what images begin to emerge? How does your internship experience play a role in creating these images? What hope can you draw from the idea that your life story is yours to create?"
- "What have you learned about yourself and the nature of HR work through your internship work and the process of reflection?"

Students have been placed in internship positions on the UConn campus as well as with organizations locally, nationally, and internationally. For more information and to read student blog posts, go to https://human-rights.uconn.edu/experiential-learning.

Appendix II

Sample Curriculum Map for Program SLOs

				Program Student Learning Outcomes				
Required courses	*HRTS regime*	*Events, theories*	*Critical evaluation*	*Develop empathy*	*Part in learning*	*Research skills*	*Communi- cation skills*	*Advocacy skills*
Intro	I	I		I	I		I	
Theories		I	I				I	
History		I		I		I	I	
Current	R	R	R		R	R	R	I
Lit/Arts				R			R	
Law			R				R	
Methods						R	A	R
Advocacy	A	A	A	R		A	A	R
Capstone	A		A	R	A	A	A	A

Note. I = introduced; R = reinforced; A = advanced.

Appendix III

Websites for HRE Resources and Syllabi

American Association for the Advancement of Science (AAAS): Offers a number of resources, including an annotated bibliography of science and human rights, guidelines for scientists working on human rights projects, examples of collaborations between scientists and human rights organizations, a primer on scientific freedom and human rights, and more.
https://www.aaas.org/coalition-resources

American Political Science Association (APSA): Has a collection of syllabi that is accessible to all (not password protected).
https://www.apsanet.org/TEACHING/Syllabi-in-Political-Science

Global Human Rights Direct (GHRD): Provides ways to connect with and hear from human rights experts from around the globe via their videoconference speakers' bureau, social media, and virtual archive.
www.globalhumanrightsdirect.com

Human Rights Consortium (HRC): At the School of Advanced Study, University of London, UK, HRC offers some open access publications in addition to publishing fee-for-access journals, *International Journal of Human Rights* and *Critical Studies in Human Rights*. (Hosts HRRN; see below.)
https://hrc.sas.ac.uk/publications/open-access-publications

Human Rights Education Associates (HREA): The global human rights education and training center.
http://www.hrea.org

Human Rights Educators USA (HRE USA): A thriving organization with a membership of over six hundred individuals and organizations. Its mission is to support HRE, and it offers many resources on its website.
https://hreusa.org

H-Human-Rights Network (HNET): "A network for scholars, policymakers, authors, historians, and other interested people devoted to the history, analysis, theory, and practice of human rights." Has resources available with no membership requirement.
https://networks.h-net.org/node/6148/h-human-rights-resources

Human Rights Researchers' Network (HRRN): A membership organization, HRRN "provides a platform to promote and facilitate interdisciplinary human rights research, including exchange between the academic and practice spheres."
https://hrrn.blogs.sas.ac.uk/about-us

International Studies Association (ISA): Has a teaching and learning site with syllabi, but one must join as member of ISA to access these.
https://www.isanet.org/Programs/PRC

University and College Consortium for Human Rights Education (UCCHRE): This organization is related to, and is an outgrowth of, HRE USA. It is a comprehensive site for higher education with resources (including syllabi and teaching activities) and networking hosted by the University of Connecticut. UCCHRE welcomes practitioners, researchers, instructors, advocates, professionals, students, administrators, alumni, and other members of the university and college communities globally that are engaged in human rights education.
https://thedoddcenter.uconn.edu/ucchre/#

Abbreviated List of Suggested Texts
for Core HRE Courses

Introduction to Human Rights Courses

Human Rights: Politics and Practice, ed. Michael Goodhart
This is an edited volume presumably meant to serve as a textbook for political science and international relations. It has about twenty different contributors and many useful chapters. However, it is a bit uneven in presentation and there is little human rights history in it.

International Human Rights, Jack Donnelly and Daniel Whelan
The first four editions of this book were authored by Jack Donnelly and were among the most oft used books in human rights courses. This was probably partially because it was one of the first human rights books for the political science student. However, the text did not seem to be intended as an introduction to human rights, because it lacked a systematic presentation of the human rights system and its history. The fifth edition has joint authorship and is greatly revised to include a more systematic introduction to human rights history, mechanisms, and current issues. Though its focus is on politics, it would make a good text for an introductory class, especially if supplemented by a compilation of primary source readings and a good newspaper.

International Human Rights: A Comprehensive Introduction, Michael Haas
About a third of this book is historical and has chapters on American, European, and "third world" approaches to human rights. Useful, if a bit dry.

25 + Human Rights Documents, Center for the Study of Human Rights
A collection of declarations, conventions, and charters. No introductions or commentary provided.

Note: Some courses use texts on the history of human rights. Memoirs, autobiographies, biographies, and other nonfiction books are also required in many introductory classes.

Theories or Philosophy of Human Rights Courses

The Philosophy of Human Rights, Patrick Hayden
> From Plato to the African Charter on Human and People's Rights, this is a compendium of readings with little commentary. The selections have brief introductions.

Philosophy of Human Rights: Theory and Practice, David Boersema
> This is a collection of selected texts but has fewer than in the Hayden volume. The primary sources are embedded in thematic chapters providing context for them, followed by discussion questions for students.

Non-introductory books about theoretical issues in human rights:
Seeing the Myth in Human Rights, Jenna Reinbold
Making Sense of Human Rights, James Nickel
On Human Rights, James Griffin

History of Human Rights Courses

The Evolution of International Human Rights: Visions Seen, Paul Gordon Lauren
> This is an excellent introduction to the history of human rights. It provides an expansive sweep of history beginning with ancient sources through modern. (Only three of ten chapters are post 1948.) Lauren includes contributions to rights from every corner of the globe and the world's major religions. As the subtitle indicates, Lauren highlights the visionaries great and small who have fought for human rights throughout history. It could be used in any college-level course.

The History of Human Rights: From Ancient Times to the Globalization Era, Micheline Ishay
> A thorough history of human rights with a useful chronology at the end of the book.

The Human Rights Reader: Major Political Essays, Speeches, and Documents from Ancient Times to the Present, Micheline Ishay
> This volume is organized around topics and ideas. After a presentation of many sacred scriptures, the focus becomes almost entirely on Western sources.

The International Human Rights Movement: A History, Aryeh Neier
> As a former executive director of Human Rights Watch, the author includes a focus on civil society and NGOs as well as legal developments.

Note: These texts are often supplemented by other nonfiction sources that provide glimpses into current issues. See recommended texts below.

Current Issues Courses

If the course is not part of a sequential degree program and has to provide an introduction to the field, faculty use chapters from the above-cited history and introductory books. Other useful books include:

Alison Brysk (*Speaking Rights to Power: Constructing Political Will*; *Global Good Samaritans: Human Rights as Foreign Policy*; and *The Future of Human Rights*, for example)

Kathryn Sikkink (*Evidence for Hope: Making Human Rights Work in the 21st Century*; *The Justice Cascade: How Human Rights Prosecutions are Changing World Politics*; *Activists Beyond Borders: Advocacy Networks in International Politics*, Margaret Keck coauthor).

Because of their excellent research, these are highly cited scholars whose books introduce people to the work being done on current human rights problems.

Books that I have used to get students to reflect on the world of charitable giving and service, and that also expose them to many human rights problems, are two ultimately upbeat books and two with less hopeful conclusions.

More hopeful:

A Path Appears: Transforming Lives, Creating Opportunities, Nicholas Kristof and Sheryl WuDunn

The International Bank of Bob: Connecting Our Worlds One $25 Kiva Loan at a Time, Bob Harris

Two presenting problematic responses:
Hoping to Help: The Promises and Pitfalls of Global Health Volunteering, Judith Lasker
The Idealist: Jeffrey Sachs and the Quest to End Poverty, Nina Munk
Exploring International Human Rights: Essential Readings, ed. Rhonda Callaway and Julie Harrelson-Stephens
> This is a short collection of excerpts from numerous scholars on nine topics, including the law, human rights organization, children, torture, and globalization.

Books with a positive take, because it's important to teach students about the incredible strides humanity has made:
Factfulness: Ten Reasons We're Wrong About the World—and Why Things Are Better Than You Think, Hans Rosling, Anna Rosling Rönnlund, and Ola Rosling
> By far the best book of this genre, as it is bound to fundamentally change one's perspective by providing a more balanced view of the state of humanity composed in eleven quick reading chapters. See also the accompanying website, Gapminder, https://www.gapminder.org, and the web page Dollar Street, "Where country stereotypes fall away."
Enlightenment Now: The Case for Reason, Science, Humanism, and Progress, Steven Pinker
> Pinker's style is readable, but this is a hefty five-hundred-page-plus tome.
Progress: Ten Reasons to Look Forward to the Future, Johan Norberg
> Norberg devotes a chapter each to ten areas in which human beings have made great progress, including sanitation, poverty, literacy, freedom, and equality. He hosts a documentary made years earlier, *Why Globalization Is Good*, which compares the level of economic progress in several countries, including Taiwan, Vietnam, and Kenya.

Note: Other nonfiction sources are used to tell first-person accounts. See recommendations below. Requiring students read the newspaper is also important for this course.

Human Rights in Literature and Theater Courses

Teaching Human Rights in Literary and Cultural Studies, ed. Alexandra Schultheis Moore and Elizabeth Swanson Goldberg.
Not necessarily to be used for an undergraduate text, but a useful resource for faculty.

Theatre and Human Rights, Paul Rae

Imagining Human Rights in Twenty-First-Century Theater: Global Perspectives, ed. Florian N. Becker, Paola S. Hernandez, and Brenda Werth

Speaking Rights to Power: Constructing Political Will, Alison Brysk

Theatres of Struggle and the End of Apartheid, Belinda Bozzoli

The Ascent of Angels in America: The World Only Spins Forward, Isaac Butler and Dan Kois

Waiting for Godot, Samuel Beckett

Mother Courage and Her Children, Bertolt Brecht

Fefu and Her Friends, Maria Irene Fornes

"Master Harold" . . . and the Boys: A Play, Athol Fugard

Angels in America: Part 1: Millennium Approaches, Tony Kushner

Angels in America: Part 2: Perestroika, Tony Kushner

The Crucible, Arthur Miller

For Colored Girls Who Have Considered Suicide/When the Rainbow Is Enuf, Ntozake Shange

Fences, August Wilson

The Freedom of the City, Brian Friel

Pantomime, Derek Walcott, from *The Longman Anthology of Modern and Contemporary Drama,* ed. Michael Greenwald, Roberto Dario Pomo, Roger Schultz, and Anne Marie Welsh

"Friday," from *Robinson Crusoe,* Daniel Defoe

Zoot Suit, from *Zoot Suit and Other Plays,* Luis Valdez

The Bus Stop, Gao Xingjian, from *The Longman Anthology of Modern and Contemporary Drama,* ed. Michael Greenwald, Roberto Dario Pomo, Roger Schultz and Anne Marie Welsh

Miss Saigon, Alain Boublil and Claude-Michel Schönberg

The Story of Miss Saigon, excerpts from Edward Behr and Mark Steyn

Only Drunks and Children Tell the Truth, Drew Hayden Taylor, from *Seventh Generation: An Anthology of Native American Plays,* ed. Mimi Gisolfi D'Aponte

Note: See the list of other nonfiction sources below for additional relevant titles.

Human Rights Law Courses

Textbook on International Human Rights, Rhona K. M. Smith
  Reasonably sized introduction to human rights law with good historical background.

International Human Rights in a Nutshell, Thomas Buergenthal, Dinah Shelton, and David Stewart.
  Part of the Nutshell book series, this is a small, thick paperback that describes itself as a reference for students or lawyers.

International Human Rights in Context: Law, Politics, Morals, Henry Steiner, Philip Alston, and Ryan Goodman
  A giant tome aimed at law students but useful for others with its presentation and documentation of laws, organizations, and topics. Every chapter filled with legal and nonlegal sources.

Mobilizing for Human Rights: International Law in Domestic Politics, Beth Simmons
  This much cited text makes the argument for the value of human rights law.

International Human Rights Law: Returning to Universal Principles, Mark Gibney
  This is a short text arguing four ways of strengthening human rights law.

Grassroots Activism and the Evolution of Transnational Justice: Families of the Disappeared, Iosif Kovras
  Short, interesting study of how and why the families of the disappeared in various countries have used the justice system successfully or not.

Shifting Legal Visions: Judicial Change and Human Rights Trials in Latin America, Ezequiel A. Gonzalez-Ocantos
  This book focuses on how activists influenced judges who were then able to mold transitional justice to successfully hold Latin American strongmen accountable.

Research Methods for Human Rights

Measuring Human Rights, Todd Landman, and *Studying Human Rights*, Todd Landman and Edzia Carvalho
  Two texts that are useful for a methods course.

Statistical Methods for Human Rights, ed. Jana Asher, David Banks, and
    Fritz Scheuren Jr.
    An edited volume with essays on the study of various human rights
    abuses.

Advocacy for Human Rights

Any of the Brysk and Sikkink books cited in the Current Issues Courses
section above would be appropriate for an advocacy course.
Campaigning for Justice: Human Rights Advocacy in Practice, Jo Becker
    Advocate and college instructor Becker brings twenty years of experi-
    ence to her book examining various campaigns for addressing human
    rights abuses, with an emphasis on successful ones. She also introduces
    students to UN mechanisms and the role of new media in advocacy.
Rhetoric in Human Rights Advocacy: A Study of Exemplars, Richard K. Ghere
    The author presents the rhetoric of both advocates and antagonists ana-
    lyzing the work of NGOs, Pussy Riot, and other individuals, famous
    and less so.
The Courage of Strangers: Coming of Age with the Human Rights Movement,
    Jeri Laber
    Memoir from a founder of Human Rights Watch describing its early
    work involving her clandestine, sometimes dangerous, visits to aid dissi-
    dents primarily in Communist Eastern Europe.

Books critical of human rights efforts include:
The Crisis Caravan: What's Wrong with Humanitarian Aid, Linda Polman
The Idealist: Jeffrey Sachs and the Quest to End Poverty, Nina Munk

Resources for Faculty

Capstone/Experiential Learning

Designing and Teaching Undergraduate Capstone Courses, Robert Hauhart
    and Jon Grahe
*Experiential Education in the College Context: What It Is, How It Works, and
    Why It Matters*, Jay W. Roberts

Teaching for Experiential Learning: Five Approaches that Work, Scott Wurdinger and Julie Carlson

Service Learning: Lesson Plans and Projects, ed. Kristine Belisle, Karen Robinson, Elizabeth Sullivan, and Felisa Tibbitts

> Published by Amnesty International and HREA, this handbook makes recommendations for designing good projects and provides assignments to assist.

Memoirs

Interventions: A Life in War and Peace, Kofi Annan

> Memoir of his tenure as secretary general of the UN with analysis of international events and the UN's successes and failures.

A Long Way Gone: Memoirs of a Boy Soldier, Ishmael Beah

> The memoir of a young man who was a child soldier in Sierra Leone and eventually became a college student in the US.

Brother, I'm Dying, Edwidge Danticat

> Memoir of a woman whose parents relocated from Haiti to the US when she was a child, and the struggles of the family she left behind when she eventually joined her parents in the States.

The Voice of Witness Reader: Ten Years of Amplifying Unheard Voices, ed. Dave Eggers

> A collection of oral stories from survivors of human rights problems and conflicts.

Zeitoun, Dave Eggers

> True story of a New Orleans man who aided others during Hurricane Katrina only to be arrested. Highly acclaimed winner of numerous accolades.

There Are No Children Here: The Story of Two Brothers Growing Up in the Other America, Alex Kotlowitz

> True story of two young brothers living in Chicago's public housing projects.

Zami: A New Spelling of My Name, Audre Lorde

> The weaving of history, memory, and myth into a genre the author calls "biomythography."

Slave: My True Story, Mende Nazer and Damien Lewis

> The biography of a young woman's enslavement as a young child in the Sudan, her being taken to London as a slave, and her eventual escape.

Reading Lolita in Tehran, Azar Nafisi

Enrique's Journey: The Story of a Boy's Dangerous Odyssey to Reunite with His Mother, Sonia Nazario

A journalist's account of the treacherous journey from Central America that many young people make. It is primarily told through the experience of one boy, Enrique.

In Order To Live: A North Korean Girl's Journey to Freedom, Yeonmi Park and Maryanne Vollers

My Name is Jody Williams: A Vermont Girl's Winding Path to the Nobel Peace Prize, Jody Williams

I Am Malala: The Girl Who Stood Up for Education and Was Shot by the Taliban, Malala Yousafzai

Fiction

Half of a Yellow Sun, Chimamanda Ngozi Adichie

The 1960s Biafran War through the eyes of four characters.

Breath, Eyes, Memory, Edwidge Danticat

The story of a Haitian child's relocation in New York.

Here Comes the Sun, Nicole Dennis-Benn

This novel's heroine is struggling to protect her little sister and survive in impoverished Jamaica.

Zahra's Paradise, Amir Soltani and Khalil

Graphic novel about 2009 post-election Iran and a mother's search for her arrested protester son.

Film

Watching Human Rights: The 101 Best Films, Mark Gibney

Not a film itself, but about half this book is devoted to feature films and the other half to documentaries. Gibney provides more than 101 titles, because in addition to those listed as "the best," he has a category called "also of note."

Poverty, Inc.: Fighting Poverty Is Big Business, but Who Profits the Most?, Michael Matheson Miller

Excellent 2016 documentary with case studies, interviews, and footage from many countries problematizing the aid industry.

Books on Course Design, Active Learning, and Assessment

On design:

Designing and Assessing Courses and Curricula: A Practical Guide, Robert M. Diamond

Creating Significant Learning Experiences: An Integrated Approach to Designing College Courses, L. Dee Fink

For active learning and assessment:

Classroom Assessment Techniques: A Handbook for College Teachers, Thomas A. Angelo and K. Patricia Cross

This book has fifty activities for active learning/assessment in the college classroom.

Engaging Ideas: The Professor's Guide to Integrating Writing, Critical Thinking, and Active Learning in the Classroom, John C. Bean

Student Engagement Techniques: A Handbook for College Faculty, Elizabeth F. Barkley

This book provides fifty ideas for engaging students.

The Human Rights Education Handbook: Effective Practices for Learning, Action, and Change, Nancy Flowers

Useful text including methods, techniques, and activities for various educational settings.

Bringing Human Rights to US Classrooms: Exemplary Models from Elementary Grades to University, ed. Susan Roberts Katz and Andrea McEvoy Spero

The first part of the book is about the history of HRE, including the drawbacks of neoliberalism for HRE. The second part is written by teachers, and each chapter provides an example of teaching a human rights topic in the classroom. Many of these models focused on K–12 environments can be adapted to the college level.

Assessment Clear and Simple: A Practical Guide for Institutions, Departments, and General Education, Barbara E. Walvoord

An (Incomplete) List for Educating Faculty

The Evolution of International Human Rights: Visions Seen, Paul Gordon Lauren

International Human Rights, Jack Donnelly and Daniel Whelan

A World Made New: Eleanor Roosevelt and the Universal Declaration of Human Rights, Mary Ann Glendon
This book captures the drama of the writing of UDHR with Eleanor Roosevelt at the helm.

The Courage of Strangers: Coming of Age with the Human Rights Movement, Jeri Laber
Memoir described above under Advocacy for Human Rights.

Joyful Human Rights, William Simmons
Human rights is not only depressing.

The Last Utopia: Human Rights in History, Samuel Moyn
The most popular book of the genre arguing against an evolutionary history and questioning the lasting power of human rights.

The Aspiring Thinker's Guide to Critical Thinking, Richard W. Paul and Linda Elder
Short, inexpensive pamphlet to use with students. The authors have published about fourteen pamphlets on critical thinking with much overlap in them.

Thinking, Fast and Slow, Daniel Kahneman
Everyone should read this book. The author won the Nobel Prize for his research on biases and heuristics. It is very readable and can be assigned to students.

Why People Believe Weird Things: Pseudoscience, Superstition, and Other Confusions of Our Time, Michael Shermer
The author is the founder of the magazine *Skeptic*. It is light read with a serious message. A main point is the need for critical thinkers to understand the scientific method.

Notes

Preface

1. Samuel Moyn, *The Last Utopia: Human Rights in History* (Cambridge: Belknap Press, 2010).

2. Jack Donnelly, *Universal Human Rights in Theory and Practice* (Ithaca: Cornell University Press, 1989); and Jack Donnelly, *International Human Rights* (Boulder: Westview Press, 1993).

3. Paul Gordon Lauren, *The Evolution of International Human Rights: Visions Seen* (Philadelphia: University of Pennsylvania Press, 1998).

4. Davydd J. Greenwood and Morten Levin, *Introduction to Action Research: Social Research for Social Change* (Thousand Oaks: Sage, 2007).

5. Betty A. Reardon and Dale T. Snauwaert, *Betty A. Reardon: A Pioneer in Education for Peace and Human Rights* (London: Springer, 2015), 146.

6. Antonia Darder, Marta P. Baltodano, and Rodolfo D. Torres, "Critical Pedagogy: An Introduction," in *The Critical Pedagogy Reader*, ed. Antonia Darder, Marta P. Baltodano, and Rodolfo D. Torres (New York: Routledge, 2017), 9.

Chapter 1

1. United Nations High Commissioner for Refugees, "Global Trends: Forced Displacement in 2016," June 19, 2017, http://www.unhcr.org/5943e8a34.pdf.

2. Henry Louis Gates Jr., "Slavery, by the Numbers," *The Root*, February 10, 2014, https://www.theroot.com/slavery-by-the-numbers-1790874492.

3. Alliance 8.7, "Global Estimates of Modern Slavery 2017," http://www .alliance87.org/2017ge/modernslavery#!section = 10.

4. Human Rights Watch, "Annual Report 2016," https://www.hrw.org/sites/ default/files/news_attachments/english_annual_report-2016.pdf.

5. Meghan Henry et al., "The 2016 Annual Homeless Assessment Report (AHAR) to Congress," 2016, https://www.hudexchange.info/resources/documents/2016 -AHAR-Part-1.pdf.

6. UN General Assembly, "Universal Declaration of Human Rights," 1948 (217 [III] A), http://www.un.org/en/universal-declaration-human-rights.

7. International Covenant on Civil and Political Rights; International Covenant on Economic, Social, and Cultural Rights; Convention on the Elimination of All Forms of Racial Discrimination; Convention on the Elimination of All Forms of Discrimination Against Women; Convention Against Torture and Other Cruel, Inhuman, or Degrading Treatment or Punishment; Convention on the Rights of the Child; International Convention on the Protection of the Rights of All Migrant Workers and Members of Their Families; International Convention for the Protection of All Persons from Enforced Disappearance; Convention on the Rights of Persons with Disabilities.

8. Mark Philip Bradley, *The World Reimagined: Americans and Human Rights in the Twentieth Century* (Cambridge: Cambridge University Press, 2016), 130, 214–15.

9. Johannes Morsink, *The Universal Declaration of Human Rights: Origins, Drafting, and Intent* (Philadelphia: University of Pennsylvania Press, 2000), 4.

10. Two excellent books on the topic are Daniel C. Thomas's *The Helsinki Effect: International Norms, Human Rights, and the Demise of Communism* (Princeton: Princeton University Press, 2001), and Sarah B. Snyder's *Human Rights Activism and the End of the Cold War: A Transnational History of the Helsinki Network* (New York: Cambridge University Press, 2013).

11. Thomas, *Helsinki Effect*, 28.

12. Amnesty International, Greenpeace, and Médecins Sans Frontières also started in the 1970s.

13. Thomas, *Helsinki Effect*, 137.

14. Sarita Cargas, "Questioning Samuel Moyn's Revisionist History of Human Rights," *Human Rights Quarterly* 38, no. 2 (2016): 423.

15. United Nations Human Rights Office of the High Commissioner, "United Nations Declaration on Human Rights Education and Training [UNDHRET]," adopted by the Human Rights Council, April 8, 2011, Article 3, Section 2, http://www .ohchr.org/EN/Issues/Education/Training/Pages/UNDHREducationTraining.aspx.

16. George Andreopoulos and Richard Pierre Claude, *Human Rights Education for the Twenty-First Century* (Philadelphia: University of Pennsylvania Press, 1997).

17. Monisha Bajaj, ed. *Human Rights Education: Theory, Research, Praxis* (Philadelphia: University of Pennsylvania Press, 2017).

18. Joseph Zadja and Sev Ozdowski, eds. *Globalisation, Human Rights Education, and Reforms* (Dordrecht: Springer Netherlands, 2017).

19. HRE USA evolved from a national meeting at the Harvard Graduate School of Education organized by Felisa Tibbitts and Nancy Flowers in 2011. (Personal communication, January 9, 2018).

20. UN Human Rights Office of the High Commissioner, "UNDHRET," Articles 2c, 4e, 4c.

21. Betty A. Reardon and Dale T. Snauwaert, *Betty A. Reardon: A Pioneer in Education for Peace and Human Rights* (London: Springer, 2015), 145.

22. Southern Poverty Law Center, "New SPLC Reports Reveal Alarming Pattern of Hate Incidents and Bullying Across Country Since Election," November 29, 2016,

https://www.splcenter.org/news/2016/11/29/new-splc-reports-reveal-alarming
-pattern-hate-incidents-and-bullying-across-country.

23. John Dear, "Human Rights and Nonviolence: Testament of a Christian Peace Activist," in *Christianity and Human Rights*, ed. Frances Adeney and Arvind Sharma (New York: SUNY Press, 2007), 183.

24. Daniel F. Polish, "Judaism and Human Rights," in *Human Rights in Religious Traditions*, ed. Arlene Swidler (New York: Pilgrim Press, 1982), 48.

25. Haim Cohen, *Human Rights in Jewish Law* (New York: Ktav Publishing House, 1984).

26. Mohammed Abed Al-Jabri, *Democracy, Human Rights, and Law in Islamic Thought* (New York: I. B. Tauris, 2009), 51.

27. Frances Adeney, "Human Rights and Responsibilities: Christian Perspectives," in Adeney and Sharma, *Christianity and Human Rights*, 19.

28. A thorough examination of the relationship of religion and human rights would include the perpetration of violence by religions as well. That topic is a digression from the point I am making in this chapter, however.

29. United Nations Human Rights Office of the High Commissioner, "Universal Human Rights Instruments," http://www.ohchr.org/EN/ProfessionalInterest/Pages/UniversalHumanRightsInstruments.aspx, accessed April 14, 2017.

30. Paula Gerber, *Understanding Human Rights: Educational Challenges for the Future* (Northampton: Edward Elgar Publishing, 2013), 5.

31. United Nations Human Rights Office of the High Commissioner, "Basic Facts About the UPR," http://www.ohchr.org/EN/HRBodies/UPR/Pages/BasicFacts.aspx, accessed April 14, 2017.

32. Human Rights Educators USA, "Human Rights Education: Submission to the UN Mid-Term Review of Recommendations from the 22nd Session of the Universal Periodic Review," 2017 (para. 1.1), https://hreusaorg.files.wordpress.com/2017/05/hre-usa-ushrn_stakeholder-submission_us-upr_sept-2014.pdf.

33. Ibid. (para. 2.4).

34. Ibid. (para. 3.2).

35. Gerber, *Understanding Human Rights*, 88.

36. Bureau of Democracy, Human Rights, and Labor, "Human Rights,", US Department of State, https://www.state.gov/j/drl/hr, accessed April 14, 2017.

37. Ibid.

38. Columbia Law School Human Rights Institute and International Association of Official Human Rights Agencies, "Ensuring Human Rights Implementation at the Federal, State, and Local Levels," 2017, http://www.law.columbia.edu/sites/default/files/microsites/human-rights-institute/files/subnational_fact_sheet.pdf.

39. Ibid.

40. Kansas Human Rights Commission, "FAQS," http://www.khrc.net/faq.html, accessed April 14, 2017.

41. Bradley, *World Reimagined*, 131.

42. Charles Tilly and Lesley Wood, *Social Movements: 1768–2012* (Abingdon: Routledge, 2012), 117–18.

43. Nonprofit Action, "Facts and Stats about NGOs Worldwide," September 4, 2015, http://nonprofitaction.org/2015/09/facts-and-stats-about-ngos-worldwide.

44. Maximpact Ecosystems, "What Challenges Do NGO's Face and What Are the Solutions?," *Maximpact Blog* March 20, 2017, http://maximpactblog.com/what-challenges-do-ngos-face-and-what-are-the-solutions.

45. Bureau of Democracy, Human Rights, and Labor, "Non-Governmental Organizations (NGOs) in the United States," US Department of State, January 20, 2017, https://www.state.gov/j/drl/rls/fs/2017/266904.htm.

46. Ibid.

47. World Vision, "2015 Annual Review," November 2, 2016, https://www.worldvision.org/wp-content/uploads/2015-annual-report-brochure-F3.pdf.

48. CARE USA, "CARE USA 2016 Annual Report," http://www.care.org/sites/default/files/care_2016_annual_report_2017_14_04.pdf, accessed April 14, 2017.

49. Save the Children Federation, "Results for Children: Annual Report 2016," https://www.savethechildren.org/content/dam/usa/reports/advocacy/annual-report/sc-2016-annualreport.pdf.

50. Médecins Sans Frontières, "International Financial Report 2016," http://www.msf.org/sites/msf.org/files/msf_financial_report_2016_final.pdf.

51. BRAC, "BRAC Annual Report 2016," http://www.brac.net/publications/annual-report/2016.

52. Joelle Tanguy and Fiona Terry, "Humanitarian Responsibility and Committed Action," *Ethics & International Affairs* 13, no. 1 (1999): 29–34.

53. Linda Polman, *The Crisis Caravan: What's Wrong with Humanitarian Aid?* (New York: Metropolitan Books, 2010), chapter 3.

54. China Labor Watch, "Something's Not Right Here: Poor Working Conditions Persist at Apple Supplier Pegatron," October 22, 2015, http://www.chinalaborwatch.org/report/109.

55. Richard Eells and Clarence Walton, *Conceptual Foundations of Business* (Homewood: Richard D. Irwin, 1974), 245.

56. Governance and Accountability Institute, "This Year's Tally of S&P 500 Company Disclosures—81% Now Publishing Sustainability/Responsibility Reports," March 14, 2016, https://www.ga-institute.com/newsletter/press-release/npage/7/article/this-years-tally-of-sp-500-company-disclosures-81-now-publishing-sustainability-responsibilit.html.

57. Extractive Industries Transparency Initiative (EITI), "Who We Are," https://eiti.org/who-we-are, accessed April 14, 2017.

58. International Organization for Standardization, "ISO 26000—Social Responsibility," https://www.iso.org/iso-26000-social-responsibility.html, accessed April 14, 2017.

59. Fair Labor Association, "Code of Conduct," http://www.fairlabor.org/our -work/code-of-conduct (last modified 2012).

60. Nancy Flowers, *The Human Rights Education Handbook: Effective Practices for Learning, Action, and Change* (Minneapolis: Human Rights Resource Center, 2000), 8.

61. UN General Assembly, "Report of the United Nations High Commissioner for Human Rights on the Implementation of the Plan of Action for the United Nations Decade for Human Rights Education," December 12, 1996, https://www.ohchr.org/ EN/Issues/Education/Training/Compilation/Pages/PlanofActionfortheUnited NationsDecadeforHumanRightsEducation,1995-2004(1996).aspx.

62. United Nations Human Rights Office of the High Commissioner, "United Nations Declaration on Human Rights Education and Training (2011)," Article 2, para. 2, https://www.ohchr.org/EN/Issues/Education/Training/Compilation/Pages/ UnitedNationsDeclarationonHumanRightsEducationandTraining(2011).aspx. Emphasis added.

63. United Nations Human Rights Office of the High Commissioner, "World Programme for Human Rights Education Second Phase Plan of Action," July 2012, http://www.ohchr.org/Documents/Publications/WPHRE_Phase_2_en.pdf. Emphasis added.

64. Nancy Flowers, "What Is Human Rights Education?", in *A Survey of Human Rights Education* (Hamburg: BertelsmannVerlag, 2003): 14–15.

65. Felisa Tibbitts, "Understanding What We Do: Emerging Models for Human Rights Education," *International Review of Education* 48, nos. 3/4 (2002): 164.

66. Paulo Freire, *Pedagogy of the Oppressed*, 2nd ed. (London: Penguin, 1996).

67. Garth Meintjes, "Human Rights Education as Empowerment: Reflections on Pedagogy," in *Human Rights Education for the Twenty-First Century*, ed. George Andreopoulos and Richard Pierre Claude (Philadelphia: University of Pennsylvania Press, 1997), 66.

68. Anja Mihr and Hans Peter Schmitz, "Human Rights Education (HRE) and Transnational Activism," *Human Rights Quarterly* 29, no. 4 (2007): 978.

69. Robin Wilson, "Social Change Tops Classic Books in Professors' Teaching Priorities," *Chronicle of Higher Education*, March 5, 2009, http://chronicle.com/article/ Social-Change-Tops-Classic/1564.

70. Monisha Bajaj, "Human Rights Education: Ideology, Location, and Approaches," *Human Rights Quarterly* 33, no. 2 (2011): 483.

71. Colin Bonnycastle, "Social Justice Along a Continuum: A Relational Illustrative Model," *Social Service Review* 85, no. 2 (2011): 269.

72. Flowers, *Human Rights Education*, 2.

73. André Keet, "Does Human Rights Education Exist?," *International Journal of Human Rights Education* 1, no. 1 (2017): 2.

74. Meintjes, "Human Rights Education," 78.

75. Henry Steiner, "The University's Crucial Role in the Human Rights Movement," *Harvard Human Rights Journal* 15 (2002): 325.

76. Michalinos Zembylas, "Emotions, Critical Pedagogy, and Human Rights Education," in *Human Rights Education: Theory, Research, Praxis*, ed. Monisha Bajaj (Philadelphia: University of Pennsylvania Press, 2017: 63.

77. Ron Dudai, "Introduction—Rights Choices: Dilemmas of Human Rights Practice," *Journal of Human Rights Practice* 6, no. 3 (2014).

78. Keet, "Does Human Rights Education Exist?," 3, 5.

79. Ibid., 11.

80. Steiner, "University's Crucial Role," 319.

81. Zembylas, "Emotions, Critical Pedagogy," 63.

82. Meintjes, "Human Rights Education," 77–78.

83. Dudai, "Introduction," 389.

84. HRE itself will also be subject to contention because of the debates inherent in a large field involving theory and praxis.

85. See, for example, Paul Gordon Lauren's *The Evolution of Human Rights: Visions Seen* (Philadelphia: University of Pennsylvania Press, 1998) and Kathryn Sikkink's *Evidence for Hope: Making Human Rights Work in the 21st Century* (Princeton: Princeton University Press, 2017).

86. Stephen Hopgood, *The Endtimes of Human Rights* (Ithaca: Cornell University Press, 2013).

87. Moyn, *Last Utopia*.

88. Makua Mutua, *Human Rights: A Political and Cultural Critique* (Philadelphia: University of Pennsylvania Press, 2002).

89. Marie-Benedicte Dembour, *Who Believes in Human Rights? Reflections on the European Convention* (Cambridge: Cambridge University Press, 2006).

90. David Rieff, *A Bed for the Night: Humanitarianism in Crisis* (London: Vintage, 2002).

91. Polman, *Crisis Caravan*.

92. Antonia Darder, Marta P. Baltodano, and Rodolfo D. Torres, "Critical Pedagogy: An Introduction," in *The Critical Pedagogy Reader*, ed. Antonia Darder, Marta P. Baltodano, and Rodolfo D. Torres (New York: Routledge, 2017), 13.

93. Ibid., 9.

Chapter 2

1. You can find the OHCHR Database at http://hre.ohchr.org/hret/intro.aspx.

2. David Suárez and Patricia Bromley, "Professionalizing a Global Social Movement: Universities and Human Rights," *American Journal of Education* 118, no. 3 (2012): 253.

3. University of Essex, "Human Rights Centre: Our Courses," https://www.essex .ac.uk/centres-and-institutes/human-rights/our-courses, accessed January 2019; University of Minnesota, "Grad Minor in Human Rights Program," https://cla.umn.edu/ human-rights/grad-minor-human-rights-program, accessed January 2019; University of Indiana, "PhD Minor in Human Rights," http://www.indiana.edu/~intlweb/gradu

ate/hrminor.shtml, accessed January 2019; Columbia University, "Graduate Studies," http://www.humanrightscolumbia.org/education/graduate, accessed January 2019.

4. Sue Shellenbarger, "Can't Pick a College Major? Create One," *Wall Street Journal*, November 17, 2010, https://www.wsj.com/articles/SB100014240527487036 28204575618622095004264.

5. *US News and World Report*, "National University Rankings," https://www .usnews.com/best-colleges/rankings/national-universities, accessed April 2017.

6. University of Ottowa, "Honours in Conflict Studies and Human Rights," https://socialsciences.uottawa.ca/programs/undergraduate-course-sequences/ honours-conflict-studies-human-rights, accessed January 2019.

7. Carleton University, "Human Rights and Social Justice," https://admissions .carleton.ca/programs/human-rights-ba/, accessed January 2019.

8. York University, "Human Rights and Equity Studies," https://futurestudents .yorku.ca/program/human-rights-equity-studies, accessed January 2019.

9. Wilfrid Laurier University, "Human Rights and Human Diversity," https:// www.wlu.ca/programs/liberal-arts/undergraduate/human-rights-and-human -diversity-ba/index.html, accessed January 2019.

10. University of Winnipeg, "Bachelor of Arts in Human Rights," https:// www.uwinnipeg.ca/global-college/ba-in-human-rights/index.html, accessed January 2019.

11. Aristotle University of Thessoloniki, "UNESCO Chair on Education for Human Rights, Democracy and Peace," https://www.auth.gr/en/units/8187, accessed January 2019.

12. Makerere University, "Bachelor of Ethics and Human Rights," https://courses- .mak.ac.ug/programmes/bachelor-ethics-and-human-rights, accessed January 2019.

13. SMU requires none of the core courses mentioned above in its BA in human rights.

14. The syllabi of many courses reveal that some assignments are focused on human rights abuses in the US or perpetrated by the US government abroad. SMU requires a course titled America's Dilemma: The Struggle for Human Rights.

15. Robert M. Diamond, *Designing and Assessing Courses and Curricula: A Practical Guide* (San Francisco: Jossey-Bass, 2008), 4.

16. University of Dayton, "Human Rights Studies Program," https://www .udayton.edu/artssciences/academics/humanrights/welcome/index.php, accessed May 2017.

17. Dedman College of Humanities and Sciences, Southern Methodist University, "Embrey Human Rights Program," http://www.smu.edu/Dedman/Academics/Insti tutesCenters/EmbreyHumanRights/know, accessed May 2017.

18. Trinity College, "Human Rights Program," http://www.trincoll.edu/Aca demics/SpecialPrograms/HumanRights/Pages/default.aspx, accessed May 2017.

19. Columbia University, "Institute for the Study of Human Rights," http://www .humanrightscolumbia.org/education/undergraduate, accessed May 2017.

20. University of Essex, "Human Rights Centre: Study with Us," http://www.essex.ac.uk/hrc/study-with-us/default.aspx, accessed May 2017.

21. Carleton University Undergraduate Admissions, "Human Rights and Social Justice (BA)," https://admissions.carleton.ca/programs/human-rights-ba, accessed May 2017.

22. Australian National University College of Arts and Social Sciences, "Human Rights," https://programsandcourses.anu.edu.au/major/HMRT-MAJ, accessed May 2017.

23. Malmo University, "Human Rights," http://edu.mah.se/en/Program/SGMRE, accessed May 2017.

24. Nancy Flowers, *The Human Rights Education Handbook: Effective Practices for Learning, Action, and Change*. Minneapolis: Human Rights Resource Center.

25. OSCE Office for Democratic Institutions and Human Rights, *Human Rights Education in the School Systems of Europe, Central Asia and North America: A Compendium of Good Practice* (Warsaw: OSCE Office for Democratic Institutions and Human Rights, 2009).

26. Council of Europe, "Charter on Education for Democratic Citizenship and Human Rights Education," https://rm.coe.int/16803034e5, accessed May 2017.

27. Organization for Security and Co-operation in Europe (OSCE), *Guidelines on Human Rights Education for Secondary School Systems* (Vienna: Organization for Security and Co-operation in Europe, 2012).

28. Asia Pacific Forum, *Human Rights Education: A Manual for National Human Rights Institutions* (Sydney: Asia Pacific Forum of National Human Rights Institutions, 2013), http://www.asiapacificforum.net/media/resource_file/Human_Rights_Education_Manual_for_NHRIs_ejmumah.pdf, updated January 2017.

Chapter 3

1. Robert Frodeman, introduction to *The Oxford Handbook of Interdisciplinarity*, ed. Robert Frodeman (Oxford: Oxford University Press, 2010), xxv.

2. Peter Weingart, "A Short History of Knowledge Formations," in Frodeman, *Oxford Handbook of Interdisciplinarity*, 10.

3. Interdisciplinarity is claimed on the websites of Bard, Barnard, Trinity, University of Dayton, University of Connecticut, and Webster University (six of the eight US BA programs), and on the websites of Carleton, St. Thomas, Ottawa, and Winnipeg (Canada), Monash University (Australia) and Essex (England).

4. Committee on Facilitating Interdisciplinary Research, Committee on Science, Engineering, and Public Policy, *Facilitating Interdisciplinary Research*, National Academies (Washington: National Academy Press, 2004), 2.

5. Harvey J. Graff, *Undisciplining Knowledge: Interdisciplinarity in the Twentieth Century* (Baltimore: Johns Hopkins University Press, 2015), 4.

6. Julie Thompson Klein, "A Taxonomy of Interdisciplinarity," in Frodeman, *Oxford Handbook of Interdisciplinarity*, 17.

7. Michael Crow and William Dabars, "Towards Interdisciplinarity by Design in the American Research University," in *University Experiments in Interdisciplinarity*, ed. Peter Weingart and Britta Padberg (Bielefeld: Transcript Verlag, 2014), 27.

8. Frodeman, introduction to *Oxford Handbook of Interdisciplinarity*, xxxv.

9. Jerry A. Jacobs, *In Defense of Disciplines: Interdisciplinarity and Specialization in the Research University* (Chicago: University of Chicago Press, 2014), 61–67.

10. Tony Becher and Paul R. Trowler, *Academic Tribes and Territories* (Buckingham: Open University Press, 2001), 28.

11. Ibid., 59.

12. Andrew Abbott, *Chaos of Disciplines* (Chicago: University of Chicago Press, 2014), 6.

13. Graff, *Undisciplining Knowledge*, 129.

14. Ibid., 139.

15. Ibid., 159.

16. Ibid., 146.

17. Others argue that cognitive science is a discipline. See, for example, José Luis Bermúdez, *Cognitive Science: An Introduction to the Science of the Mind* (Cambridge: Cambridge University Press, 2010).

18. Jacobs, *In Defense of Disciplines*, 126–27.

19. Ibid., 81.

20. Becher and Trowler, *Academic Tribes*, 43.

21. Jacobs, *In Defense of Disciplines*, 85.

22. Ibid.

23. Julie Thompson Klein, *Creating Interdisciplinary Campus Cultures: A Model for Strength and Sustainability* (San Francisco: Jossey-Bass, 2010), 20.

24. Jacobs, *In Defense of Disciplines*, 89.

25. Becher and Trowler, *Academic Tribes*, 20.

26. Mark William Roche, *Realizing the Distinctive University: Vision and Values, Strategy and Culture* (Notre Dame: University of Notre Dame Press, 2017), 33.

27. Thomas Kuhn, *The Structure of Scientific Revolutions* (Chicago: University of Chicago Press, 1970), 24–25.

28. National Academies of Sciences, Engineering, and Medicine, *The Integration of the Humanities and Arts with Sciences, Engineering, and Medicine in Higher Education: Branches from the Same Tree* (Washington, D.C.: National Academies Press, 2018), 171.

29. Jerry Jacobs and Scott Frickel, "Interdisciplinarity: A Critical Assessment," *Annual Review of Sociology* 35 (2009): 48.

30. Michael Crow and William Dabars, *Designing the New American University* (Baltimore: Johns Hopkins University Press, 2014), viii.

31. Robert Frodeman, *A Sustainable Knowledge: A Theory of Interdisciplinarity* (New York: Palgrave Macmillan, 2014), 87.

32. Quoted in Intelligence Squared (IQ2) Debates, "Too Many Kids Go to College," October 12, 2011, http://intelligencesquaredus.org/debates/past-debates/item/550-too-many-kids-go-to-college-our-first-debate-in-chicago.

33. Alan Marcus, ed. *Science as Service: Establishing and Reformulating American Land Grant Universities, 1865–1930* (Tuscaloosa: University of Alabama Press, 2015).

34. Jonathan Cole, *The Great American University: Its Rise to Prominence, Its Indispensable Role, and Why It Must Be Protected* (New York: Public Affairs, 2010).

35. Jonathan Cole, *Toward a More Perfect University* (New York: Public Affairs, 2016).

36. Klein, *Creating Interdisciplinary Campus Cultures*, 107.

37. Ibid., 115.

38. William H. Newell, "The Case for Interdisciplinary Studies: Response to Professor Benson's Five Arguments," *Issues in Integrative Studies* 2 (1998): 117.

39. Klein, *Creating Interdisciplinary Campus Cultures*, 32.

40. Lennard J. Davis, "A Grand Unified Theory of Interdisciplinarity," *Chronicle of Higher Education* 53, no. 40 (2007): B9, as cited in Jacobs and Frickel, "Interdisciplinarity," 51–52.

41. Veronica Boix Mansilla and Howard Gardner, "Assessing Interdisciplinary Work at the Frontier: An Empirical Exploration of "Symptoms of Quality," Interdisciplines.org, https://www.mtu.edu/research/administration/enhancement/pdf/assessing-interdisciplinary-work.pdf, as cited in Jacobs and Frickel, "Interdisciplinarity," 51–52.

42. Robert Frodeman, "The End of Disciplinarity," in *University Experiments in Interdisciplinarity*, ed. Peter Weingart and Britta Padberg (New York: Columbia University Press, 2014), 187.

43. Ethan Kleinberg, "Interdisciplinary Studies at a Crossroads," *Liberal Education* 94, no. 1 (2008): 8.

44. Frodeman, "End of Disciplinarity," 189.

45. Kleinberg, "Interdisciplinary Studies," 6.

46. Ibid., 9.

47. National Center for Educational Statistics, "Fast Facts, Back to School Statistics," https://nces.ed.gov/fastfacts/display.asp?id=372 (last modified 2017).

48. Abbott, *Chaos of Disciplines*, 135.

49. Ibid., 135.

50. Ibid., 171.

51. Jacobs, *In Defense of Disciplines*, 77.

52. Richard Paul and Linda Elder, *The Aspiring Thinker's Guide to Critical Thinking* (Dillon Beach: Foundation for Critical Thinking, 2009), 20.

53. Karri Holley, "Understanding Interdisciplinary Challenges and Opportunities in Higher Education," *ASHE Higher Education Report* 35, no. 2 (2009): 14.

54. William H. Newell and William J. Green, "Defining and Teaching Interdisciplinary Studies," *Improving College and University Teaching* 30, no. 1 (1982): 25.

55. Eloise Buker, "Is Women's Studies a Disciplinary or an Interdisciplinary Field of Inquiry?," *NWSA Journal* 15, no. 1 (2003): 73.

56. Francesca Klug, *A Magna Carta for All Humanity: Homing in on Human Rights* (Abingdon: Routledge, 2015), 19.

57. The books include Todd Landman, *Studying Human Rights* (Abingdon: Routledge 2006); Todd Landman and Edzia Carvalho, *Measuring Human Rights* (Abingdon: Routledge 2009); and two edited volumes: Jana Asher, David Banks, and Fritz Scheuren Jr., *Statistical Methods for Human Rights* (New York: Springer US, 2008), and Fons Coomans, Fred Grunfeld, and Menno Kamminga, eds. *Methods of Human Rights Research* (Cambridge: Intersentia, 2009).

58. Coomans et al., *Methods of Human Rights Research*, 32.

59. Stephen Golub, "What Is Legal Empowerment? An Introduction," in *Legal Empowerment: Practitioners' Perspectives*, ed. Stephen Golub (Rome: International Development Law Organization, 2010).

60. Kathryn Sikkink, *Evidence for Hope: Making Human Rights Work in the 21st Century* (Princeton: Princeton University Press, 2017), 24.

61. Tony Becher and Paul Trowler, *Academic Tribes and Territories*. (Ballmoor, UK: Open University Press, 2001), 59.

62. Micheline Ishay, *The History of Human Rights: From Ancient Times to the Globalization Era* (Berkeley: University of California Press, 2008).

63. Peter Uvin, *Human Rights and Development* (Bloomfield: Kumarian Press, 2004).

64. Tove Skutnabb-Kangas and Robert Phillipson in collab. with Martin Rannut, *Linguistic Human Rights* (New York: Mouton de Gruyter, 1995).

65. Dorothee Baumann-Pauly and Justine Nolan, *Business and Human Rights: From Principles to Practice* (New York: Routledge, 2016).

66. Aoife Nolan, Rory O'Connell, and Colin Harvey, eds., *Human Rights and Public Finance: Budgets and the Promotion of Economic and Social Rights* (Oxford: Hart Publishing, 2013).

67. Jim Ife, *Human Rights and Social Work* (New York: Cambridge, 2012).

68. Gerhard Bos and Marcus Duwell, eds., *Human Rights and Sustainability: Moral Responsibilities for the Future* (Abingdon, UK: Routledge, 2016).

69. David Forsythe, *Human Rights in International Relations* (New York: Cambridge University Press, 2006).

70. Mark Frezzo. *The Sociology of Human Rights* (Cambridge: Polity Press, 2015).

71. Kate Nash, *The Political Sociology of Human Rights* (Cambridge: Cambridge University Press, 2015).

72. John Witte and M. Christian Green, *Religion and Human Rights: An Introduction* (New York: Oxford University Press, 2012).

73. Michael Freeman, *Human Rights: An Interdisciplinary Approach* (Cambridge: Polity, 2002), 78.

74. Ibid.

75. Richard Claude, *Comparative Human Rights* (Baltimore: Johns Hopkins University Press, 1976).

76. Ibid., 3–84.

77. Ibid., 91.

78. American Anthropological Association, "1947 Statement on Human Rights," June 24, 1947, http://humanrights.americananthro.org/1947-statement-on-human-rights, accessed June 1, 2018.

79. My comparison of HRE to religious studies is indebted to Sarah E. Fredericks's essay, "Religious Studies and Religious Practice," in Frodeman, *Oxford Handbook of Interdisciplinarity*, 385–96.

80. Sikkink, *Evidence for Hope*, 24.

Chapter 4

Note to epigraph: Michael B. Smith, Rebecca S. Nowacek, and Jeffrey L. Bernstein, *Citizenship Across the Curriculum* (Bloomington: Indiana University Press, 2010), 2.

1. See books such as L. Dee Fink's *Creating Significant Learning Experiences: An Integrated Approach to Design in College Course* (San Francisco: Jossey-Bass, 2013) and Richard Arum and Josipa Roksa's *Academically Adrift: Limited Learning on College Campuses* (Chicago: University of Chicago Press, 2010).

2. Arum and Roksa, *Academically Adrift*.

3. Derek Bok, *Our Underachieving Colleges: A Candid Look at How Much Students Learn and Why They Should Be Learning More* (Princeton: Princeton University Press, 2006).

4. Ibid., 49. Emphasis in original.

5. Ibid., 145.

6. Douglas Belkin, "Exclusive Test Data: Many Colleges Fail to Improve Critical-Thinking Skills," *Wall Street Journal*, June 5, 2017, https://www.wsj.com/articles/exclusive-test-data-many-colleges-fail-to-improve-critical-thinking-skills-1496686662.

7. Bok, *Our Underachieving Colleges*, 114.

8. Arum and Roksa, *Academically Adrift*, 36.

9. See Bok's chapters 4 and 5 of *Our Underachieving Colleges* for data on graduates' writing abilities and quantitative literacy.

10. Heather Hackman, "Five Essential Components for Social Justice Education," *Equity & Excellence in Education* 38, no. 2 (2005): 103–9.

11. Nicole Stedman and Brittany Adams, "Identifying Faculty's Knowledge of Critical Thinking Concepts and Perceptions of Critical Thinking Instruction in Higher Education," *North American Colleges and Teachers of Agriculture* 58, no. 2 (2012): 9.

12. Arum and Roksa, *Academically Adrift*, 35.

13. Mark Halx and L. Earle Reybold, "A Pedagogy of Force: Faculty Perspectives of Critical Thinking Capacity in Undergraduate Students," *Journal of General Education* 54, no. 4 (2005): 313.

14. See Margaret Lloyd and Nan Bahr, "Thinking Critically about Critical Thinking in Higher Education," *International Journal for the Scholarship of Teaching and Learning* 4, no. 2 (2010): 18; Tim van Gelder, "Teaching Critical Thinking: Some Lessons from Cognitive Science," *College Teaching* 53, no. 1 (2005): 41–46, and Sharon Bailin, Roland Case, Jerrold R. Coombs, and Leroi B. Daniels, "Common Misconceptions of Critical Thinking," *Journal of Curriculum Studies* 31, no. 3 (1999): 269–83.

15. See Daniel Willingham, "Critical Thinking: Why Is It So Hard to Teach?," *Arts Education Policy Review* 109, no. 4 (2008): 21–32, and Daniel Kahneman, *Thinking, Fast and Slow* (New York: Farrar, Straus, and Giroux, 2011).

16. Kahneman, *Thinking, Fast and Slow*.

17. Robert Ennis, "Critical Thinking and Subject Specificity: Clarification and Needed Research," *Educational Researcher* 18, no. 3 (1989): 4.

18. Richard Paul quoted in Gerald Nosich, *Learning to Think Things Through: A Guide to Critical Thinking Across the Curriculum* (London: Pearson, 2009), 2.

19. Willingham, "Critical Thinking"

20. Bok, *Our Underachieving Colleges*, 109.

21. Hackman, "Five Essential Components," 103.

22. Philip Abrami et al., "Instructional Interventions Affecting Critical Thinking Skills and Dispositions: A Stage 1 Meta-Analysis," *Review of Educational Research* 78, no. 4 (2008): 1108.

23. Washington State University, "Guide to Rating Critical Thinking," 2001, http://learning.colostate.edu/files/classes/42/File_385B9007-C87B-4164-4101084A4BD20704.pdf.

24. Ibid.

25. Van Gelder, "Teaching Critical Thinking."

26. Stephen Brookfield and Stephen Preskill, *Discussion as a Way of Teaching: Tools and Techniques for Democratic Classrooms* (San Francisco: Jossey-Bass, 2005).

27. Fink, *Creating Significant Learning Experiences*, xi.

28. Terrel L. Rhodes, *Assessing Outcomes and Improving Achievement: Tips and Tools for Using Rubrics.* Washington, D.C.: Association of American Colleges and Universities, 2009.

29. Some resources on this topic are listed in Appendix IV.

30. For example, Smith, Nowacek, and Bernstein, *Citizenship Across the Curriculum*, and Nadine Dolby, *Rethinking Multicultural Education for the Next Generation: The New Empathy and Social Justice* (Abingdon: Routledge, 2012).

31. Özlem Sensoy and Robin DiAngelo, *Is Everyone Really Equal: An Introduction to Key Concepts in Social Justice Education* (New York: Teachers College Press, 2012).

32. Lauren Bialystok, "Politics Without "Brainwashing": A Philosophical Defence of Social Justice Education," *Curriculum Inquiry* 44, no. 3 (2014): 418.

33. Dolby, *Rethinking Multicultural Education*, 7.

34. Maxine Greene, introduction to *Teaching for Social Justice*, ed. William Ayers, Jean Ann Hunt, and Therese Quinne (New York: New Press, 1998).

35. Hackman, "Five Essential Components," 104.

36. Ibid., 105.

37. Robin DiAngelo and Özlem Sensoy, " 'We Don't Want Your Opinion': Knowledge Construction and the Discourse of Opinion in the Equity Classroom," *Equity & Excellence in Education* 42, no. 4 (2009): 443–55.

38. Jill Marshall and Ana Maria Klein, "Lessons in Social Action: Equipping and Inspiring Students to Improve Their World," *Social Studies* 100, no. 5 (2009): 218–21.

39. Ibid., 219.

40. Ibid., 220.

41. Freeman et al., "Active Learning Increases Student Performance in Science, Engineering, and Mathematics," *Proceedings of the National Academy of Sciences of the United States of America* 111, no. 23 (2010): 8414.

42. Elizabeth Barkley, *Student Engagement Techniques: A Handbook for College Faculty* (San Francisco: Jossey-Bass, 2009), 17.

43. Ibid., 18.

44. Freeman et al., "Active Learning," 8410.

45. José Antonio Bowen, *Teaching Naked: How Moving Technology out of your College Classroom Will Improve Student Learning* (New York: John Wiley, 2012), 196.

46. Brookfield and Preskill, *Discussion as a Way.*

47. Ibid., xv.

48. Ibid., 20.

49. Ibid., 6.

50. Ibid., 7.

51. Ibid., 8.

52. Ibid., 23.

53. Ibid., 69.

54. Ibid., 105.

Chapter 5

1. United Nations Human Rights Office of the High Commissioner, "World Programme for Human Rights Education Second Phase Plan of Action," July 2012, http://www.ohchr.org/Documents/Publications/WPHRE_Phase_2_en.pdf.

2. Nancy Flowers, *The Human Rights Education Handbook: Effective Practices for Learning, Action, and Change* (Minneapolis: Human Rights Resource Center, 2000), 14.

3. David Suárez, "Education Professionals and the Construction of Human Rights Education," *Comparative Education Review* 51, no.1 (2007): 48–70.

4. Felisa Tibbitts and Peter G. Kirchschläger, "Perspectives of Research on Human Rights Education," *Journal of Human Rights Education* 2, no. 1 (2010): 8–29.

5. Anne Becker, Annamagriet de Wet, and Willie van Vollenhoven, "Human Rights Literacy: Moving Towards Rights-Based Education and Transformative Action

Through Understandings of Dignity, Equality, and Freedom," *South African Journal of Education* 35, no. 2 (2015): 1–12.

6. Monisha Bajaj, "Human Rights Education: Ideology, Location, and Approaches," *Human Rights Quarterly* 33, no. 2 (2011): 481–508.

7. University of Dayton, "Human Rights Studies Program," https://www.udayton.edu/artssciences/academics/humanrights/welcome/index.php, accessed May 2017.

8. April Kelly-Woessner and Matthew C. Woessner, "My Professor Is a Partisan Hack: How Perceptions of a Professor's Political Views Affect Student Course Evaluations," *Political Science and Politics* 39, no. 3 (2006): 498.

9. Bureau of Democracy, Human Rights, and Labor, "Human Rights," US Department of State, https://www.state.gov/j/drl/hr, accessed April 14, 2017.

10. Ibid.

11. Matthew C. Woessner, "Rethinking the Plight of Conservatives in Higher Education," *Academe* 98, no. 1 (2012), https://www.aaup.org/article/rethinking-plight-conservatives-higher-education#.XCkl_1VKiJA.

12. "Research shows that more than a third of the public believes political 'bias' in higher education to be a 'very serious' problem," writes Neil Gross in *Why Are Professors Liberal and Why Do Conservatives Care?* (Cambridge: Harvard University Press, 2013).

13. Henry Steiner, "The University's Crucial Role in the Human Rights Movement," *Harvard Human Rights Journal* 15, 325.

14. Peter Rosenblum, "Teaching Human Rights: Ambivalent Activism, Multiple Discourses, and Lingering Dilemmas," *Harvard Human Rights Journal* 15 (2002): 305.

15. For an excellent guide to involving students in advocacy projects, see William Paul Simmons's forthcoming 2018 "Problem Based Learning Without Borders: Impact and Potential for University-Level Human Rights Education," *Journal of Human Rights*. See https://www.williampaulsimmons.com/problem-based-learning-without-borders.html.

16. Lauren Bialystok, "Politics Without 'Brainwashing': A Philosophical Defence of Social Justice Education," *Curriculum Inquiry* 44, no. 3 (2014): 430–31.

17. Richard Rorty, *Truth and Progress: Philosophical Papers*, vol. 3 (Cambridge: Cambridge University Press, 1998), 185.

18. Martin Puchner, *The Written World* (New York: Random House, 2017), 1.

19. Alexandra Schultheis Moore and Elizabeth Swanson Goldberg, *Teaching Human Rights in Literary and Cultural Studies* (New York: Modern Language Association of America, 2015), 217.

20. Michalinos Zembylas, *Emotion and Traumatic Conflict: Reclaiming Healing in Education* (New York: Oxford University Press, 2015).

21. Michalinos Zembylas, "Emotions, Critical Pedagogy, and Human Rights Education," in *Human Rights Education: Theory, Research, Praxis*, edited by Monisha Bajaj," 47–68.

22. Sara H. Konrath, Edward H. O'Brien, and Courtney Hsing, "Changes in Dispositional Empathy in American College Students over Time: A Meta-Analysis," *Personality and Social Psychology Review* 15, no. 2 (2010).

23. Philip L. Jackson, Pierre Rainville, and Jean Decety, "To What Extent Do We Share the Pain of Others? Insight from the Neural Bases of Pain Empathy," *Pain* 125, no. 1 (2006): 5–9.

24. Nadine Dolby, *Rethinking Multicultural Education for the Next Generation: The New Empathy and Social Justice* (Abingdon: Routledge, 2012), 58.

25. Lynn Hunt, *Inventing Human Rights: A History* (New York: W. W. Norton, 2008), 55.

26. Jean Decety, Stephanie Echols, and Joshua Correll, "The Blame Game: The Effect of Responsibility and Social Stigma on Empathy for Pain," *Journal of Cognitive Neuroscience* 22, no. 5 (2010): 985–97.

27. Anneke E. K. Buffone and Michael J. Poulin, "Empathy, Target Distress, and Neurohormone Genes Interact to Predict Aggression for Others—Even Without Provocation," *Personality and Social Psychology Bulletin* 40, no. 11 (2014): 1406–422.

28. Ibid.

29. Ibid., 1419.

30. Zembylas, "Emotions, Critical Pedagogy," 63.

31. Dolby, *Rethinking Multicultural Education*, 69.

32. Tania Singer and Olga Klimecki, "Empathy and Compassion," *Current Biology* 24, no. 18 (2014): R875–78.

33. Jack Donnelly, *Universal Human Rights in Theory and Practice*, 3rd ed. (Ithaca: Cornell University Press, 2003), 9.

34. Dolby, *Rethinking Multicultural Education*, 22.

35. United Nations Human Rights Office of the High Commissioner, "United Nations Declaration on Human Rights Education and Training," https://ohchr.org/EN/Issues/Education/Training/Pages/UNDHREducationTraining.aspx.

36. Plan of Action for the First Phase (2005–2007) of the World Programme for Human Rights Education (2005), https://www.ohchr.org/EN/Issues/Education/Training/Compilation/Pages/PlanofActionforthefirstphase(2005-2007)oftheWorldProgrammeforHumanRightsEducation(2005).aspx, accessed January 2019.

37. Nancy Flowers. *The Human Rights Education Handbook: Effective Practices for Learning, Action, and Change* (Minneapolis: Human Rights Resource Center, 2000), 59.

38. See Jay Roberts, *Experiential Education in the College Context: What It Is, How It Works, and Why It Matters* (New York: Routledge, 2016); Scott Wurdinger and Julie Carlson, *Teaching for Experiential Learning: Five Approaches That Work* (Lanham: R& L Education, 2009).

39. Association for Experiential Education, "What Is Experiential Education?," http://www.aee.org/what-is-ee.

40. Roberts, *Experiential Education*, and Association of American Colleges & Universities, "About LEAP," June 29, 2017, https://www.aacu.org/leap, accessed February 1, 2018.

41. Jo Becker, *Campaigning for Justice: Human Rights Advocacy in Practice* (Palo Alto: Stanford University Press, 2012).

42. Jody Williams, *My Name Is Jody Williams: A Vermont Girl's Winding Path to the Nobel Peace Prize* (Berkeley: University of California Press, 2013).

43. Susan Albertine and Tia Brown McNair, "Seeking High-Quality, High-Impact Learning: The Imperative of Faculty Development and Curricular Intentionality," *Peer Review* 14, no. 3 (2012): 3.

44. Robert C. Hauhart and Jon E. Grahe, *Designing and Teaching Undergraduate Capstone Courses* (San Francisco: Jossey-Bass, 2015), 66.

45. Gary Goldstein and Peter Fernald, "Humanistic Education in a Capstone Course," *College Teaching* 57, no. 1 (2009): 28.

46. Robert C. Hauhart and Jon E. Grahe, *Designing and Teaching Undergraduate Capstone Courses* (San Francisco: Jossey-Bass, 2015).

47. Ibid., 125.

Chapter 6

1. Felisa Tibbitts, "Understanding What We Do: Emerging Models for Human Rights Education," *International Review of Education* 48, nos. 3/4 (2002): 169.

2. United Nations Human Rights Office of the High Commissioner, "UNDHRET," Article 2, Section 2a, 2017, http://www.ohchr.org/EN/Issues/Education/Training/Pages/UNDHREducationTraining.aspx.

3. United Nations Human Rights Office of the High Commissioner, "World Programme for Human Rights Education Second Phase Plan of Action," July 2012, http://www.ohchr.org/Documents/Publications/WPHRE_Phase_2_en.pdf, 5.

4. WSD Handa Center for Human Rights and International Justice, "Minor Requirements," Stanford University, https://handacenter.stanford.edu/academics/minor-human-rights/minor-requirements, accessed May 1, 2017.

5. University of Iowa, "Human Rights, Certificate," http://catalog.registrar.uiowa.edu/law/university-center-human-rights/human-rights-certificate/, accessed January 2019.

6. Science and Human Rights Coalition, "Syllabi on Science and Human Rights," American Association for the Advancement of Science, 2017, https://www.aaas.org/page/syllabi-science-and-human-rights.

7. L. Dee Fink, *Creating Significant Learning Experiences: An Integrated Approach to Designing College Courses* (San Francisco: Jossey-Bass, 2013), 34.

8. Ibid., 36. Emphasis in original.

9. Nicholas Kristof and Sheryl WuDunn, *A Path Appears: Transforming Lives, Creating Opportunity* (New York: Vintage, 2015).

10. Nina Munk, *The Idealist: Jeffrey Sachs and the Quest to End Poverty* (New York: Anchor, 2014).

11. Michael Matheson Miller, *Poverty Inc.: Fighting Poverty Is Big Business, but Who Profits the Most?* Directed by Michael Matheson Miller (Action Institute, 2014).

12. Global Human Rights Direct, http://globalhumanrightsdirect.com.

13. Ibid., 63.

14. Robert M. Diamond, *Designing and Assessing Courses and Curricula: A Practical Guide* (San Francisco: Jossey-Bass, 2008), 11.

15. David Suárez, "Education Professionals and the Construction of Human Rights Education," *Comparative Education Review* 51, no. 1 (2007): 48–70.

Afterword

1. UN General Assembly, "Universal Declaration of Human Rights," 1948, http://www.un.org/en/universal-declaration-human-rights.

2. Patrick Hayden, *The Philosophy of Human Rights* (St. Paul: Paragon House, 2001); David Boersema, *Philosophy of Human Rights: Theory and Practice* (Boulder: Westview Press, 2011).

3. Eleanor Roosevelt, *You Learn by Living: Eleven Keys for a More Fulfilling Life* (New York: Harper Perennial, 1960), 168.

Appendix I

1. All excerpts from the syllabus in Appendix I courtesy of Rachel Jackson.

Bibliography

Abbott, Andrew. *Chaos of Disciplines*. Chicago: University of Chicago Press, 2001.

Abrami, Philip, Robert Bernard, Evgueni Borokhovski, Anne Wade, Michael Surkes, Rana Tamim, and Dai Zhang. "Instructional Interventions Affecting Critical Thinking Skills and Dispositions: A Stage 1 Meta-Analysis." *Review of Educational Research* 78, no. 4 (2008): 1102–34.

Adeney, Frances. "Human Rights and Responsibilities: Christian Perspectives." In *Christianity and Human Rights*, edited by Frances Adeney and Arvind Sharma, 19–41. New York: SUNY Press, 2007.

Adichie, Chimamanda Ngozi. *Half of a Yellow Sun*. New York: Anchor, 2007.

Al-Jabri, Mohammed Abed. *Democracy, Human Rights, and Law in Islamic Thought*. New York: I. B. Tauris, 2009.

Alliance 8.7. "Global Slavery Estimates 2017." Global Estimates of Modern Slavery: Forced Labour and Forced Marriage. 2017. http://www.alliance87.org/2017ge/modernslavery#!section = 10.

American Anthropological Association. "1947 Statement on Human Rights." June 24, 1947. http://humanrights.americananthro.org/1947-statement-on-human-rights. Accessed June 2018.

Andrade, H. G. "Using Rubrics to Promote Thinking and Learning." *Educational Leadership* 57, no. 5(2000): 13–18. Retrieved from http://www.ascd.org/publications/educational-leadership/feb00/vol 57/num05/.

Andreopoulos, George, and Richard Pierre Claude. *Human Rights Education for the Twenty-First Century*. Philadelphia: University of Pennsylvania Press, 1997.

Angelo, Thomas A., and K. Patricia Cross. *Classroom Assessment Techniques: A Handbook for College Teachers*. San Francisco: Jossey-Bass, 1993.

Annan, Kofi. *Interventions: A Life in War and Peace*. London: Penguin, 2013.

Aristotle University of Thessoloniki. "UNESCO Chair on Education for Human Rights, Democracy and Peace." https://www.auth.gr/en/units/8187. Accessed January 2019.

Arum, Richard, and Josipa Roksa. *Academically Adrift: Limited Learning on College Campuses*. Chicago: University of Chicago Press, 2010.

Asher, Jana, David Banks, and Fritz Scheuren Jr. *Statistical Methods for Human Rights.* New York: Springer US, 2008.

Asia Pacific Forum. *Human Rights Education: A Manual for National Human Rights Institutions.* Sydney: Asia Pacific Forum of National Human Rights Institutions, 2013. http://www.asiapacificforum.net/media/resource_file/Human_Rights_Education_Manual_for_NHRIs_ejmumah.pdf, updated January 2017.

Association for Experiential Education. "What Is Experiential Education?" http://www.aee.org/what-is-ee. Accessed February 1, 2018.

Association of American Colleges & Universities. "About LEAP." June 29, 2017. https://www.aacu.org/leap.

Australian National University College of Arts and Social Sciences. "Human Rights." Australian National Institute. https://programsandcourses.anu.edu.au/major/HMRT-MAJ. Accessed May 2017.

Bailin, Sharon, Roland Case, Jerrold R. Coombs, and Leroi B. Daniels. "Common Misconceptions of Critical Thinking." *Journal of Curriculum Studies* 31, no. 3 (1999): 269–83.

Bajaj, Monisha, ed. *Human Rights Education: Theory, Research, Praxis.* Philadelphia: University of Pennsylvania Press, 2017.

Bajaj, Monisha. "Human Rights Education: Ideology, Location, and Approaches." *Human Rights Quarterly* 33, no. 2 (2011): 481–508.

Barkley, Elizabeth F. *Student Engagement Techniques: A Handbook for College Faculty.* 1st ed. San Francisco: Jossey-Bass, 2009.

Baumann-Pauly, Dorothee, and Justine Nolan. *Business and Human Rights: From Principles to Practice.* New York: Routledge, 2016.

Beah, Ishmael. *A Long Way Gone: Memoirs of a Boy Soldier.* New York: Sarah Crichton Books, 2008.

Bean, John C. *Engaging Ideas: The Professor's Guide to Integrating Writing, Critical Thinking, and Active Learning in the Classroom.* San Francisco: Jossey-Bass, 2011.

Becher, Tony, and Paul R. Trowler. *Academic Tribes and Territories.* Ballmoor, UK: Open University Press, 2001.

Becker, Anne, Annamagriet de Wet, and Willie van Vollenhoven. "Human Rights Literacy: Moving Towards Rights-Based Education and Transformative Action Through Understandings of Dignity, Equality, and Freedom." *South African Journal of Education* 35, no. 2 (2015): 1–12.

Becker, Florian N., Paola S. Hernandez, and Brenda Werth, eds. *Imagining Human Rights in Twenty-First-Century Theater: Global Perspectives.* New York: Palgrave Macmillan, 2013.

Becker, Jo. *Campaigning for Justice: Human Rights Advocacy in Practice.* Palo Alto: Stanford University Press, 2012.

Beckett, Samuel. *Waiting for Godot.* New York: Grove, 1954.

Behr, Edward, and Mark Steyn. *The Story of Miss Saigon*. New York: Arcade, 1991.

Belisle, Kristine, and Elizabeth Sullivan. "Service-Learning Lesson Plans and Projects: Human Rights Resources for Educators." Ed. Kristine Belisle, Karen Robinson, Elizabeth Sullivan, and Felisa Tibbitts. Amnesty International–USA, HREA. May 2007. https://www.amnestyusa.org/pdfs/HumanRightsAndServiceLearningPt1.pdf.

Belkin, Douglas. "Exclusive Test Data: Many Colleges Fail to Improve Critical-Thinking Skills." *Wall Street Journal*, June 5, 2017.

Bermúdez, José Luis. *Cognitive Science: An Introduction to the Science of the Mind*. Cambridge: Cambridge University Press, 2010.

Bialystok, Lauren. "Politics Without 'Brainwashing': A Philosophical Defence of Social Justice Education." *Curriculum Inquiry* 44, no. 3 (2014): 413–40.

Bok, Derek. *Our Underachieving Colleges: A Candid Look at How Much Students Learn and Why They Should Be Learning More*. Princeton: Princeton University Press, 2006.

Bonnycastle, Colin. "Social Justice Along a Continuum: A Relational Illustrative Model." *Social Service Review* 85, no. 2 (2011): 267–95.

Boersema, David. *Philosophy of Human Rights: Theory and Practice*. Boulder: Westview Press, 2011.

Bos, Gerhard, and Marcus Duwell, eds. *Human Rights and Sustainability: Moral Responsibilities for the Future*. Abingdon, UK: Routledge, 2016.

Boublil, Alain, and Claude-Michel Schönberg. *Miss Saigon*. New York: Decca Broadway, 1991.

Bowen, José Antonio. *Teaching Naked: How Moving Technology out of Your College Classroom Will Improve Student Learning*. New York: John Wiley, 2012.

Bozzoli, Belinda. *Theatres of Struggle and the End of Apartheid*. Athens: Ohio University Press, 2004.

BRAC. "BRAC Annual Report 2016." 2017. http://www.brac.net/publications/annual-report/2016.

Bradley, Mark Philip. *The World Reimagined: Americans and Human Rights in the Twentieth Century*. Human Rights in History series. Cambridge: Cambridge University Press, 2016.

Brecht, Bertolt. *Mother Courage and Her Children*. New York: Grove, 1955.

Brookfield, Stephen, and Stephen Preskill. *Discussion as a Way of Teaching: Tools and Techniques for Democratic Classrooms*. San Francisco: Jossey-Bass, 2005.

Brysk, Alison. *The Future of Human Rights*. Cambridge: Polity, 2018.

Brysk, Alison. *Global Good Samaritans: Human Rights as Foreign Policy*. Oxford: Oxford University Press, 2009.

Brysk, Alison. *Speaking Rights to Power: Constructing Political Will*. Oxford: Oxford University Press, 2013.

Buergenthal, Thomas, Dinah Shelton, and David Stewart. *International Human Rights in a Nutshell.* St. Paul: West Academic Publishing, 2009.

Buffone, Anneke E. K., and Michael J. Poulin. "Empathy, Target Distress, and Neurohormone Genes Interact to Predict Aggression for Others—Even Without Provocation." *Personality and Social Psychology Bulletin* 40, no. 11 (2014): 1406–422.

Buker, Eloise. "Is Women's Studies a Disciplinary or an Interdisciplinary Field of Inquiry?" *NWSA Journal* 15, no. 1 (2003): 73–93.

Bureau of Democracy, Human Rights, and Labor. "Human Rights." US Department of State. 2017. https://www.state.gov/j/drl/hr. Accessed April 14, 2017.

Bureau of Democracy, Human Rights, and Labor. "Non-Governmental Organizations (NGOs) in the United States." US Department of State. 2017. https://www.state.gov/j/drl/rls/fs/2017/266904.htm.

Butler, Isaac, and Dan Kois. *The Ascent of Angels in America: The World Only Spins Forward.* New York: Bloomsbury USA, 2018.

Callaway, Rhonda L., and Julie Harrelson-Stephens, eds. *Exploring International Human Rights: Essential Readings.* Boulder: Lynne Rienner Publishers, 2007.

CARE USA. "CARE USA 2016 Annual Report." 2017. http://www.care.org/sites/default/files/care_2016_annual_report_2017_14_04.pdf. Accessed April 14, 2017.

Cargas, Sarita. "Questioning Samuel Moyn's Revisionist History of Human Rights." *Human Rights Quarterly* 38, no. 2 (2016): 411–25.

Cargas, Sarita, Sheri Williams, and Martina Rosenberg, "An Approach to Teaching Critical Thinking Across Disciplines Using Performance Tasks with a Common Rubric." *Thinking Skills and Creativity* 26 (2017): 24–37.

Carleton University Undergraduate Admissions. "Human Rights and Social Justice (BA)." https://admissions.carleton.ca/programs/human-rights-ba. Accessed May 2017.

China Labor Watch. "Something's Not Right Here: Poor Working Conditions Persist at Apple Supplier Pegatron." October 22, 2015. http://www.chinalaborwatch.org/report/109.

Claude, Richard. *Comparative Human Rights.* Baltimore: Johns Hopkins University Press, 1976.

Cohen, Haim. *Human Rights in Jewish Law.* New York: Ktav Publishing House, 1984.

Cole, Jonathan. *The Great American University: Its Rise to Prominence, Its Indispensable Role, and Why It Must Be Protected.* New York: Public Affairs, 2010.

Cole, Jonathan. *Toward a More Perfect University.* New York: Public Affairs, 2016.

Columbia Law School Human Rights Institute and International Association of Official Human Rights Agencies. "Ensuring Human Rights Implementation at the Federal, State, and Local Levels." 2017. http://www.law.columbia.edu/sites/default/files/microsites/human-rights-instit ute/files/subnational_fact_sheet.pdf.

Columbia University. "Graduate Studies." http://www.humanrightscolumbia.org/education/graduate. Accessed January 2019.

Columbia University. "Institute for the Study of Human Rights." http://www.human
    rightscolumbia.org/education/undergraduate. Accessed May 2017.

Committee on Facilitating Interdisciplinary Research, Committee on Science, Engi-
    neering, and Public Policy. *Facilitating Interdisciplinary Research*. National Acade-
    mies. Washington: National Academy Press, 2004.

Condon, Paul, Gaelle Desbordes, Willa Miller, and David DeSteno. "Meditation
    Increases Compassionate Responses to Suffering." *Psychological Science* 24, no. 10
    (2013): 2115–27.

Coomans, Fons, Fred Grunfeld, and Menno Kamminga. *Methods of Human Rights
    Research*. Cambridge: Intersentia, 2009.

Council of Europe. "Charter on Education for Democratic Citizenship and Human
    Rights Education." https://rm.coe.int/16803034e5. Accessed May 2017.

Crow, Michael, and William Dabars. *Designing the New American University*. Balti-
    more: Johns Hopkins University Press, 2014.

Crow, Michael, and William Dabars. "Towards Interdisciplinarity by Design in the
    American Research University." In *University Experiments in Interdisciplinarity*,
    edited by Peter Weingart and Britta Padberg, 13–36. Bielefeld: Transcript Verlag,
    2014.

Danticat, Edwidge. *Breath, Eyes, Memory*. New York: Soho Press, 2015.

Danticat, Edwidge. *Brother, I'm Dying*. New York: Vintage, 2008.

Darder, Antonia, Marta P. Baltodano, and Rodolfo D. Torres. "Critical Pedagogy: An
    Introduction." In *The Critical Pedagogy* Reader, 1–23. New York: Routledge, 2017.

Dear, John. "Human Rights and Nonviolence: Testament of a Christian Peace Activ-
    ist." In *Christianity and Human Rights*, edited by Frances Adeney and Arvind
    Sharma, 183–97. New York: SUNY Press, 2007.

Decety, Jean, Stephanie Echols, and Joshua Correll. "The Blame Game: The Effect
    of Responsibility and Social Stigma on Empathy for Pain." *Journal of Cognitive
    Neuroscience* 22, no. 5 (2009): 985–97.

Dedman College of Humanities and Sciences. "Embrey Human Rights Program."
    Southern Methodist University. https://www.smu.edu/Dedman/Academics/Insti
    tutesCenters/EmbreyHumanRights. Accessed May 2017.

Defoe, Daniel. "Friday." In *Robinson Crusoe*. New York: Penguin, 2013.

Dembour, Marie-Benedicte. *Who Believes in Human Rights? Reflections on the Euro-
    pean Convention*. Cambridge: Cambridge University Press, 2006.

Dennis-Benn, Nicole. *Here Comes the Sun*. New York: Liveright Publishing, 2017.

Diamond, Robert M. *Designing and Assessing Courses and Curricula: A Practical Guide*.
    San Francisco: Jossey-Bass, 2008.

DiAngelo, Robin, and Özlem Sensoy. "'We Don't Want Your Opinion': Knowledge
    Construction and the Discourse of Opinion in the Equity Classroom." *Equity &
    Excellence in Education* 42, no. 4 (2009): 443–55.

Dolby, Nadine. *Rethinking Multicultural Education for the Next Generation: The New
    Empathy and Social Justice*. Abingdon: Routledge, 2012.

Donnelly, Jack. *International Human Rights.* 4th ed. Boulder: Westview Press, 2012. First published 1993.

Donnelly, Jack. *Universal Human Rights in Theory and Practice.* 3rd ed. Ithaca: Cornell University Press, 2003. First published 1989.

Dudai, Ron. "Introduction—Rights Choices: Dilemmas of Human Rights Practice." *Journal of Human Rights Practice* 6, no. 3 (2014): 389–98.

Eells, Richard, and Clarence Walton. *Conceptual Foundations of Business.* 3rd ed. Irwin Series in Management and the Behavioral Sciences. Homewood: Richard D. Irwin, 1974.

Eggers, Dave, ed. *The Voice of Witness Reader: Ten Years of Amplifying Unheard Voices.* San Francisco: McSweeney's, 2015.

Eggers, Dave. *Zeitoun.* New York: Vintage, 2010.

Ennis, Robert. "Critical Thinking and Subject Specificity: Clarification and Needed Research." *Educational Researcher* 18, no. 3 (1989): 4–10.

Extractive Industries Transparency Initiative (EITI). "Who We Are." https://eiti.org/who-we-are. Accessed April 14, 2017.

Fair Labor Association. "Code of Conduct." http://www.fairlabor.org/our-work/code-of-conduct. Last modified 2012.

Fink, L. Dee. *Creating Significant Learning Experiences: An Integrated Approach to Designing College Courses.* San Francisco: Jossey-Bass, 2013.

Flowers, Nancy. *The Human Rights Education Handbook: Effective Practices for Learning, Action, and Change.* Minneapolis: Human Rights Resource Center, 2000.

Flowers, Nancy. "What Is Human Rights Education?" In *A Survey of Human Rights Education.* Hamburg: BertelsmannVerlag, 2003. 107–18.

Fornes, Maria Irene. *Fefu and Her Friends.* New York: PAJ Publications, 1978.

Forsythe, David. *Human Rights in International Relations.* New York: Cambridge University Press, 2006.

Foucault, Michel. *Discipline and Punish: The Birth of the Prison*, trans. Alan Sheridan. New York: Vintage Books, 1995.

Fredericks, Sarah E. "Religious Studies and Religious Practice." In *The Oxford Handbook of Interdisciplinarity*, edited by Robert Frodeman, 385–96. Oxford: Oxford University Press, 2010.

Freeman, Michael. *Human Rights: An Interdisciplinary Approach.* Cambridge: Polity, 2002.

Freeman, Scott, Sarah L. Eddy, Miles McDonough, Michelle K. Smith, Nnadozie Okoroafor, Hannah Jordt, and Mary Pat Wenderoth. "Active Learning Increases Student Performance in Science, Engineering, and Mathematics." *Proceedings of the National Academy of Sciences of the United States of America* 111, no. 23 (2014): 8410–15.

Freire, Paulo. *Pedagogy of the Oppressed.* 2nd ed. London: Penguin, 1996.

Frezzo, Mark. *The Sociology of Human Rights.* Cambridge: Polity Press, 2015.

Friel, Brian. *The Freedom of the City.* New York: Samuel French, 1973.

Frodeman, Robert. "The End of Disciplinarity." In *University Experiments in Interdisciplinarity*, edited by Peter Weingart and Britta Padberg, 175–98. New York: Columbia University Press, 2014.

Frodeman, Robert. Introduction to *The Oxford Handbook of Interdisciplinarity*. Edited by Robert Frodeman. Oxford: Oxford University Press, 2010.

Frodeman, Robert. *A Sustainable Knowledge: A Theory of Interdisciplinarity*. New York: Palgrave Macmillan, 2014.

Fugard, Athol. *"Master Harold" . . . and the Boys: A Play*. New York: Vintage, 2009.

Gates, Henry Louis, Jr. "Slavery, by the Numbers." *The Root*, February 10, 2014. https://www.theroot.com/slavery-by-the-numbers-1790874492.

Gerber, Paula. *Understanding Human Rights: Educational Challenges for the Future*. Northampton: Edward Elgar Publishing, 2013.

Ghere, Richard K. *Rhetoric in Human Rights Advocacy: A Study of Exemplars*. Lanham: Lexington Books, 2016.

Gibney, Mark. *International Human Rights Law: Returning to Universal Principles*. Lanham: Rowman & Littlefield, 2015.

Gibney, Mark. *Watching Human Rights: The 101 Best Films*. Abingdon: Routledge, 2013.

Glendon, Mary Ann. *A World Made New: Eleanor Roosevelt and the Universal Declaration of Human Rights*. 1st ed. New York: Random House, 2002.

Global Human Rights Direct. http://globalhumanrightsdirect.com

Goldstein, Gary, and Peter Fernald. "Humanistic Education in a Capstone Course." *College Teaching* 57, no. 1 (2009): 27–36.

Golub, Stephen. "What Is Legal Empowerment? An Introduction." In *Legal Empowerment: Practitioners' Perspectives*, edited by Stephen Golub, 9–18. Rome: International Development Law Organization, 2010.

González-Ocantos, Ezequiel A. *Shifting Legal Visions: Judicial Change and Human Rights Trials in Latin America*. Cambridge: Cambridge University Press, 2016.

Governance and Accountability Institute. "This Year's Tally of S&P 500 Company Disclosures—81% Now Publishing Sustainability/Responsibility Reports." March 14, 2016. https://www.ga-institute.com/newsletter/press-release/npage/7/article/this-years-tally-of-sp-500-company-disclosures-81-now-publishing-sustainability-responsibilit.html

Graff, Harvey J. *Undisciplining Knowledge: Interdisciplinarity in the Twentieth Century*. Baltimore: Johns Hopkins University Press, 2015.

Greene, Maxine. Introduction to *Teaching for Social Justice*. Edited by William Ayers, Jean Ann Hunt, and Therese Quinne. New York: New Press, 1998.

Greenwood Davydd J., and Morten Levin. *Introduction to Action Research: Social Research for Social Change*. Thousand Oaks: Sage, 2007.

Gross, Neil. *Why Are Professors Liberal and Why Do Conservatives Care?* Cambridge: Harvard University Press, 2013.

Hackman, Heather. "Five Essential Components for Social Justice Education." *Equity & Excellence in Education* 38 (2005): 103–9.

Halx, Mark, and L. Earle Reybold. "A Pedagogy of Force: Faculty Perspectives of Critical Thinking Capacity in Undergraduate Students." *Journal of General Education* 54, no. 4 (2005): 293–315.

Harris, Bob. *The International Bank of Bob: Connecting Our Worlds One $25 Kiva Loan at a Time.* London: Bloomsbury USA, 2014.

Hauhart, Robert C., and Jon E. Grahe. *Designing and Teaching Undergraduate Capstone Courses.* San Francisco: Jossey-Bass, 2015.

Hayden, Patrick. *The Philosophy of Human Rights.* St. Paul: Paragon House, 2001.

Henry, Meghan, Rian Watt, Lily Rosenthal, and Azim Shivji. "The 2016 Annual Homeless Assessment Report (AHAR) to Congress." November 2016. https://www.hudexchange.info/resources/documents/2016-AHAR-Part-1.pdf.

Holley, Karri. "Understanding Interdisciplinary Challenges and Opportunities in Higher Education." *ASHE Higher Education Report* 35, no. 2 (2009): 140.

Hopgood, Stephen. *The Endtimes of Human Rights.* Ithaca: Cornell University Press, 2013.

Human Rights Educators USA. "Human Rights Education: Submission to the UN Universal Periodic Review 22nd Session." 2017. https://hreusaorg.files.wordpress.com/2017/05/hre-usa-ushrn_stakeholder-submission_us-upr_sept-2014.pdf.

Human Rights Watch. "Defending Our Values: Annual Report 2016." https://www.hrw.org/sites/default/files/news_attachments/english_annual_report-2016.pdf.

Hunt, Lynn. *Inventing Human Rights, A History.* New York: W. W. Norton, 2008.

Ife, Jim. *Human Rights and Social Work.* New York: Cambridge, 2012.

Intelligence Squared (IQ2) Debates. "Too Many Kids Go to College." October 12, 2011. https://www.intelligencesquaredus.org/debates/too-many-kids-go-college.

International Organization for Standardization. "ISO 26000—Social Responsibility." 2017. https://www.iso.org/iso-26000-social-responsibility.html. Accessed April 14, 2017.

Ishay, Micheline. 2008. *The History of Human Rights: From Ancient Times to the Globalization Era.* Berkeley: University of California Press, 2008.

Ishay, Micheline. *The Human Rights Reader: Major Political Essays, Speeches, and Documents from Ancient Times to the Present.* Abingdon: Routledge, 2007.

Jackson, Phillip, Pierre Rainville, and Jean Decety. "To What Extent Do We Share the Pain of Others? Insight from the Neural Bases of Pain Empathy." *Pain* 125, no. 1 (2006): 5–9.

Jacobs, Jerry A. *In Defense of Disciplines: Interdisciplinarity and Specialization in the Research University.* Chicago: University of Chicago Press, 2014.

Jacobs, Jerry, and Scott Frickel. "Interdisciplinarity: A Critical Assessment." *Annual Review of Sociology* 35 (2009): 43–65.

Kahneman, Daniel. *Thinking, Fast and Slow.* New York: Farrar, Straus, and Giroux, 2011.

Kansas Human Rights Commission. "FAQS." *Kansas Human Rights Commission.* http://www.khrc.net/faq.html. Accessed April 14, 2017.

Katz, Susan Roberta, and Andrea McEvoy Spero. *Bringing Human Rights to US Classrooms: Exemplary Models from Elementary Grades to University.* New York: Palgrave Macmillan, 2015.

Keck, Margaret, and Kathryn Sikkink. *Activists Beyond Borders: Advocacy Networks in International Politics.* Ithaca: Cornell University Press, 1998.

Keet, Andre'. "Does Human Rights Education Exist?" *International Journal of Human Rights Education* 1, no. 1 (2017): 1–18.

Kelly-Woessner, April, and Matthew C. Woessner. "My Professor Is a Partisan Hack: How Perceptions of a Professor's Political Views Affect Student Course Evaluations." *Political Science and Politics* 39, no. 3 (2006): 495–501.

King, Thomas. *The Truth About Stories: A Native Narrative.* Toronto: Anansi Press, 2003.

Klein, Julie Thompson. *Creating Interdisciplinary Campus Cultures: A Model for Strength and Sustainability.* San Francisco: Jossey-Bass, 2010.

Klein, Julie Thompson. "A Taxonomy of Interdisciplinarity." In Frodeman, *Oxford Handbook of Interdisciplinarity,* 15–30.

Kleinberg, Ethan. "Interdisciplinary Studies at a Crossroads." *Liberal Education* 94, no. 1 (2008): 6–11.

Klug, Francesca. *A Magna Carta for All Humanity: Homing in on Human Rights.* Abingdon: Routledge, 2015.

Konrath, Sara, Edward H. O'Brien, and Courtney Hsing. "Changes in Dispositional Empathy in American College Students over Time: A Meta-Analysis." *Personality and Social Psychology Review* 15, no. 2 (2011): 180–98.

Kotlowitz, Alex. *There Are No Children Here: The Story of Two Boys Growing Up in the Other America.* New York: Doubleday, 1992.

Kottler, J. A., and M. Marriner. *Changing People's Lives While Transforming Your Own: Paths to Social Justice and Global Human Rights.* Hoboken: John Wiley & Sons, 2009.

Kovras, Iosif. *Grassroots Activism and the Evolution of Transitional Justice: The Families of the Disappeared.* Cambridge: Cambridge University Press, 2017.

Kristof, Nicholas, and Sheryl WuDunn. *A Path Appears: Transforming Lives, Creating Opportunity.* New York: Vintage, 2015.

Kuhn, Thomas. *The Structure of Scientific Revolutions.* Chicago: University of Chicago Press, 1970.

Kushner, Tony. *Angels in America: Part 1: Millennium Approaches.* New York: TCG, 1992.

Kushner, Tony. *Angels in America: Part 2: Perestroika.* New York: TCG, 1992.

Laber, Jeri. *The Courage of Strangers: Coming of Age with the Human Rights Movement.* New York: PublicAffairs, 2005.

Landman, Todd. *Studying Human Rights.* Abingdon: Routledge, 2006.

Landman, Todd, and Edzia Carvalho. *Measuring Human Rights*. Abingdon: Routledge, 2009.

Lasker, Judith. *Hoping to Help: The Promises and Pitfalls of Global Health Volunteering*. Ithaca: ILR Press, 2016.

Lauren, Paul Gordon. *The Evolution of International Human Rights: Visions Seen*. 1st ed. Philadelphia: University of Pennsylvania Press, 1998.

Lloyd, Margaret, and Nan Bahr. "Thinking Critically about Critical Thinking in Higher Education." *International Journal for the Scholarship of Teaching and Learning* 4, no. 2 (2010): 18.

Loeb, Paul. *The Impossible Will Take a Little While*. New York: Perseus Books Group, 2004.

Lohrenscheit, Claudia. "International Approaches in Human Rights Education." *International Review of Education* 48 (2002): 173–85.

Lorde, Audre. *Zami: A New Spelling of My Name*. Toronto: Crossing Press, 1982.

Makerere University. "Bachelor of Ethics and Human Rights." https://courses.mak.ac .ug/programmes/bachelor-ethics-and-human-rights. Accessed January 2019.

Malmo University. "Human Rights." https://edu.mah.se/en/Program/SGMRE. Accessed May 2017.

Marcus, Alan, ed. *Science as Service: Establishing and Reformulating American Land-Grant Universities, 1865–1930*. Tuscaloosa: University of Alabama Press, 2015.

Marshall, Jill, and Ana Maria Klein. "Lessons in Social Action: Equipping and Inspiring Students to Improve Their World." *Social Studies* 100, no. 5 (2009): 218–21.

McNair, Tia Brown and Susan Albertine. "Seeking High-Quality, High-Impact Learning: The Imperative of Faculty Development and Curricular Intentionality." *Peer Review* 14, no. 3 (2012): 4–5.

Mutua, Makau. *Human Rights: A Political and Cultural Critique*. Philadelphia: University of Pennsylvania Press, 2002.

Maximpact Ecosystems. "What Challenges Do NGO's Face and What Are the Solutions?" *Maximpact Blog*. March 20, 2017. http://maximpactblog.com/what-chal lenges-do-ngos-face-and-what-are-the-solutions.

Mayotte, Cliff, ed. *The Power of the Story: The Voice of Witness Teacher's Guide to Oral History*. San Francisco: McSweeney's and Voice of Witness, 2013.

Médecins San Frontières. "International Financial Report 2016." http://www.msf.org/ sites/msf.org/files/msf_financial_report_2016_final.pdf.

Meintjes, Garth. "Human Rights Education as Empowerment: Reflections on Pedagogy." In *Human Rights Education for the Twenty-First Century*, edited by George Andreopoulos and Richard Pierre Claude, 64–79. Philadelphia: University of Pennsylvania Press, 1997.

Mihr, Anja, and Hans Peter Schmitz. "Human Rights Education (HRE) and Transnational Activism." *Human Rights Quarterly* 29, no. 4 (2007): 973–93.

Miller, Arthur. *The Crucible*. New York: Random House, 1976.

Miller, Michael Matheson. *Poverty Inc.: Fighting Poverty Is Big Business, but Who Profits the Most?* Directed by Michael Matheson Miller. Action Institute, 2014.

Moore, Alexandra Schultheis, and Elizabeth Swanson Goldberg, eds. *Teaching Human Rights in Literary and Cultural Studies.* New York: Modern Language Association of America, 2015.

Morsink, Johannes. *The Universal Declaration of Human Rights: Origins, Drafting, and Intent.* Philadelphia: University of Pennsylvania Press, 2000.

Moyn, Samuel. *The Last Utopia: Human Rights in History.* Cambridge: Harvard University Press, 2012.

Munk, Nina. *The Idealist: Jeffrey Sachs and the Quest to End Poverty.* New York: Anchor, 2014.

Nafisi, Azar. *Reading Lolita in Tehran.* New York: Random House, 2008.

Nash, Kate. *The Political Sociology of Human Rights.* Cambridge: Cambridge University Press, 2015.

National Academies of Sciences, Engineering, and Medicine. *The Integration of the Humanities and Arts with Sciences, Engineering, and Medicine in Higher Education: Branches from the Same Tree.* Washington, D.C.: National Academies Press, 2018.

National Center for Educational Statistics. "Fast Facts, Back to School Statistics." Institute of Educational Sciences. https://nces.ed.gov/fastfacts/display.asp?id = 372. Last modified 2017.

Nazario, Sonia. *Enrique's Journey: The Story of a Boy's Dangerous Odyssey to Reunite with His Mother.* New York: Random House, 2007.

Nazer, Mende, and Damien Lewis. *Slave: My True Story.* New York: PublicAffairs, 2005.

Neier, Aryeh. *The International Human Rights Movement: A History.* Princeton: Princeton University Press, 2013.

Newell, William H. "The Case for Interdisciplinary Studies: Response to Professor Benson's Five Arguments." *Issues in Integrative Studies* 2 (1983): 1–19.

Newell, William H., and William J. Green. "Defining and Teaching Interdisciplinary Studies." *Improving College and University Teaching* 30, no. 1 (1982): 23–30.

Nolan, Aoife, Rory O'Connell, and Colin Harvey, eds. *Human Rights and Public Finance: Budgets and the Promotion of Economic and Social Rights.* Oxford: Hart Publishing, 2013.

Nonprofit Action. "Facts and Stats about NGOs Worldwide." September 4, 2015. http://nonprofitaction.org/2015/09/facts-and-stats-about-ngos-worldwide.

Norberg, Johan, dir. *Globalization Is Good.* Freedom Productions, 2003.

Norberg, Johan. *Progress: Ten Reasons to Look Forward to the Future.* London: Oneworld Publications, 2016.

Nosich, Gerald. *Learning to Think Things Through: A Guide to Critical Thinking Across the Curriculum.* London: Pearson, 2009.

Opitz, Florian, dir. *The Big Sellout.* California Newsreel, 2006

Organization for Security and Co-operation in Europe (OSCE). *Guidelines on Human Rights Education for Secondary School Systems.* September 24, 2012 http://www.osce.org/odihr/93969.

OSCE Office for Democratic Institutions and Human Rights. *Human Rights Education in the School Systems of Europe, Central Asia, and North America: A Compendium of Good Practice.* Warsaw: OSCE Office for Democratic Institutions and Human Rights, 2009. http://www.ohchr.org/Documents/Publications/Compendium HRE.pdf.

Park, Yeonmi, and Maryanne Vollers. *In Order to Live: A North Korean Girl's Journey to Freedom.* London: Penguin.

Parker, Theodore. *Ten Sermons of Religion. Sermon III: Of Justice and Conscience.* Ann Arbor: University of Michigan Library, 1852/2005.

Paul, Richard W., and Linda Elder. *The Aspiring Thinker's Guide to Critical Thinking.* Dillon Beach, Calif.: Foundation for Critical Thinking, 2009.

Perkins, John. *Confessions of an Economic Hitman.* New York: Plume, 2006.

Pinker, Steven. *Enlightenment Now: The Case for Reason, Science, Humanism, and Progress.* New York: Viking, 2018.

Polish, Daniel F. "Judaism and Human Rights." In *Human Rights in Religious Traditions,* edited by Arlene Swidler, 40–50. New York: Pilgrim Press, 1982.

Polman, Linda. *The Crisis Caravan: What's Wrong with Humanitarian Aid?* New York: Metropolitan Books, 2010.

Puchner, Martin. *The Written World.* New York: Random House, 2017.

Rae, Paul. *Theatre and Human Rights.* Basingstoke: Palgrave Macmillan, 2009.

Reardon, Betty A., and Dale T. Snauwaert. *Betty A. Reardon: A Pioneer in Education for Peace and Human Rights.* London: Springer, 2015.

Rhodes, Terrel L. *Assessing Outcomes and Improving Achievement: Tips and Tools for Using Rubrics.* Washington, D.C.: Association of American Colleges and Universities. 2009.

Rieff, David. *A Bed for the Night: Humanitarianism in Crisis.* London: Vintage, 2002.

Roberts, Jay W. *Experiential Education in the College Context: What It Is, How It Works, and Why It Matters.* New York: Routledge, 2016.

Roche, Mark William. *Realizing the Distinctive University: Vision and Values, Strategy and Culture.* Notre Dame: University of Notre Dame Press, 2017.

Roosevelt, Eleanor. *You Learn by Living: Eleven Keys for a More Fulfilling Life.* New York: Harper Perennial, 2011. First published by Westminster John Knox Press, 1960.

Rorty, Richard. *Truth and Progress: Philosophical Papers.* Vol. 3. Cambridge: Cambridge University Press, 1998.

Rosenblum, Peter. "Teaching Human Rights: Ambivalent Activism, Multiple Discourses, and Lingering Dilemmas." *Harvard Human Rights Journal* 15 (2002): 301–16.

Rosling, Hans, Anna Rosling Rönnlund, and Ola Rosling. *Factfulness: Ten Reasons We're Wrong About the World—and Why Things Are Better Than You Think*. New York: Flatiron Books, 2018.

Save the Children Federation. "Results for Children: Annual Report 2016." https://www.savethechildren.org/content/dam/usa/reports/advocacy/annual-report/sc-2016-annualreport.pdf.

Science and Human Rights Coalition. "Syllabi on Science and Human Rights." American Association for the Advancement of Science. 2017. https://www.aaas.org/page/syllabi-science-and-human-rights.

Sensoy, Özlem, and Robin DiAngelo. *Is Everyone Really Equal: An Introduction to Key Concepts in Social Justice Education*. New York: Teachers College Press, 2011.

Shange, Ntozake. *For Colored Girls Who Have Considered Suicide/When the Rainbow Is Enuf*. New York: Simon and Schuster, 1975.

Shellenbarger, Sue. "Can't Pick a College Major? Create One." *Wall Street Journal*, November 17, 2010.

Shermer, Michael. *Why People Believe Weird Things: Pseudoscience, Superstition, and Other Confusions of Our Time*. New York: Henry Holt, 1997.

Sikkink, Kathryn. *Evidence for Hope: Making Human Rights Work in the 21st Century*. Princeton, N.J.: Princeton University Press, 2017.

Sikkink, Kathryn. *The Justice Cascade: How Human Rights Prosecutions Are Changing World Politics*. New York: W. W. Norton, 2011.

Simmons, Beth. *Mobilizing for Human Rights: International Law in Domestic Politics*. Cambridge: Cambridge University Press, 2009.

Simmons, William Paul. *Joyful Human Rights*. Philadelphia: University of Pennsylvania Press, 2018.

Simmons, William Paul. "Problem Based Learning Without Borders: Impact and Potential for University-Level Human Rights Education." *Journal of Human Rights* (2019).

Singer, Tania, and Olga Klimecki. "Empathy and Compassion." *Current Biology* 24, no. 18 (2014): R875–78.

Skutnabb-Kangas, Tove, and Robert Phillipson in collab. with Martin Rannut. *Linguistic Human Rights*. New York: Mouton de Gruyter, 1995.

Smith, Michael, Rebecca Nowacek, and Jeffery L. Bernstein. *Citizenship Across the Curriculum*. Bloomington: Indiana University Press, 2010.

Smith, Rhona K. M. *Textbook on International Human Rights*. 5th ed. Oxford: Oxford University Press, 2012.

Snyder, Sarah B. *Human Rights Activism and the End of the Cold War: A Transnational History of the Helsinki Network*. New York: Cambridge University Press, 2013.

Soltani, Amir, and Khalil. *Zahra's Paradise*. New York: First Second Publishing, 2011.

Southern Poverty Law Center. "New SPLC Reports Reveal Alarming Pattern of Hate Incidents and Bullying Across Country Since Election." November 29, 2016.

https://www.splcenter.org/news/2016/11/29/new-splc-reports-reveal-alarming
-pattern-hate-incidents-and-bullying-across-country.

Stedman, Nicole, and Brittany Adams. "Identifying Faculty's Knowledge of Critical
Thinking Concepts and Perceptions of Critical Thinking Instruction in Higher
Education." *North American Colleges and Teachers of Agriculture* 58, no. 2 (2012):
9–14.

Steiner, Harry, Philip Alston, and Ryan Goodman. *International Human Rights in Context: Law, Politics, Morals.* 2nd ed. Oxford: Oxford University Press, 2000.

Steiner, Henry. "The University's Critical Role in the Human Rights Movement." *Harvard Human Rights Journal* 15 (2002): 317–28.

Suárez, David. "Education Professionals and the Construction of Human Rights Education." *Comparative Education Review* 51, no. 1 (2007): 48–70.

Suárez, David, and Patricia Bromley. "Professionalizing a Global Social Movement:
Universities and Human Rights." *American Journal of Education* 118, no. 3 (2012):
253–80.

Tanguy, Joelle, and Fiona Terry. "Humanitarian Responsibility and Committed
Action." *Ethics & International Affairs* 13, no. 1 (1999): 29–34.

Taylor, Drew Hayden. *Only Drunks and Children Tell the Truth.* In *Seventh Generation:
An Anthology of Native American Plays,* edited by Mimi Gisolfi D'Aponte. New
York: TCG, 1999.

Thomas, Daniel. *The Helsinki Effect: International Norms, Human Rights, and the
Demise of Communism.* Princeton: Princeton University Press, 2001.

Tibbitts, Felisa. "Understanding What We Do: Emerging Models for Human Rights
Education." *International Review of Education* 48, nos. 3/4 (2002): 159–71.

Tibbitts, Felisa, and Peter G. Kirchschläger. "Perspectives of Research on Human
Rights Education." *Journal of Human Rights Education* 2, no. 1 (2010): 8–29.

Tilly, Charles, and Lesley Wood. *Social Movements 1768–2012.* 1st ed. Abingdon:
Routledge, 2012.

Trinity College. "Human Rights Program." https://www.trincoll.edu/Academics/Spe-
cialPrograms/HumanRights. Accessed May 2017.

UN General Assembly. "Universal Declaration of Human Rights." 1948. http://
www.un.org/en/universal-declaration-human-rights.

UN General Assembly. "Report of the United Nations High Commissioner for Human
Rights on the Implementation of the Plan of Action for the United Nations Decade for Human Rights Education." December 12, 1996. https://documents-dds
-ny.un.org/doc/UNDOC/GEN/N97/008/02/PDF/N9700802.pdf?OpenElement.

United Nations High Commissioner for Refugees. "Global Trends: Forced Displacement in 2016." June 19, 2017. http://www.unhcr.org/5943e8a34.pdf.

United Nations Human Rights Office of the High Commissioner. "Basic Facts About
the UPR." http://www.ohchr.org/EN/HRBodies/UPR/Pages/BasicFacts.aspx.
Accessed April 14, 2017.

United Nations Human Rights Office of the High Commissioner. "United Nations Declaration on Human Rights Education and Training (UNDHRET)." 2017. http://www.ohchr.org/EN/Issues/Education/Training/Pages/UNDHREducation Training .aspx.

United Nations Human Rights Office of the High Commissioner. "Universal Human Rights Instruments." http://www.ohchr.org/EN/ProfessionalInterest/Pages/UniversalHumanRightsInstruments.aspx. Accessed April 14, 2017.

United Nations Human Rights Office of the High Commissioner. "United Nations Declaration on Human Rights Education and Training (2011)." https://www.ohchr.org/EN/Issues/Education/Training/Compilation/Pages/UnitedNationsDeclarationonHumanRightsEducationandTraining(2011).aspx.

United Nations Human Rights Office of the High Commissioner. "World Programme for Human Rights Education, First Phase Plan of Action." 2012. https://www.ohchr.org/EN/Issues/Education/Training/Compilation/Pages/PlanofActionforthefirstphase(2005-2007)oftheWorldProgrammeforHumanRightsEducation(2005).aspx.

United Nations Human Rights Office of the High Commissioner. "World Programme for Human Rights Education Second Phase Plan of Action." July 2012. http://www.ohchr.org/Documents/Publications/WPHRE_Phase_2_en.pdf.

University of Dayton. "Human Rights Studies Program." https://www.udayton.edu/artssciences/academics/humanrights/welcome/index.php. Accessed May 2017.

University of Essex. "Human Rights Centre: Study with Us." https://www.essex.ac.uk/centres-and-institutes/human-rights/our-courses. Accessed May 2017.

University of Indiana. "PhD Minor in Human Rights." http://www.indiana.edu/~intlweb/graduate/hrminor.shtml. Accessed January 2019.

University of Iowa. "Human Rights, Certificate." http://catalog.registrar.uiowa.edu/law/university-center-human-rights/human-rights-certificate/. Accessed January 2019.

University of Minnesota. "Grad Minor in Human Rights Program." https://cla.umn.edu/human-rights/grad-minor-human-rights-program. Accessed January 2019.

University of Ottowa. "Honours in Conflict Studies and Human Rights." https://socialsciences.uottawa.ca/programs/undergraduate-course-sequences/honours-conflict-studies-human-rights. Accessed January 2019.

University of Winnipeg. "Bachelor of Arts in Human Rights." https://www.uwinnipeg.ca/global-college/ba-in-human-rights/index. html. Accessed January 2019.

US News and World Report. "National University Rankings." https://www.usnews.com/best-colleges/rankings/national-universities. Accessed April 2017.

Uvin, Peter. *Human Rights and Development*. Bloomfield: Kumarian Press, 2004.

Valdez, Luis. *Zoot Suit*. In *Zoot Suit and Other Plays*. Houston: Arte Publico Press, 1992.

Van Gelder, Tim. "Teaching Critical Thinking: Some Lessons from Cognitive Science." *College Teaching* 53, no. 1 (2005): 41–46.

Walcott, Derek. "Pantomime." In *The Longman Anthology of Modern and Contemporary Drama*, edited by Michael Greenwald, Roberto Dario Pomo, Roger Schultz, and Anne Marie Welsh, 690–714. New York: Longman, 2004.

Walvoord, Barbara E. *Assessment Clear and Simple: A Practical Guide for Institutions, Departments, and General Education*. San Francisco: Jossey-Bass, 2010.

Washington State University. "Guide to Rating Critical Thinking." 2001. http://learning.colostate.edu/files/classes/42/File_385B9007-C87B-4164-4101084A4BD20704.pdf.

Weingart, Peter. "A Short History of Knowledge Formations." In Frodeman, *Oxford Handbook of* Interdisciplinarity, 3–14.

Wilfrid Laurier University. "Human Rights and Human Diversity." https://www.wlu.ca/programs/liberal-arts/undergraduate/human-rights-and-human-diversity-ba/index.html. Accessed January 2019.

Williams, Jody. *My Name Is Jody Williams: A Vermont Girl's Winding Path to the Nobel Peace Prize*. Berkeley: University of California Press, 2013.

Willingham, Daniel. "Critical Thinking: Why Is It So Hard to Teach?" *Arts Education Policy Review* 109, no. 4 (2008): 21–32.

Wilson, A. S., A. Barham, and J. Hammock. *Practical Idealists*. Cambridge: Harvard University Press, 2008.

Wilson, August. *Fences*. New York: Samuel French, 1986.

Wilson, Robin. "Social Change Tops Classic Books in Professors' Teaching Priorities." *Chronicle of Higher Education*. March 5, 2009. https://www.chronicle.com/article/Social-Change-Tops-Classic/1564 .

Witte, John, and M. Christian Green. *Religion and Human Rights: An Introduction*. New York: Oxford University Press, 2012.

Woessner, Matthew C. "Rethinking the Plight of Conservatives in Higher Education." *Academe* 98, no. 1 (2012). https://www.aaup.org/article/rethinking-plight-conservatives-higher-education#.XCkl_1VKiJA.

World Vision US. "2015 Annual Review." November 2, 2016. https://www.worldvision.org/wp-content/uploads/2015-annual-report-brochure-F3.pdf.

WSD Handa Center for Human Rights and International Justice. "Minor Requirements." Stanford University. https://handacenter.stanford.edu/academics/minor-human-rights/minor-requirements. Accessed May 1, 2017.

Wurdinger, Scott, and Julie Carlson. *Teaching for Experiential Learning: Five Approaches That Work*. Lanham: R&L Education, 2009.

Xingjian, Gao. *The Bus Stop*. In *The Longman Anthology of Modern and Contemporary Drama*, edited by Michael Greenwald, Roberto Dario Pomo, Roger Schultz, and Anne Marie Welsh. New York: Longman, 2004.

York University. "Human Rights and Equity Studies." https://futurestudents.yorku.ca/program/human-rights-equity-studies. Accessed January 2019.

Yousafzai, Malala. *I Am Malala: The Girl Who Stood Up for Education and Was Shot by the Taliban*. Boston: Little, Brown, 2015.

Zadja, Joseph, and Sev Ozdowski, eds. *Globalisation, Human Rights Education, and Reforms*. Dordrecht: Springer Netherlands, 2017.

Zembylas, Michalinos. *Emotion and Traumatic Conflict: Reclaiming Healing in Education*. New York: Oxford University Press, 2015.

Zembylas, Michalinos. "Emotions, Critical Pedagogy, and Human Rights Education." In *Human Rights Education: Theory, Research, Praxis*, edited by Monisha Bajaj, 47–68. Philadelphia: University of Pennsylvania Press, 2017.

Index

Abbott, Andrew, 55
about (educating *about* HRTS). *See* educating *about* HRTS
academia and academics: critical pedagogy of HRTS, 22–24; definition of HRE, 20–21
active learning: benefits, 70, 83–84, 86, 87; definitions, 83; learning and teaching, 69, 83–87, 88; publications, 155
activism, 41–42, 95
activities. *See* teaching activities
advocacy in HRTS: assignments, 105–6, 107–9; educating *for* HRTS courses, 95, 102, 105–6; in HRTS vocabulary, 60; in programs, 41–42; publications, 152
Al-Jabri, Mohammed Abed, 10
American Anthropological Association, 64–65
American Association for the Advancement of Science (AAAS), 122–23
anthropology, and HRTS study, 64–65
Argentina, BAs in HRTS, 28
Arizona State University, interdisciplinarity, 48–49
art courses, and educating *for* HRTS, 95, 96–100
arts, contribution to HRTS, 65
Arum, Richard, 71
assessment of courses: in course design, 123, 132; examples, 128, 129, 130, 131, 132; in HRE, 132, 134–36; publications, 155
assessment of programs in HRE, 136
assessment of students' work, 135–36
assignments: advocacy in HRTS, 105–6, 107–9; in critical thinking, 75–76, 77–78; educating *about* HRTS, 133–34; educating *for* HRTS, 98, 107–9; educating *through* HRTS, 77–78
Association for Experiential Education, 104

Association of American Colleges and Universities (AAC&U), VALUE rubrics for CT teaching, 76, 78, 80
attitudes for HRTS, 41–42, 90, 91
Australia, BAs in HRTS, 28
Australian National University, goal of HRE program, 41
availability bias, 73–74

Bajaj, Monisha, 21
Bard College, HRTS program, 28, 31
Barnard College, HRTS program, 28, 30, 31
BAs in HRTS: *vs.* biology BSc, 38; programs worldwide, 27–28, 30, 33–35; in US, 28–9, 31–32, 54
Becker, Jo, 105–6, 107
Bialystok, Lauren, 94–95
Bok, Derek, 71, 74
books, xi, 6, 60, 63; suggested texts, 146–56
Brecht, Bertold, 101
Brookfield, Stephen, 85–86, 87
Buffone, Anneke E. K., 99
Bureau of Democracy, Human Rights, and Labor (US), 13, 94
business, and HRTS, 16–18
Buti, Antonio, ix

Canada, BAs in HRTS, 28, 30, 33–35
Canadian Human Rights Foundation, 6. *See also* Equitas's International Centre for Human Rights Education
capstone courses: description and types, 106, 109–10; educating *for* HRTS, 95, 102, 106, 109–10; example, 141–42; for minor in HRE, 121; publications about, 152–53
Cargas, Sarita: course design example, 126–32; critical pedagogy in HRE, 24–25; education in HRE, ix

A c k n o w l e d g m e n t s

To write a scholarly book is to enter into a dialogue, and in this case it is about human rights education, HRE. Not only am I now participating in this discussion in print, but I have also spent dozens of hours in conversation with fellow scholars, all of whom I call friends. To them I want to say thank you—you have made this a better book. I begin by expressing gratitude to my colleagues from the Honors College at the University of New Mexico: the most dependable research assistants Shoshana Adler and Darrell Horton; and my writing group Myrriah Gomez, Amaris Ketcham, Ryan Swanson; and especially Marygold Walsh-Dilley, a tough critic, but kind friend throughout. Thank you to those who took the time to be interviewed and allowed me to supplement the text with their contributions to human rights education: Kristina Eberbach, Columbia University; Susan Katz, University of San Francisco; Glenn Mitoma, University of Connecticut; Shayna Plaut, Winnipeg University; Kristi Rudelius-Palmer, University of Minnesota; William Simmons, University of Arizona; Sandra Sirota, University of Connecticut; and Maria Szasz, University of New Mexico. I am grateful to one of the matriarchs of HRE, Nancy Flowers, for helpful feedback on part of the manuscript. A special acknowledgment to Cece Shantzek, my stellar Albuquerque editor, with whom I spent many stimulating hours debating ideas in HRE. I am indebted to my editor at the University of Pennsylvania Press, Peter Agree, for thinking my ideas worthy of a book. To my stalwart companion and husband, Gruia Catalin Roman, thank you for your loving support (and never complaining as the book receipts piled up). And finally, to my parents, Millie and Harry Cargas, for imbuing with me their love and their love of education.